Historic Denali National Park and Preserve

Tracy Salcedo

Guilford, Connecticut

For Sara Hesse Bergendahl
From Evergreen to the Misty to Fairbanks, our adventures continue

An imprint of Globe Pequot

Distributed by NATIONAL BOOK NETWORK

British Library Cataloguing in Publication Information available

Library of Congress Cataloging-in-Publication Data

Names: Salcedo, Tracy, author.
Title: Historic Denali National Park and Preserve / by Tracy Salcedo.
Description: Guilford, Connecticut : Lyons Press, 2017.
Identifiers: LCCN 2017023904 (print) | LCCN 2017025157 (ebook) | ISBN 9781493028924 (e-book) | ISBN 9781493028917 (paperback : alkaline paper)
Subjects: LCSH: Denali National Park and Preserve (Alaska)—History. | Denali National Park and Preserve (Alaska)—Centennial celebrations, etc.
Classification: LCC F912.M23 (ebook) | LCC F912.M23 S25 2017 (print) | DDC 979.8/3—dc23
LC record available at https://lccn.loc.gov/2017023904

∞™ The paper used in this publication meets the minimum requirements of American National Standard for Information Sciences—Permanence of Paper for Printed Library Materials, ANSI/NISO Z39.48-1992.

Printed in the United States of America

Contents

Preface: A Walk on the Wild Side vi
Introduction xi

Chapter One: The Native Name 1
Chapter Two: Denali's First People 8
Chapter Three: Mountaineering: First to the Top 26
Chapter Four: Kantishna 46
Chapter Five: Denali in Two Steps: Defining and Redefining a National Park 59
Chapter Six: Of Sheep, Wolves, and Men: Charles Sheldon, Adolph Murie, and Gordon Haber 80
Chapter Seven: Mountaineering: The Second Wave 93
Chapter Eight: Supermen: Harry Karstens and Grant Pearson 113
Chapter Nine: On Denali's Skirts: Superwomen 130
Chapter Ten: Let the Big Dogs Run 148
Chapter Eleven: Planes, Trains, and Automobiles 159
Chapter Twelve: Denali's Natural History 175
Chapter Thirteen: Rock and Ice: A Mountain of Science 200
Chapter Fourteen: Defining Wilderness: A Different Kind of National Park 220
Chapter Fifteen: Denali by the Numbers. 225

Acknowledgments 227
Resources and Further Reading 229
Index 239
About the Author 249

Preface: A Walk on the Wild Side

I'd been googled.

The backcountry rangers at the boardroom table were friendly but wary. Here was the author of a slew of hiking guides to trails in the Lower 48, come to write about their trailless wilderness. They were probably thinking about me in the same way naturalist Kennan Ward assumed rangers were thinking about him when he arrived in Denali National Park and Preserve: that I was just another yahoo from California with sand for brains. I like to imagine myself a deeper thinker than that, but I got the point. I had to explain myself.

No, I assured them. I was in Denali to do research for a book of essays about its history, and was hoping they could help me zero in on the people, places, and events visitors might want to read about. Their relief was audible, but the rangers remained cautious. What they believe in, what they love, is besieged, and they are ready to wield words, passion, and experience to defend it.

The thing is, there are only about thirty miles of trails in all of Denali's six million acres. And for these rangers, developed trails are the least interesting thing the park has to offer. Wilderness is what Denali is all about.

For a hiker, a new universe opens in Denali's backcountry. You can wander off in any direction, up any gravel bar, across any expanse of tundra, to any ridgetop, to any mountaintop—even to the top of the High One, if you are so inclined. No one's going to admonish you to stay on a designated footpath. In fact, parties of hikers are encouraged to fan out and walk side by side so they don't beat social paths into the tundra.

It's a tough thing for a veteran of national parks like Yosemite, or Lassen Volcanic, or Rocky Mountain, to wrap her head around. You see, earlier that day I had driven up to the Savage River, where the pavement ends and the Denali Park Road is closed to vehicle traffic. It was late September; no one was there. I parked my car at the trailhead—one of Denali's few trailheads—and started down the gravel path toward the fast-flowing stream. Then I paused. The river was low, but the force of the flow in each channel made the water jump and rumble. The sky was thick and gray. Dustings of snow capped the peaks. The lower slopes of the river canyon were steep and shadowy. And I was alone.

Denali checked in. Denali asked the question: Are you safe? I considered it. I'm not afraid to hike alone. It's my modus operandi when I'm researching guidebooks. I carry a giant day pack, the bottom filled with basic survival gear, just in case. But that was at home. Here, in this enormous empty place, I had nothing but desire, a jacket, waterproof hiking shoes, and my wits. I was completely unprepared. If I walked into Denali, I'd almost certainly come out alive. But I could also be unlucky and get lost; startle a grizzly; maybe trip, smack my head on a rock, pass out, and freeze to death. These things happen here; I'd been reading about them. One mistake, and Denali would ship my desiccated bones home, perhaps in a day, or a week, or two weeks or ten, after I'd been picked clean by its hungry, thrifty residents.

I told the backcountry rangers about this. They were curious: Why did I seek out a trail? Because I felt safer there, I said. Well, they explained, in Denali a trail doesn't translate to safety. The Yosemite rules don't apply. Moreover, being safe is not the point. Being open and exposed and awed and enervated—that's the point.

It's an extraordinary idea for an Outsider, considering the emphasis in other national parks on compliance to a trail-centric convention, and hypersensitivity to accommodating every need of a visitor. But then Denali is an extraordinary park.

In the Lower 48 walking off-trail is, for the most part, anathema. Walking off-trail causes erosion, is disruptive to habitat, and constitutes bad human behavior. It's easier to manage people when they stay on a trail. It's easier to find them when they get lost or hurt. In the busiest national parks in the busiest seasons, it's easier to educate visitors about proper etiquette if there's a trailhead with ample signage or, better yet, a

Views that inspire: Denali from Stony Hill in 1967.
PHOTO COURTESY OF THE NATIONAL PARK SERVICE, DENALI NATIONAL PARK AND PRESERVE MUSEUM COLLECTIONS. PHOTO BY PETER SANCHEZ.

trailhead staffed by a ranger offering advice and supervision. Most of the time visitors are fairly prepared, but in the Lower 48 the level of stupid, oblivious, and dangerous can be staggering.

Those rules don't apply in Denali. Denali is *wilderness*, even where it's not designated Wilderness. In this place a person is on his or her own. There should be no expectation of rescue. Feeling vulnerable, being prepared, and being constantly attuned to the surroundings is the expectation. The wild is one of the most valuable things Denali has to offer.

Echoing Gifford Pinchot, who maintained that public lands should be managed for the best and highest use, I argued that Denali must prepare to meet the expectations of a public that will descend upon it in ever greater numbers—a public accustomed to Yosemite and Yellowstone, to being guided by rangers who can point them in the right direction and

Denali rises above the Chulitna River.
PHOTO BY TRACY SALCEDO.

pluck them off rocks with helicopters if they get in over their heads. The mountain is a magnet. The hordes will come.

And the rangers, most convincingly echoing John Muir, who clashed with Pinchot by maintaining that public lands should be preserved untouched, argued that Denali is now, and should remain, different. Let the people come. They will be liberated here, knowing that as they crest a ridge or skirt a crevasse on a trackless slope they might be the first to have done this thing. They might be the first to have seen the massive vista from that nameless peak. They might have crossed a pass that no one has crossed before. Instead of following in another person's footsteps, they walk paths followed by the wild creatures that make their homes here; creatures who know the best way, who are the pathfinders.

What the rangers argue for is a delicate thing. Even as they channel Muir, other forces channel Pinchot. A new trails plan is under consideration for the park, and conservation versus preservation will play out over this boardroom table and others. What will be, will be. There is no right or wrong.

But the arguments of the ardent defenders of Denali's wildness swayed this guidebook writer. Before I left the park, I drove back up toward the Savage River under a lifting sky. In the filtered sunlight I could just make out the bulk of Denali, far distant, unmistakable, awesome. I stepped out of the car, alone again. I walked to the side of the road, off the road, onto a gravel bar in a stream that I didn't know the name of. One step, two steps, three steps, stop. Off the trail, walking on the wild side. I felt the void on my packless back, a heightened awareness, a thrilling spark of tempered fear and freedom. This was not the time; I was still unprepared. But with the right gear, and my wits, I could wander in any direction. My path in six million acres could be mine alone. I felt liberated.

Introduction

Every visitor lucky enough to see Denali has this moment. An "aha" moment, when the mountain reveals itself and all becomes clear.

This is why. This explains everything.

For Grant Pearson the moment came at the end of a long patrol to Kantishna. Charles Sheldon had a moment too, as did Harry Karstens, Adolph Murie, Fannie Quigley, Belmore Browne, and all the characters who figure in the history of Denali National Park and Preserve. For the host of nameless Athabascans who lived near the base of the mountain for thousands of years, the High One was part of a heritage passed down from generation to generation. They were born into the aha moment.

There is no adequate way to capture that moment in an essay. Denali must be seen to be believed. But to get an idea, imagine the mountains framing its base as the Rockies or the Sierra Nevada, snow-capped peaks of stunning proportions skirted with dense forest and bleeding braided rivers. Then stack another mountain on top, another 10,000 feet of snow and ice, miles around, streaked with glaciers, twin summits shooting streamers of cloud into a layer of atmosphere so rarefied it strips the breath away.

Aha.

The stories of mountaineers who wanted to stand, breathless, atop the roof of the North American continent drive the history of Denali National Park. But other stories have unfolded within the park's borders, of miners and naturalists and scientists and conservationists. This book comprises essays about their experiences and motivations, as well as about the natural world that shaped those experiences. The essays are built on the research and writings of the explorers and scientists themselves, interviews with Denali's rangers, and National Park Service publications,

Taking in the views from Sable Pass in winter.
PHOTO COURTESY OF THE NATIONAL PARK SERVICE, DENALI NATIONAL PARK AND PRESERVE MUSEUM COLLECTIONS.

as well as on the work of historians who've plumbed newspapers, journals, superintendents' reports, and government records to flesh out the details.

The essays, as they evolved, refused to confine themselves to a linear format. Even the park historian wavered as he considered how best to order them. It's hard to say what came first: Kantishna? The mountaineers? Thus, mentions of Denali's influential characters, significant places, defining events, and signature attributes are interwoven throughout. The players diverge and converge and diverge again, like the channels in the streams flowing from the toes of Denali's glaciers.

Each of these short excursions into Denali's history is also informed by the experience of today's park, because what came before is still being lived in Denali in the present moment. From subsistence to dogsledding

Denali on a clear day: You have to see it to believe it.
PHOTO BY TRACY SALCEDO.

to patrolling a mostly empty wilderness in the dead of winter, aspects of Denali's present day aren't far removed from its first day. In that regard it presents a different national park experience than that found in sister parks in the Lower 48—or, as Alaskans would put it, Outside. Bringing stories into the present also acknowledges that history is made, or revised, day to day.

Given that Denali is a wilderness park, of all the themes that run through these essays, wilderness is the most pervasive. The wild creatures and wild places that the Sourdoughs encountered on their donut-fueled summit assault in 1910 are still on the mountain today, some hardly altered, some embattled. But they endure, for the enjoyment of the visitor and the benefit of the generations to come.

The other theme that runs through the stories is obsession. Perhaps Belmore Browne's Denali experience encapsulates this best: He came back to the mountain again and again and again, and though he wasn't destined to be first to the summit—or reach the summit at all—he wasn't defeated. In fact, he battled to ensure the mountain that turned him away was preserved for posterity so that others could be enthralled by its power and beauty. I hope these essays capture some of that magic, and that even if readers never see Denali unveiled, in reading they are gifted with a bit of the passion that inspired Browne and so many others.

My aha moment came during my second trip to Denali National Park and Preserve. As they had on my first visit, clouds hovered on the ridges of the Alaska Range for days on end, and Denali remained hidden, which is not unusual. But then the sky lifted, and there it was. A mountain stacked on mountains, so huge and white and incredible that I swerved into the first pullout I reached, stepped out of the car, and gaped. I had appointments. Those no longer mattered. Around each bend of the long highway through the Chulitna river valley, a new vista opened, and I was compelled, Belmore Browne–style, to stop again and again and again. That was a gift.

And I've been given another: the opportunity to delve into the evolution of the amazing park inspired by the mountain. This has only enhanced my aha moment, allowing me to live it again and again and again through the stories of those who've come before. Whether your moment has happened or lies in the future, my hope is that these essays may do the same for you.

Chapter One

The Native Name

For the record, Denali is now formally Denali. President Barack Obama made it official in August 2015. Mount McKinley and Mount McKinley National Park are no more. Search the official database maintained by U.S. Geological Survey's Board on Geographic Names for Mount McKinley, and you get Denali.

The funny thing is, Denali has always been Denali. Even after a white prospector pinned the name of a presidential candidate on a peak that candidate would never see, those who knew the mountain, even those not from Alaska, called it Denali.

So, what's in a name? In this case, the history of the place. In researching this book, it became clear pretty quickly that the importance of place names in Denali National Park and Preserve reaches far beyond the iconic peak at its heart. The names represent survival, landscape, and memory. I'd be remiss if I didn't elaborate on their origins and applications.

For the Athabascan bands—Koyukon, Ahtna, Lower Tanana, Dena'ina, Upper Kuskokwim—who lived on the land prior to the arrival of white men, names were richly descriptive. More than eighty native names within and surrounding the park are thought to describe hunting grounds; others describe travel routes; still others describe events that occurred in that place. "A long time ago, if a native person were told, 'I went to Yedatene Na,' the name would conjure up a picture of the entire area, including the rivers, mountains, valleys," Brenda Rebne wrote in her history of the Cantwell-Denali band. "It would be just as clear a directive as giving someone directions to a store in Fairbanks using street names."

Minchumina was recorded by Lieutenant Joseph Herron, who was exploring the region in 1899, as the Tanana word for "clear lake." Explorer Belmore Browne relays the translation of *Susitna* as "river of sand." In park literature *Teklanika* is "glacier creek." *Nenana* is "stopping while migrating river." *Toklat* is "headwaters river." *Telida* translates to "whitefish place."

Denali, in Koyukon Athabascan, is the High, Tall One.

Of course, it's more complicated than that. Our *Denali* is based on the Koyukon name for the mountain, Deenaalee; variations in spelling are inherent when rendering an unwritten Native language into written American English. Other bands had other names for the mountain, all relating in some way to its physical dominance: Dinadhi, Denaze, Dghelay Ka'a; the Tall One, the Big Mountain. Denali, according to one geographer, has nearly fifty variant names. And as one journalist quipped, you could combine the translations as "Mount Big High One."

The Russian colonists followed the Native lead when they called the peak Bolshaya or Bolshaya Gora, translating to "big mountain."

Then came American prospectors and explorers, who, with a few exceptions, had no use for Native (or Russian) names. For them the landscape was a blank slate. As they had done across the American West, Alaska's new pioneers hurled names at every feature they encountered as if they were the first to see them. This led to redundancy: You can find an Emerald Lake, a Clearwater Creek, a Cathedral Peak, even a Sugarloaf, in states and parks from coast to coast. Thankfully, some are evocative in the way of Native American names: the Never Summer Range, Clouds Rest, the Devils Kitchen; the Canyonlands, the Badlands, Death Valley, the Great Smoky Mountains.

In the early days of the national parks, it was also common to jettison Native names in favor of monikers commemorating significant American politicians, scientists, and explorers: Mount Rainier (for Rear Admiral Peter Rainier via Captain George Vancouver), General Grant (for President Ulysses S. Grant; later Sequoia & Kings Canyon National Parks), and, of course, Mount McKinley. A handful of the early parks were blessed with an apt descriptive moniker: think the Grand Canyon, Crater Lake, and Yellowstone. Yosemite is the sole Native survivor from those days.

The crazy thing about McKinley is that William McKinley wasn't even president when prospector and Princeton alum William Dickey dubbed the mountain in his honor in 1896. Forget Denali, forget Densmore's Mountain (so called for a prospector who couldn't stop talking about the magnificent peak). The story goes that Dickey chose the McKinley moniker to settle an argument with other prospectors about the superiority of the gold standard as monetary policy, which McKinley backed, versus "free silver," the monetary policy backed by his opponent, Democrat William Jennings Bryan. Dickey promoted the name in an article he wrote for the *New York Sun*, and "McKinley" stuck.

The fixation of geographers and explorers on naming landmarks for powerful friends and colleagues is widespread within the park. Thus, there's Mount Foraker (for another politician, though this impressive peak was already known as Denali's Wife or the Wife); Mount Mather (for the first head of the National Park Service); Mount Brooks (for pioneering geologist Alfred Brooks, whose name is also on Alaska's Brooks Range); Mount Dan Beard (bestowed by mountaineer Belmore Browne for an illustrator and one of the movers and shakers in the early Boy Scouts); and the list goes on.

In some cases, in those early days, features likely didn't have native names, such as the glacier in the Great Basin high on Denali's northeast face, which Archdeacon Hudson Stuck named Harper Glacier for Walter Harper, the Native Alaskan to first step onto the summit, and for prospector and explorer Arthur Harper, his father. Stuck named Karstens Ridge for the acclaimed coleader of the first ascent party, Harry Karstens, who went on to become Mount McKinley National Park's first superintendent.

But even for the climbers who first stood on the summit in 1913, the mountain was Denali. Stuck begins his account of the mountain's first ascent with this statement: "Forefront in the book, because forefront in the author's heart and desire, must stand a plea for the restoration to the greatest mountain in North America of its immemorial native name."

Belmore Browne, who made three attempts on the mountain's summit and later championed its preservation as a national park, also stood behind the Native name, and Native names in general. "These great mountains, rivers, and glaciers are firstly the property of all the people,

Denali and Reflection Pond in 1963.
PHOTO COURTESY OF THE NATIONAL PARK SERVICE, DENALI NATIONAL PARK AND PRESERVE MUSEUM COLLECTIONS. PHOTO BY VERDE WATSON.

and secondly, as they form important geographical monuments or dividing lines, they should when possible be given historical or descriptive names," he wrote in *The Conquest of Mount McKinley*.

And Charles Sheldon, the hunter/naturalist who spearheaded the park's establishment, "made several appeals for 'Denali National Park' during the park's establishment and in his memoir," writes park historian Erik Johnson. Sheldon argued for Denali in the epilogue of his memoir, *Wilderness of Denali*, as well as "in some of the letters to Thomas Riggs when they [were] drafting the legislation."

Denali National Park and Preserve isn't devoid of modern descriptive names, ones that hint at the experiences or impressions of latecomers. Wonder Lake, according to one-time superintendent Grant Pearson, didn't get its name as some kind of "travel-folder puffery." Instead, it's

Following the Denali Park Road toward the fog-shrouded Teklanika River.
PHOTO COURTESY OF THE NATIONAL PARK SERVICE, DENALI NATIONAL PARK AND PRESERVE MUSEUM COLLECTIONS.

derived from the musings of prospectors who stumbled across the three-mile-long lake while surveying possibilities in the Kantishna District. "One miner said, 'I wonder how we missed this before?' With frontier humor, the lake came to be called 'I Wonder Lake,'" Pearson wrote in *My Life of High Adventure*. "When maps of the region were drawn up, the name apparently looked like a typographical error to the cartographer, who cut out the 'I.'"

When a sled dog named Muckluck died on the trail in 1912, Browne named Muckluck Pass after the animal, noting that in the "savage life" of a mountaineer "so little tenderness or affection enters into the daily grind that a man loves his dogs passionately."

Controversial wildlife biologist Gordon Haber, who studied wolves in Denali for decades starting in the mid-twentieth century, had strong opinions about naming features on the landscape. In *Among Wolves*, pilot Troy Dunn recounted how naming a landmark after a person "really got [Haber's] goat." Instead, the scientist would bestow names "based on his experiences there: Ass-kicker Canyon, Mudslump Valley," Dunn told writer Marybeth Holleman.

Other names that have stuck memorialize those who've lost their lives on the mountain, or whose lives were interwoven with the place. Theodore Koven and Allen Carpé, two members of the 1932 Cosmic Ray expedition who were the first to die on Denali, have lesser peaks named in their memory. Point Farine was named for Jacques "Farine" Batkin, who died in the first winter ascent of Denali in 1967. Copper Mountain was renamed Mount Eielson for pioneering bush pilot Ben Eielson, who was first to land a plane in the park.

These names have stuck with little controversy attached. Not so McKinley. Alaska's state legislature officially renamed the mountain Denali in 1975, but the change didn't translate to the national arena. Despite public opinion the U.S. Board of Geographic Names remained silent on the matter. Repeated efforts by Alaskan lawmakers to get a bill renaming the peak through Congress were thwarted by their colleagues from Ohio, McKinley's home state. Renaming the mountain got a boost in 1980, with the passage of the Alaska National Interest Lands Conservation Act (ANILCA); that legislation essentially recreated Mount McKinley National Park, adding millions of acres and designating the original park a Wilderness. The vast reserve surrounding the roof of North America was now Denali National Park and Preserve.

But the mountain stayed McKinley.

What Sally Jewell, President Obama's Secretary of the Interior, did when she issued her order to restore Denali's Native name was honor the mountain's history and prehistory. The change recognized the sovereignty of the place and of Native Alaskans, as well as the arrogance of colonialism.

The change remains controversial. William McKinley was, after all, an American president, and deserves to be remembered and celebrated. Republican politicians from Ohio have expressed outrage, and there have been rumblings about changing the mountain's name back again.

But Denali is Denali. And the upshot is to let you, the reader, know why that's the name I use, as often as I can, in these essays. There are times when, in the storytelling, the names Mount McKinley and Mount McKinley National Park must be used. But otherwise it's all Denali. It may not be strictly historically correct, but I am not a historian. I'm a writer, and as I've pored through the literature and experienced the peak and park, Denali is the only name I hear.

Denali has music. It has power. It shines. It transcends politics. It has history.

Chapter Two

Denali's First People

When people first crossed the land bridge linking the Old World to the New, they encountered things that would be strange and fantastic to their descendants: woolly mammoths, prehistoric bison, horses, camels, and scimitar cats, all roaming a steppe that was ice-free even as the rest of the north froze. The one fantastic thing that would be familiar is the massive rock-and-ice mountain barricading the tundra realm on its south side: Denali.

The question is: Why would anyone call a place like Denali home? The landscapes are formidable. Winter brings endless nights and bitter cold. Summer, a season of blooms, berries, and bugs, is short. Game migrates mile over endless mile, and the hunter must follow. Rivers in flood, encounters with bears, and sudden storms can all turn deadly. To the modern sensibility Alaska's interior is inhospitable at best and uninhabitable at worst: a nice place to visit, but you wouldn't want to live there.

Yet people have been at home in Denali for thousands of years. Yes, some moved on—the rest of the Americas would not have been populated if someone hadn't thought there was something better over the next hill or around the next river bend. But others were satisfied and sustained by the vast wilderness that surrounds the High One. They put down roots, migrated with the caribou, preserved the berries when they ripened, and endured winter's darkness, knowing that, come summer, there would be a midnight sun.

A sun dog (also called a mock sun, parhelion, and phantom sun) lights the horizon above the Savage River in 1966.
PHOTO COURTESY OF THE NATIONAL PARK SERVICE, DENALI NATIONAL PARK AND PRESERVE MUSEUM COLLECTIONS. PHOTO BY PETER SANCHEZ.

A Matter of Archaeological Record

It's generally accepted that people migrated into Alaska from Siberia at the end of the last ice age, when both were part of a vast northern steppe-tundra known as Beringia. Sea levels had dropped as water from the oceans was bound up in the ice sheets that covered much of North America and Europe, opening the bridge. When the ice melted, water flooded back into the oceans, filling the Bering and Chukchi Seas and creating a barrier to further land-based migration.

While dating the appearance of the Bering Land Bridge has been established—it was exposed between forty thousand and fifteen thousand years ago—pinning down migration dates is like pinning down a cloud by throwing darts into the sky. Given the current evidence, it's generally accepted that colonization of the New World first occurred about fifteen thousand years ago. It's also possible that the timeline could change as new anthropological evidence is revealed.

How these migrants lived once they arrived in Alaska is answerable through archaeology. Uncover a stone tool, and a skilled archaeologist can determine if that tool was used to kill an animal, or to skin it, or to butcher it, or to stitch its hide into clothing. Other artifacts, like fragments of bone found around a hearth, are clues to what the people ate and how the food was prepared. Where the hearths are located offers insight into where people lived, whether seasonally or in more permanent camps.

Denali National Park's proximity to the ephemeral land bridge upped the odds that some remnant of the continent's first peoples would be found here. Archaeology in the park began in the early 1960s, when a party from the University of Alaska discovered a pair of prehistoric sites on the Teklanika River. Teklanika West is the better known of the two sites, and excavations have revealed both how the first people used the land and a timeline of prehistoric occupation. Called a "lookout site" in park literature, Teklanika West's location was ideal for scouting game. People using the site also worked on (or discarded) the stone tools they used to kill and slaughter game. Sharpening or reshaping the tools would have been a constructive way to pass the time while waiting for caribou or sheep to migrate through.

Later excavations revealed a pair of hearths surrounded by bone fragments and pieces of stone worked by human hands, suggesting long-term occupation of the site in successive seasons. Advanced scientific tools including radiocarbon analysis, as well as the presence of bone from an extinct species of bison, have been used to assign dates to the different levels of occupation. Artifacts in the lowest levels date back more than twelve thousand years; the most recent occupation of the site took place about fourteen hundred years ago.

Teklanika East is a quarry site containing an outcrop of chert, which is ideal for toolmaking; like obsidian, chert can be worked predictably and produces a sharp edge when fractured. At Bull River, a more remote alpine site in the park, an archaeological survey and excavation in 2007

Excavations at Teklanika West in the 1960s revealed clues about prehistoric occupations in Denali National Park.
PHOTO COURTESY OF THE NATIONAL PARK SERVICE, DENALI NATIONAL PARK AND PRESERVE MUSEUM COLLECTIONS. PHOTO BY RON BOYCE AND BERYL BEARD.

uncovered both stone tools and the litter created by flint-knapping (tool-making), as well as charcoal that could have come from a campfire. The site dates back about 12,400 years—the oldest yet in the park—and contains "compelling evidence" that prehistoric hunters inhabited Denali's uplands as the ice age waned, which would have been "a time of drastic global warming and environmental change," according to park literature. Archaeologists have also located what is believed to be a hunting blind, constructed of stone in the shelter of a rock alcove, along with stone tools, in Denali's alpine reaches.

Another significant find—one that allows archaeologists to hypothesize about cultural connections—was made when the skull of a bison, part of Denali's museum collection, was reexamined. It was painted with ochre, a red pigment used by prehistoric peoples around the world for decoration and in religious and ceremonial contexts. One idea posed in park literature: that the dots on the bison skull were made by a shaman in a trance state, since "visions at the early stages of a trance are universally manifested as dots, zig-zags, and meandering lines."

In Denali, as elsewhere around the world, stone and bone are the most likely artifacts to have survived into the modern era. Time consumes the perishable: clothing; basketry; wooden objects; structures made of ice, timber, or earth; and flesh. But in Denali, as elsewhere in the northern latitudes, ice patches present an opportunity for discovery of more fragile artifacts. The patches—not glaciers, given their crevasses and constant movement—have long been used by caribou and sheep as islands of refuge from summertime's bugs. The congregations of game make the patches prime sites for finding evidence of prehistoric hunters as well. Artifacts have been recovered from ice patches in other Alaskan national parks, from resilient atlatl darts fashioned from stone to fragile basketry.

Nothing has been found yet in Denali's ice patches, but surveys are ongoing. And there's a new sense of urgency to this research as the Arctic and sub-Arctic regions grow warmer and the ice melts. Once exposed, the more fragile artifacts will break down and disappear. Locating, mapping, and preserving resources found in the patches will not only help fill in the blanks in the archaeological record, but also present a way to monitor the effects of climate change in the park.

The archaeological record currently indicates that there was a limit to how high prehistoric peoples and precolonial Athabascans ranged in Denali. Though sites have been found above tree line, given the wealth of the lowlands, there was no need for the people to frequent the snowy heights, according to park anthropologists. The glaciers and high, stony ridges on Denali itself hold few practical resources.

But what is known about the reach of human exploration and occupation of Denali in prehistory, like the timing of the original colonization of Beringia, could change as the science advances. Archaeology may even lead to revision of the record of first ascents on the peak itself, given recent finds on a mountaintop in Argentina, where archaeologists have uncovered Incan mummies at 22,100 feet, as well as textiles, pottery, and food. Though Teklanika and other sites in and around Denali have confirmed about twelve thousand years of occupation, each new year brings the potential for discovery of new sites and a new understanding of the Denali cultural complex.

The Athabascans

Fitting the prehistoric people of the New World into discrete cultural boxes has long preoccupied anthropologists and linguists. To help make sense of precolonial cultures, scholars assigned tribes and bands to language groups. The Athabascan language family overlies vast tracts of territory, encompassing groups that settled Interior Alaska, the Yukon Territory, the Northwest Territory, and the upper reaches of British Columbia, Saskatchewan, and Alberta; it also reaches into the American Southwest and can be found among tribes that occupied portions of coastal Oregon and northern California.

But language alone doesn't define a people. English-speaking San Franciscans, for example, can converse with—and thus trade with, marry, and make war on—the people of Los Angeles, but the two populations differ, their worldviews dictated by the landscapes and resources that surround them, and by their cultural memories. Likewise in Alaska, where Athabascans differentiate into smaller groups, the Tanana, Dena'ina, Ahtna, Upper Kuskokwim, and Koyukon among them. The bands are defined more by place than by the language roots they share, or categorizations imposed by academia.

No Athabascan band is exclusively associated with what is now Denali National Park and Preserve: The Dena'ina (Tanaina) and Ahtna live south of the Alaska Range, the Tanana to the north and east, and the Koyukon and Upper Kuskokwim to the north and west. And these associations break down still further. As described by a student of Cantwell's Native history, the Western Ahtna, with homelands tucked into Denali's south and east sides, comprise three distinct bands, the Tyone Lake, the Talkeetna, and the Cantwell-Denali, which have ties to Ahtna bands at Tazlina Lake and Valdez Creek, farther removed from the Alaska Range. Bands from each group moved between camps in territories that ranged across the lowlands within and surrounding the park.

Bands crossed great distances to trade with each other. Lake Minchumina, located outside the park boundary northwest of the range, was in the Koyukon homeland, and Cantwell, located along a migration route that would later become the Denali Highway, was in Ahtna territory. Hundreds of miles and thousands of feet of elevation gain separate the two communities, but the connections were made and sustained.

Athabascans also came together for potlatches, ceremonial gatherings that celebrated major life events including births, namings, weddings, and deaths. Feasting, singing, storytelling, and gift-giving were all part of the potlatch tradition, which could last for days or weeks, depending on how wealthy the family hosting the potlatch was. Potlatches, once outlawed because whites viewed gatherings of Natives as a threat, have been revived in modern times, though the practices, from the method of gift-giving to the kinds of food served, have changed.

On the Table

> *Denali is a wilderness park. But when you overlay the place names and how the land was utilized, it becomes a grocery store.*
>
> —Amy Craver, cultural anthropologist for Denali National Park and Preserve

The early Athabascans who lived around Denali were nomadic, following game from camp to camp in the spring, summer, and early fall, and then settling into a winter village for the better part of that long season. Dogs and sleds were integral to travel in winter before the advent of snow machines; in summer the people traveled by foot. On the lowlands winter homes were semipermanent and built mostly below ground, the pyramid-shaped roofs insulated with sod and outfitted with a smoke hole to vent the central fire. In spring, summer, and fall, people erected shelters of skin or bark in their camps. When camps moved, the women and dogs carried the loads while the men, with their weapons, scouted for game.

Big game, such as caribou and sheep, were premium targets for Native people living near Denali, who mostly forayed into what would become the park in late summer and early autumn, before streams and rivers froze, so they could float their harvest downriver. Caribou was a staple. In addition to hunting individuals, Athabascans drove small numbers into confined areas, using fencing and snares to corner them for harvest. No part of any animal went to waste. When caribou (or moose) were killed, whatever wasn't eaten right away was dried and cached for the winter. The head was used to make soup; bones were roasted and cracked open so the marrow could be eaten, but they could also be fashioned into weapons and tools. Brains were used to tan hides. The hides, in turn, were used for shelter; stitched into clothing (using tendons as thread); or stretched over a spruce frame, fastened with spruce roots, and sealed with spruce gum to make a canoe.

Big game was augmented with smaller animals, such as snowshoe hares, grouse and ptarmigan, and ducks and geese. The pelts of marten, lynx, wolf, beaver, and muskrat were used to trim clothing. Even salmon skin was a valuable resource, used to make waterproof moccasins and other gear. Fish was another staple: Whitefish was harvested from the lakes and streams around Denali, along with some salmon, and ice fishing was a commonly used technique. The fish was dried and smoked to preserve it. In other regions, men and women employed dip nets, gill nets, and fish traps fashioned from willow and spruce to catch fish.

The Athabascan table was laden with more than meat and fish. Berries were gathered in season and in profusion: blueberry, lingonberry (also known as lowbush cranberry), raspberry, and highbush cranberry, along with some salmonberry and bog cranberry. Lamb's quarter, young willow, and young fireweed were among the wild greens harvested for food. Bands also used spruce, willow, birch bark, and other plants to make basketware, snowshoes, hunting gear, sleds and boats, and housing.

Storytellers

Athabascan stories that describe how things came to be, or contain moral messages, or possess the power to protect, have passed orally from generation to generation for centuries. With the lives of the storytellers so entwined with the forces and creatures of the natural world, it's no surprise that the tales revolve around the adventures and lessons learned by characters like Raven, Porcupine, Willow Grouse Woman, Fox, Beaver, and Brown Bear.

Raven is central to Athabascan mythology, figuring in such monumental events as the creation of the sun and moon and the formation of Denali and the Alaska Range. The story of the High One varies in the telling. Anthropologist Miranda Wright, a native of Nulato, located north and west of the range, called Denali "that shiny place in the sky where all the spirits go to." *The Legend of Denali*, as told by Chief Mitch Demientieff of Nenana and presented on the park's website, goes this way:

> *Long before Denali was created, there lived in Alaska an Indian named Yahoo. He possessed great power but had no wife. Yahoo built a canoe and paddled west to find one. As he approached the raven chief village, he began singing a song that explained he was seeking a wife.*
>
> *The wife of the second chief spoke softly. "You may have my daughter for your wife, but take her and go quickly. The raven chief is preparing to kill you!"*
>
> *Yahoo began to paddle away with the young woman. The raven chief was right behind him. The raven chief caused a great storm. The water became very rough. Yahoo took out a powerful stone and threw it ahead of him, calming the waters, but mountainous green waves continued to roll behind him.*
>
> *Next, the raven chief threw his great spear straight at Yahoo, but Yahoo, using medicine, changed the large wave behind him into a mountain of stone, just in time. The great spear glanced off the crest of the stone mountain.*
>
> *There was a second tremendous wave of water, even greater than the first. Yahoo used all his medicine to turn this wave into a tremendous mountain of stone. When the great spear hit the top of the mountain there was a crash of breaking rock, and the great spear flew off into the sky.*
>
> *The raven chief was paddling so quickly his canoe struck the second great mountain of stone. The raven chief was thrown onto the rocks, where he changed instantly into a raven and flapped to the top of the mountain.*
>
> *Exhausted, Yahoo fell asleep. When he awoke he was back at home with his new wife at his side. Gazing around, Yahoo saw the two mountains he had created. There was a smaller one to the west, now called Foraker, but the larger one, the one the great war spear*

glanced off before shooting into the stars, that mighty dome would be called—Denali! The great one!

Yahoo looked at the sky to see the great raven happy to be back with his people, dancing his approval in the wind.

In stories recounted in ethnographer Frederica de Laguna's *Tales from the Dena*, Raven determines the flows of rivers, he makes ground out of driftwood, he fashions the first canoe out of birch bark, and he makes islands by paddling energetically. He marries and is spurned; he exacts revenge and sometimes kills when crossed. Raven is not predictable: He is a creative force and also destructive; he's calculating and clever; his ingenuity gets him both into trouble and out of it.

The Traveler is also integral to Athabascan folklore. Like Raven, he is destructive at times, but de Laguna writes that the Traveler also "dreamed in advance of all the places he would visit and of the adventures he would encounter, and [he] had the mission of correcting things in the world that were wrong." He journeys from place to place, learning how to build a better canoe, how to make a better fish net, and how to navigate the dangers posed by animals and rivers. And he walks a lot, like the nomads who tell his stories. De Laguna quotes a Tlingit woman, who observed of her neighbors in the Interior: "All they have to do is walk around."

Specific behaviors accompany the taboo surrounding Athabascan women and bears. Young women weren't permitted to confront the bear spirit; if a bear approached a camp, they were taught to not look at it or talk about it, and to hide until the bear was chased away. One story describes a woman who disguises herself as a bear to uncover her husband's infidelities with two other women. In her fury the woman-disguised-as-bear kills all three. On her way home, still wearing the bear skin, the woman is distracted by Raven and the skin sticks to her forever; angry woman becomes angry bear. The wisdom of teaching women to distance themselves from bears makes sense: Any person is in mortal danger if she (or he) surprises a sow with cubs in the wild, and startling a brown bear, male or female, can have deadly consequences. Stories like these reinforced a healthy and necessary respect for the creatures the people lived among.

When the White Man Came

"Once intertwined in the economic web of the Western world, there was no return to the ways of the past."

—Brenda Rebne, *Cantwell Native Village History*

The arrival of the Russians in the mid-1700s didn't have an immediate impact on Athabascan bands in the Interior, but the colonists imposed serious hardships on Alaska's coastal indigenous peoples over the next hundred years or so. The Russians knew Denali—they called it Bolshaya Gora ("big mountain")—but the mountain didn't draw them inland in great numbers. There was plenty to occupy them along the coast.

But as was the case throughout the Americas, the arrival of colonialists meant the spread of disease. Native peoples throughout Alaska were devastated by epidemics of tuberculosis, smallpox, scarlet fever, and other infectious plagues. Disease spread to the Interior Athabascans through contact with neighboring indigenous bands, decimating populations before face-to-face contact with the white man became more common.

By the early 1800s fur trappers were making inroads up the Yukon, and these traders established direct contact with Native bands in the Interior. Their arrival brought a wave of lifestyle changes to the Athabascan people, mostly in the form of novel trade goods like steel blades and woven, which subsequently pushed traditional lifeways out. By the late 1860s, as historian Raymond Collins notes, many Upper Kuskokwim had been baptized into the Russian Orthodox Church and taken Russian surnames. "Iron replaced the bone, stone and copper used in weapons and knives. Rifles were in the process of replacing the bow and arrow and spear," Collins wrote in *Dichinanek' Hwt'ana*, his history of the people of Nikolai and Telida, rural communities located north and west of Denali. "Beads replaced porcupine quills in decorations on clothing. Western clothing replaced moose and caribou skin garments with the exception of hats, gloves and footwear." Cabins replaced traditional subterranean homes and, in the new economy, "trapping became a major activity through the winter—earlier trapping had been a minor activity that took place in connection with hunting for food since only a few furs were needed for blankets and clothing."

The arrival of American prospectors in the mid- and late 1800s nailed home changes to the Native Alaskan way of life that had started with the Russians. Gold discoveries triggered stampedes, with some, like the rush to the Klondike, involving tens of thousands of immigrants. Each stampede resulted in the movement of Native populations into permanent settlements. Children were sent away to missionary schools and taught English. Fish wheels augmented the use of gill nets and traps, and wire was used in place of willow. Guns and steel replaced stone and bone in the toolkit of the hunter. In the Denali region, several thousand prospectors rushed to Kantishna. The focus was gold, but market hunters were also in the mix, harvesting great numbers of game animals, both large and small, in the Kantishna Hills. This unrestricted hunting spurred naturalist Charles Sheldon to campaign for Denali's preservation. For the local native people, it translated to increased hardship as the food sources they'd relied on for generations were massacred.

The economies of indigenous populations also changed, as the focus shifted from subsistence to working for cash that could be exchanged for goods. Ahtna men went to work for miners on Valdez Creek, southeast of Denali and Cantwell, and members of other bands worked as laborers in mining camps throughout the region. Native values, however, did not change. The Ahtna and their neighbors placed little priority on acquiring wealth. What they needed came from the land, and had always come from the land. Historian William Brown records that to the Athabascans, the idea of working for cash was "nonsensical, because one had to hunt and fish for the family's true necessities, and wage-work shortened time on the land for those activities." But with the territory's new immigrants creating competition for those resources, the Natives were forced to buy into the new cash economy. They now had to purchase much of what they needed to survive.

When mines played out, some members of Denali's local bands moved on to Mount McKinley National Park to work on construction of the Alaska Railroad, which was completed in 1923. The next great influx of Outsiders arrived about twenty years later, as the Alaska Highway forged northward during World War II. This, again, presented job opportunities for Athabascans and, again, created competition: the proverbial double-edged sword. They now had access to modern jobs and medical care, but their hunting grounds were opened to weekend warriors and vacationers, and the Outsiders also brought with them hostility and alcohol. Yet another population rush followed Alaska's statehood in 1959. With each incursion native lifeways were further displaced, and Native communities near Denali were not immune. For some, as noted in *Tales from the Dena*, "formerly self-sufficient Native families have found themselves unable to live without assistance, as the economy has shifted from that of subsistence fishing, hunting, and gathering to one increasingly based on jobs, contracts, and cash—a new life for which they were not prepared."

SUBSISTENCE

> *We feel that subsistence living offers a rare opportunity to experience some of the basic satisfactions in life, an opportunity which is becoming harder to find in our society. It seems to us important to sustain and encourage the option of this lifestyle, just as society attempts to retain a working knowledge of many other arts or crafts which, to a large extent, have been bypassed by twentieth-century technology.*
>
> —BISHOP REPORT, 1978

The word "subsistence" carries negative connotations in a society that equates happiness and success with conspicuous consumption. One dictionary definition—having "the minimum (as of food and shelter) necessary to support life"—implies a bare-bones and uncertain way to survive in the context of twenty-first-century America.

Contemplate, instead, "real being," the first definition provided by Merriam-Webster, and subsistence becomes alluring. That doesn't mean there isn't uncertainty in subsistence living; it is hard work, and requires knowledge, tools, and skills that, for Native Alaskans, have accumulated over generations. But with that experience in hand and heart, subsistence is attractive.

For many residents of the forty-ninth state, Native and non-Native, living adjacent to Denali National Park or farther afield, the "real being" definition is truest. There is richness in subsistence here, in the fish, the caribou and moose, the berries, the warmth of pelts, the timber used to build shelters and fuel fires. There is also richness in the lifestyle that subsistence living provides, in the ties that bind families, link villages, and fix people to the land. It's a lifeway that inspires deep connection to the environment.

It's also a way of life protected, and circumscribed, by law.

In 1980 the Alaska National Interest Lands Conservation Act (ANILCA) moved millions of acres in the state into the public lands system, including four million acres surrounding the original Mount McKinley National Park. As vast tracts were secured in the public domain, the rights of "ownership" shifted to the federal government, including the right to prohibit the removal of resources, such as game, from the properties. Recognizing the impact the new law would have on rural residents and the indigenous people who had relied on those resources for generations, ANILCA contains provisions that ensure the right to "conduct subsistence activities" on some of the lands. In parts of the new Denali National Park and Preserve, as in portions of other expanded national parks and in new parks created under ANILCA, hunting, trapping, fishing, and timber-cutting for shelter and firewood were permitted.

Other provisions of ANILCA—which was extremely controversial when enacted and remains subject to conflicts in interpretation—limit those activities to ensure the sustainability of resources. For instance, the harvesting of game and fish are subject to "bag limits, methods of take, [and] seasons of take," and the National Park Service and state are charged with monitoring "customary trade" of subsistence harvests, including the trapping of game for hides, to make sure it conforms to traditional subsistence uses.

When Mount McKinley National Park became Denali National Park and Preserve, the two-million-acre core of the park, which surrounds the Denali massif and includes a narrow buffer on the south slope of the Alaska Range and a broader buffer to the north, was designated Wilderness. It is completely off-limits to hunting, even by Native peoples.

Within the park and preserve at large, which spreads north and south of the Wilderness boundary, subsistence activities are permitted. In parcels specifically designated preserves—large blocks of land to the northwest and southwest—sport hunting is permitted.

For residents of the remote communities bordering Denali, like those near Lake Minchumina and Nikolai, interaction with the park proper and its designated Wilderness is ongoing. The populations of these communities are small: Nikolai, an Athabascan village on the Kuskokwim River, had fewer than a hundred residents, according to the 2010 census; Lake Minchumina was even smaller in 2010, with about fifteen year-round residents, mostly non-Native. Telida, with an "old village" dating to 1899, is now abandoned. These villages are so far distant from the core of the park that visitors might never know that their residents hunt, fish, and log within its boundaries, as permitted by ANILCA.

A relatively modern picture of the subsistence lifestyle practiced near Denali is drawn in a National Park Service research report from 1978. The Bishop report focuses on Lake Minchumina and Nikolai, where subsistence living is foundational.

The village at Lake Minchumina, north and west of the park boundary, was sparsely populated until white prospectors began to arrive in the early 1900s, according to the report. From the time the Kantishna stampede hit its height, just after the turn of the twentieth century, and into the 1920s, the community's population grew. The number of trappers living at the lake peaked at fourteen in the 1930s. There was another population "boom" in the 1940s, in conjunction with construction of an airstrip as part of the war effort, and after World War II ended, some residents stayed on to staff a Federal Aviation Administration station at the lake. In 1975, pre-ANILCA, the report cites a population of twenty-nine souls, some part-time.

Given that moose and caribou in the area were abundant in the 1950s and 1960s, hunters from Lake Minchumina had minimal impact on the robustness of the herds. Residents hunted black bears, but not grizzlies. As had been the case for native Athabascans for generations, big game was augmented with small game, including ptarmigan, hares, grouse, ducks, and geese. Fish of all kinds—"humpbacked whitefish, broad whitefish, long-nosed sucker, northern pike, and burbot"—were caught, and this bounty was used on the table, as bait, for dog food, and for fertilizer. Those living in Lake Minchumina harvested wild berries and grasses as foodstuffs and to craft into goods for sale or trade, and cultivated gardens planted with potatoes, cabbage, and carrots as primary crops, and beets, turnips, rutabagas, celery, broccoli, and other herbs and vegetables to supplement. In the black spruce bogs and flats, trappers caught wolves, lynx, wolverines, marten, mink, otters, red foxes, beavers, ermines, weasels, and "some coyote." Marten, beaver, and mink were the most valuable resources in terms of fur, which could be considered part of "customary trade."

But even "at its most intense, hunting has been relatively light," the report notes. The subsistence practices of Lake Minchumina's residents never posed a threat to the balance of wildlife populations in the broader Denali ecosystem or beyond.

The impacts of subsistence hunting out of Cantwell, a larger town in the Ahtna homeland on the south side of the Alaska Range, are much more visible in the park. Because ANILCA permits subsistence hunters access to resources, residents of Cantwell and other communities can use ATV roads to reach hunting and fishing grounds. Hunting is also allowed in Kantishna, just north of the wilderness boundary, and the few residents with inholdings in the old mining boomtown can drive private vehicles up the park road to reach their properties and harvest resources in the region. While private vehicles are typically prohibited on the park road, this ANILCA provision has an upside, according to one park ranger: Having a subsistence hunter toss a bull moose onto a Denali National Park bus loaded with tourists is just a bad idea. Better to have it in the back of a truck, covered with a tarp, so park visitors might not even know it's there.

Since ANILCA was enacted, the park has carefully monitored subsistence activities within its boundaries. A 2012 state-of-the-park report does not make note of harmful impacts to any animal populations. Instead, the report states, "There is some concern about the continuity of subsistence, because there are fewer youth in subsistence communities near the park."

Recognizing the ongoing importance of subsistence to Alaskan cultural identity and the richness of Denali's subsistence legacy, and working within the limitations of ANILCA's mandates, the park service continues to foster traditional uses on the lands it oversees. Permits are granted annually so that subsistence hunters may take caribou and moose outside designated Wilderness, and traplines extend into the preserve from traditional communities. As Raymond Collins observed in *Dichinanek Hwt'ana*:

> *One of the aspects of Denali National Park that should be remembered and honored . . . is that it is part of the heritage of the Athabaskan people of Nikolai and Telida, and other Interior Athabaskans. Their recent relatives and ancestors used these lands for hundreds, if not thousands, of years but left a very light footprint. When one travels from Denali Park down the Kuskokwim valley toward Telida and Nikolai, it is very difficult to determine any changes in the nature of the land until approaching the communities themselves. There are trapline trails and a few scattered cabins but even these trails are used more by animals than people. The Park can be considered wilderness, not because it has been protected from human use, but because the people who used it for thousands of years did not attempt to change its basic nature.*

Endurance

Though the changes have been profound, today's Athabascans share more with the first Alaskans than just proximity to the High One. Subsistence is no longer the only way to live on the land, but the tradition of hunting caribou and harvesting fish from clearwater streams remains. And Athabascans have taken back control of their own destinies in other ways. Native corporations, whose shareholders are Athabascan, Tlingit, Aleut, and Inuit, were established as part of the Alaska Native Claims Settlement Act (ANCSA) in 1971, and today play significant roles in fighting for Native rights within the state.

Specific to Denali National Park, Fairbanks-based Doyon Ltd., the corporation owned by Interior Athabascans, holds a concession in partnership with Aramark. This concession represents a financial bond to a homeland Doyon's shareholders can no longer lay claim to. The corporation also operates the Kantishna Roadhouse, a backcountry lodge on an inholding within the park boundary. Doyon owns nearly all of the land allocated to it by ANCSA outside the park, making it "the largest private landowner in the state," according to the corporation's website. Whatever wealth Doyon accumulates through its land ownership and businesses it returns to its shareholders, with the goal of ensuring that Athabascans have access to education, jobs, and the traditional, natural resources of the land that has sustained them for millennia.

Chapter Three

Mountaineering: First to the Top

As little by little we gained higher and higher eminence the view broadened, and ever new peaks and ridges thrust themselves into view. We were within the hall of the mountain kings indeed; kings nameless here, in this multitude of lofty summits, but that elsewhere in the world would have each one his name and story.

—Hudson Stuck, *The Ascent of Denali*

For most mountaineers the highest peak on any continent is, by definition, the most desirable. And the ultimate prize is to be the first.

An unknown Athabascan may have reached Denali's summit before Walter Harper and his teammates in 1913, but no story survives. Then again, perhaps in prehistory it was enough to live with the mountain; there was no need to conquer it.

Not so for the white man in the modern age of exploration. At the turn of the twentieth century, a number of expeditions set off on quests of discovery in the Arctic and Antarctic, as well as in other remote pockets of a world where unknowns were fast becoming known. The spirit that drove men to sail uncharted waters; to trek across the vast unmapped interiors of Africa, South America, and Asia; and to blaze trails through the American West found new life in journeys at the tips of the earth.

Exploration was a rich white man's game. With one notable exception those who led the earliest expeditions on Denali were wealthy, educated, and from the East Coast. They belonged to exclusive clubs, some of which survive into modern times, like the National Geographic

The mountaineer's goal: Denali's summit peaks.
PHOTO COURTESY OF THE NATIONAL PARK SERVICE, DENALI NATIONAL PARK AND PRESERVE MUSEUM COLLECTIONS. PHOTO BY P. G. SANCHEZ.

Society and the American Alpine Club. Their ambitions were informed by their reputations both as adventurers and as contributors to science. They not only had to claim the summit; they had to document what they encountered along the way. Denali's early climbers generated a treasury of volumes detailing their expeditions: what they ate, what they hunted, what they saw, what they forded, how they overcame, how they failed. They also asked and attempted to answer the bigger questions: Exactly how high is the roof of North America? What obstacles does a mountaineer face on Denali? What toll does altitude take on the human body? What is the best route to the top? What tools are best for the task?

But for all the other intentions, the main motivation was clear: These men wanted a crown. They wanted to be the first to conquer Denali.

Going Remote

It ended up being a slow race to the top. Summit attempts took months to plan and carry out. If approached from coastal ports to the south, getting to the Alaska Range required torturous trailblazing travel through thick forest, up thunderous rivers, over ridgeline after ridgeline. The journey was shorter, though not much easier, from Fairbanks in the Interior.

Once a base camp was established low on one of Denali's glaciers, a storehouse of supplies had to be ferried through a booby trap of crevasses to camps at higher and higher elevations. And that's where things got even trickier.

Mountaineering rangers at the Walter Harper Talkeetna Ranger Station say it's not uncommon for visitors to ask how climbing Denali compares to climbing Mount Everest. Such a comparison, while incomplete in terms of all the subtleties, does inform an understanding of what climbers, including those on the earliest expeditions, face on their summit bids.

The obvious place to start is height: Everest, at 29,028 feet, is the highest peak on the planet; the summit of Denali, at 20,310 feet, is nearly two miles lower. It's not as high as many peaks in the Himalayas and Karakoram, or as high as a number of Andean mountains, including Aconcagua, the highest mountain on the South American continent. On that simple score there's really no comparison.

But that doesn't begin to tell the story.

The first thing that sets Denali apart is its latitude, and the radical weather generated by this northern exposure. Rising just two hundred miles south of the Arctic Circle, Denali is the coldest and stormiest of the Seven Summits; the rest are close enough to the equator to escape the extremes of cold, snow, and wind that regularly blast the High One. Gusts exceeding one hundred miles per hour have blown climbers off the peak. Three feet of snow can fall overnight. In the spring climbing season, temperatures can drop to –40 degrees Fahrenheit; in winter temperatures famously can reach –148 degrees Fahrenheit . . . or lower. The average temperature on the summit of Everest in winter is a comparatively balmy –33 degrees Fahrenheit.

As one of the park's mountaineering volunteers put it, "The weather will do what Denali wants it to do."

Next, there's vertical relief. The distance from base to summit on Denali exceeds that of Mount Everest, and of most mountains on earth, for that matter. From the mountain's foot a climber must ascend more than 18,000 feet to reach the top. Even when deposited at 7,200 feet, the elevation of today's base camp on the Kahiltna Glacier, more than 13,000 vertical feet of rock and ice rise above. On Everest, with base camp at 17,500, climbers ascend about 11,500 feet to the summit.

Denali doesn't have a "death zone," as do Mount Everest and other peaks that exceed 8,000 meters (~26,000 feet). But that doesn't mean the air doesn't become seriously thin. Denali's climbers don't need to carry oxygen, but altitude-related illnesses are still a real possibility. At 10,000 feet it's not uncommon for those who aren't acclimated to feel the effects of altitude, including shortness of breath, headache, nausea, and general malaise. Some climbers are crippled by altitude sickness (or acute mountain sickness), forcing them to abort their missions. At Denali's summit atmospheric oxygen is less than half that at sea level, which markedly increases the risk of life-threatening altitude-related illnesses such as high-altitude pulmonary edema (fluid buildup in the lungs) and high-altitude cerebral edema (fluid buildup in the brain). The only cure for these is descent.

And mountaineers on Denali face what might be considered "standard" dangers, hazards common on Everest and other extreme peaks. Glaciers require special care and skill to safely navigate. The literature is thick with stories of experienced climbers plunging into glacial crevasses that, as one ranger described them, are "large enough to swallow a train." Avalanche is another threat: In stories, Denali's avalanches materialize as massive clouds of ice or are felt as earthquakes. On the Wickersham Wall they rain down with alarming frequency.

Combine the commonplace with the weather extremes imposed by latitude, and Denali can only be characterized as a mountain unlike any other. The variables have become better understood with time and experience, but still present formidable obstacles, even for the best prepared modern climber.

As for Denali's first mountaineers, they had no concept of what they would face on their summit attempts . . . which makes their stories all the more compelling.

The First Try

James Wickersham was one of thousands of prospectors who flooded into Alaska during the Klondike gold rush in the final years of the nineteenth century. But Wickersham set himself apart from the crowd with qualities other fortune hunters didn't possess: political savvy, staying power, and a passion for mountaineering. He didn't strike it rich in the Klondike, nor when he followed the yellow metal west to Fairbanks, but he found other ways to prosper in his adopted home. He became Interior Alaska's first district court judge, was instrumental in founding what would become the University of Alaska, served as the territory's first congressional representative, and was among those who promoted the establishment of Mount McKinley National Park. He left an indelible mark on America's northernmost territory.

He also led the first summit assault on Denali.

Wickersham was an experienced mountaineer and prospector by the time he led his expedition to Denali in 1903. Born and educated in Illinois, the judge lived for a time in Tacoma, Washington, where, according to historian Tom Walker, he climbed a number of peaks in the Olympic and Cascade mountains. Appointed to Alaska's sprawling Third Judicial District as the Klondike gold rush waned, he set up shop initially in Eagle, downstream on the Yukon River from Dawson City, in 1900. The judgeship took him to the goldfields in Nome before depositing him in Fairbanks, site of yet another gold rush. Denali and the Alaska Range are where the eye turns in Fairbanks on any sunny day, and the mountaineer in Wickersham awakened. He wanted to climb that peak.

He assembled and outfitted a team, and then employed a steamer called the *Tanana Chief* to assist in the long approach via the Tanana and Kantishna Rivers. Heading cross-country up the McKinley River toward the mountain's base, he staked mining claims on several creeks, which helped trigger the short-lived Kantishna gold rush, which in turn triggered interest in setting Denali aside as a national park. He also sprinkled names on the creeks and mountains he passed, including Mount Deborah, for his wife. Walker relates that the peak already had a name—Mount Foraker—but that another Alaska Range peak would come to bear Mrs. Wickersham's name.

The judge's Denali climb ended at one of the most impressive faces on the mountain. The Wickersham Wall, which writer Kim Heacox calls "one of the most daunting mountaineering challenges in the world," rises 14,000 feet from the Peters Glacier to the summit of the North Peak. A broad, convoluted mash-up of ice cliffs and chutes, the wall is notoriously swept by avalanches "[s]nowslides of every size, and every form of glacial movement, are on exhibition in this great natural amphitheater . . ." Wickersham wrote in his memoir, *Old Yukon: Tales, Trails, and Trials*. In 1903 it was an obstacle the judge and his team were not equipped to surmount. Wickersham turned away.

But his failed summit attempt was hardly a defeat for the lawman, who went on to champion Alaska, then still a territory, as a nonvoting delegate to Congress. In addition to backing the establishment of Mount McKinley National Park, he was also instrumental in building the Alaska Railroad. He secured home rule (an elected legislature) for the territory and proposed the first statehood bill, though that status would not be granted until 1959, long after Wickersham's death.

As for the Wickersham Wall: It wouldn't be climbed for another sixty years. In 1963 a seven-man team from the Harvard Mountaineering Club, following a scary route that had been scoped out by renowned cartographer and photographer Bradford Washburn, took more than a month to summit Denali via the Wall. It took the men "only two days to come down, taking the easy route on the other side," climber John Graham remembered.

A Most Arduous Hoax

> *I found it interesting to try to note the reasons why men go to this far-off northland to fulfill the ambitions of the prospector, the hunter, or the mountaineer . . . We were all the wildest kind of dreamers.*
>
> —Frederick Cook, *To the Top of the Continent*

Dr. Frederick Cook was a veteran Arctic and Antarctic explorer with a solid reputation, and it seemed only natural that he should claim the first ascent of the highest peak on the continent. The claim would prove false, but Cook made it anyway.

The doctor met defeat on Denali on his first summit attempt in 1903, and owned up to the failure. On that expedition he and his team of four approached from the south side and crossed the Alaska Range to the west of the massif, with the goal of attempting to summit from the north side. The journey involved weeks of challenging wayfinding and trekking through rugged woodlands plumbed with swollen rivers. The expedition was thwarted by impossible terrain at about 11,000 feet. Despite earnest scouting, "we were compelled to acknowledge defeat, for there was no way around the succession of sheer granite cliffs," Cook wrote in *To the Top of the Continent*, a chronicle of his Denali adventures.

But Cook didn't backtrack; instead, his expedition chalked up a significant first by circumnavigating the Alaska Range. It wasn't an easy exploration by anyone's reckoning. "Continued rains, thick underbrush, rapid streams, and difficult slopes, as well as horseflies and mosquitos, all combined to retard progress," Cook wrote of the trek. Robert Dunn, whose *Shameless Diary of an Explorer* is considered a classic in adventure literature, is blatantly, sometimes hilariously, forthcoming on the hardships, as well as critical of the leadership qualities of Cook, whom he refers to sardonically as "the Professor." A sample of Dunn's recollections as the men struggled to drive packhorses through the lowlands on the approach: "Oh, our beautiful oaths! Hot, hungry, dizzy, insane with mosquitoes, we struggled waist-deep in yellow muck, unsnarling slimy cinches, packing, repacking the shivering exhausted beasts. It was endless. Torture."

And this about the foiled summit attempt: "Up shot the talus, straight as Jacob's Ladder, into the clouds and we hanging to it . . . we kept now to rock slide, to snow slide, to glacier-edge. Heads bent to stomachs, sweating, gasping, we stopped to turn in silence every two hundred steps and view the poor horses, reduced to specks in their snowy purgatory, headed in on an island among crevasses. . . ."

On his second attempt to summit Denali in 1906, Cook again made the long, arduous approach from the south. He was accompanied by a solid team of adventurers and scientists and outfitted with horses and a motorboat. The journey was documented by Cook and also by Belmore Browne, who would lead two subsequent expeditions to the mountain.

Browne's account arguably does the more accurate job of laying out the trials of the trek. In *The Conquest of Mount McKinley*, he writes of crawling on "hands and knees" through the brush, body pierced by devil's club thorns, "trail chopping" through dense spruce forests, and following moose tracks and the "rut left in the wet grass by a passing grizzly." The team's horses served as pack animals and as "ferry-boats," the men clinging to their backs as they swam the swollen rivers.

In the end the great white wilderness surrounding Denali whipped the team back southward toward what passed for civilization in Alaska at the time. While the rest of the team transported horses, equipment, and stories back from the high country, Dr. Cook and a single companion, Edward Barrill, traveled back into the Alaska Range, looking for an alternative route by which to attempt the summit in another season.

In *To the Top of the Continent*, Cook describes, in what he clearly hoped was convincing detail, how he and Barrill discovered a potential route while scouting on the Ruth Glacier, which Cook named for his daughter. Carrying what Cook determined were the basic necessities, including stoves, food, sleeping bags, and ice axes—their packs, he claimed, weighed about forty-five pounds each—he and Barrill negotiated sketchy terrain, dug into a frozen mountainside to ride out a storm anchored only by their ice axes, and scaled formidable slopes in their impromptu bid. On September 16, 1906, Cook declared, the two cleared the summit.

"At last! The soul-stirring task was crowned with victory; the top of the continent was under our feet. Our hands clasped, but not a word was uttered. We felt like shouting, but we had not the breath to spare," he wrote of the pinnacle moment.

To document his achievement, Cook took a picture of Barrill planting a flag on a pyramidal, snow-covered cone that was touted among colleagues, patrons, and in the press as proof of his success.

But Cook's triumph was called out as suspect by Browne and others who had been part of the 1906 expedition. They knew from hard experience that Cook and Barrill couldn't have approached, summited, and returned in the span of time Cook reported, nor could the two have made the summit with the supplies Cook said they carried: "I knew it in the same way that any New Yorker would know that no man could walk from the Brooklyn Bridge to Grant's tomb in ten minutes," Browne wrote.

The story further unraveled when Barrill, who initially backed the explorer's story, recanted. Cook's reputation took another slam when his claim as the first to reach the North Pole in 1908 was challenged by Arctic explorer Robert Peary, who made the same claim in 1909. His reputation clouded by suspicion, the doctor had his membership in several prestigious alpine clubs rescinded, and the Explorers Club sponsored a second expedition, with Belmore Browne at the helm, to investigate Cook's first ascent claim.

Debunking Dr. Cook

The fundamental cause at the bottom of all the dissensions that have occurred in the history of exploration is selfishness.
—Belmore Browne, *The Conquest of Mount McKinley*

When the Explorers Club expedition, under the leadership of now experienced Denali climbers Belmore Browne and Professor Herschel Parker, returned to the mountain in 1910, the mission was threefold. Claiming the summit was, of course, at the fore, but the team was also charged with mapping "the impressive mass of peaks and glaciers that guard the great mountain's southern flanks," and was primed to prove Dr. Cook's fraud.

The Browne-Parker party mostly ditched the use of horses on the approach to the south side of the massif, instead traveling up the Susitna and Chulitna Rivers in a motorboat. The *Explorer*, with a few harrowing exceptions, powered up the big rivers like a champ, though the swift currents were an ongoing challenge. Browne and his men slammed the vessel into gravel bars on occasion (the team carried extra propellers just for such accidents), and in *The Conquest of Mount McKinley*, Browne describes eddy-hopping from one side of the thundering Chulitna River to the other to make progress upstream, "slowly climbing the current as a salmon climbs a fish-ladder. It was thrilling work."

By the time the team reached the Ruth Glacier, Browne knew Dr. Cook couldn't have reached the summit. He and his men had been methodically ferrying supplies from camp to camp, and given the distances involved and the difficult terrain, Cook and Barrill hadn't had enough food and fuel to summit and return alive. Adding to the evidence, another team on the mountain, from Oregon's Mazama Mountaineering Club, used the same Ruth Glacier approach and came to the same conclusion. Browne and his companions, in the process of exploring the uncharted glacier, winding around crevasses and under seracs, eventually found the point where the Cook photo had been staged. Browne pegged the point, now known as Fake Peak, at 5,300 feet in elevation and twenty miles from Denali's summit. "Our mountain detective work was based on the fact that no man can lie topographically," Browne observed.

The fraud unveiled, Browne and his team set their sights on the summit. But Denali turned them away, thwarting them with yet more impossible terrain—in this instance an obstacle dubbed "the Great Serac"—and by torturing them with snow blindness and inclement weather. It would be several years before Browne could return to the mountain for a third try. In the meantime, a ragtag crew of miners took a shot at the prize, aiming to show the hoity-toity mountaineers from Outside how it was done in Alaska.

The Sourdough Expedition

They hadn't the faintest idea of how to climb a mountain.
—Grant Pearson, *My Life of High Adventure*

The men who made up Denali's 1910 Sourdough Expedition didn't care about science. Their packs contained no instruments, no cameras, no fancy gear. They did, however, carry a singular and important tool: a fourteen-foot-long spruce pole with an American flag attached, which they planted on the summit of Denali's North Peak (a penultimate summit about eight hundred feet lower than the mountain's South Peak) to prove a point.

Prospectors from Kantishna, hardened by labor in the placers on the skirts of the great peak, the Sourdough team approached Denali with grit and disdain. Their assault on the roof of the continent was unapologetically ego-driven. Damn the fancy-pants newcomers from the East Coast; damn that poser Frederick Cook and his questionable claim to a first ascent. These four frontiersmen—Tom Lloyd, Billy Taylor, Pete Anderson, and Charley McGonagall—would climb the mountain better and faster, and would leave indisputable evidence of their conquest for all to see.

Yes, the spruce pole. The rationale was that, planted on the North Peak, it would be visible on a clear day to anyone in Fairbanks who had a good scope.

And what of equipment? The prospectors' gear was unorthodox, even for the times. They used snowshoes on the snowfields; their crampons were homemade; they wore "bib overalls, long underwear, shirts, parkas, mittens, shoepacs (insulated rubber boots), and Indian moccasins," according to journalist Bill Shernowit. The climbers ascended the Muldrow Glacier unroped, "a practice most contemporary McKinley mountaineers would consider foolhardy." And they piled snow on poles to cross crevasses they couldn't jump.

As for rations on the summit push, forget pemmican, raisins, hardtack, and tea. These guys made it to the top fueled by a thermos of coffee and donuts.

Yes, donuts.

But in some ways the outfit was proven—after all, the climbers were equipped with gear that had been used for years in the frigid goldfields of Alaska and Canada's Yukon Territory. The hard work of prospecting had conditioned the summiters well. The two men who planted the pole at 19,470 feet climbed more than 8,000 feet on the summit day and then descended the same distance, completing what one ranger described as "essentially the first flash ascent" on Denali.

The Sourdoughs' accomplishment astounds Denali's climbing and ranger community to this day. "They had clumsy home-made climbing irons strapped to their moccasins, and home-made hooked pike poles in their hands," wrote future park superintendent and climber Grant Pearson in *My Life of High Adventure*. "They didn't bother to rope themselves together, and they cut no steps. It was every man for himself, with reliance solely on crampons. They hadn't the faintest idea of how to climb a mountain."

The Muldrow Glacier flows between high peaks; this photo was taken from a plane piloted by famed Denali flier Don Sheldon.
PHOTO COURTESY OF THE NATIONAL PARK SERVICE, DENALI NATIONAL PARK AND PRESERVE MUSEUM COLLECTIONS. PHOTO BY PETER SANCHEZ.

But they had donuts . . .

Though one of their motivations had been to put Dr. Cook in his place, the singular achievement of the Sourdoughs would be called into question after the fact as well, a likely outgrowth of what journalist Shernowit calls the "barroom braggadocio" that instigated the expedition in the first place. The Kantishna miners had been outraged by "Doc Cook" and his bogus claim. Yet in his account of the expedition, published locally in Fairbanks and in the *New York Times*, leader Thomas Lloyd falsely asserted he was part of the Sourdough summit team, when in fact only Billy Taylor and Pete Anderson had reached the North Peak. Given Lloyd's unfortunate declaration, a lack of corroboration from teammates who'd returned to remote Kantishna, and a confluence of other evidence that contradicted Lloyd's account, "the team's true feat was transformed into an Alaskan tall tale," Shernowit wrote in *To the Top of Denali*.

Two years later, however, their accomplishment would be verified by the Stuck expedition. As they neared the saddle between the North and South Peaks, wrote Archdeacon Hudson Stuck in his memoir, *The Ascent of Denali*, "all at once Walter [Harper] cried out, 'I see the flagstaff.' Eagerly pointing to the rocky prominence nearest the summit—the summit itself is covered with snow—he added: 'I see it plainly!'"

The archdeacon also wrote that "the men who accomplished the astonishing feat of climbing the North Peak, in one almost superhuman march from the saddle of the Northeast Ridge, could most certainly have climbed the South Peak too."

But they may have needed another donut or two.

Almost There

The wind sang a grand, deep song among the sharp peaks and desolate gorges, and a great spout of snow shot high into the air where the narrowing mountain walls confined the wind.

—Belmore Browne, *The Conquest of Mount McKinley*

Belmore Browne and Herschel Parker returned to Denali for another attempt on the yet-unclaimed South Peak in 1912. This time the team set off from the coast in the waning months of the winter and employed sled dogs to take them up the Copper River rail line to the trail that passed through the Alaska Range via Broad Pass to the north side approach, where Wickersham and Cook had been stymied but the Sourdoughs had had their success. Warm weather rendered the trail treacherous on the south side, with dogs, sleds, cargo, mushers, and passengers all subject to "killaping" (tipping) when the snow was too soft. When the trail was properly iced over, however, the going was swift and easy.

The team arrived on the north side in April, where Browne was "delighted" to discover that one branch of the Muldrow Glacier "made a roadway to the very base of Mount McKinley." The team established a base camp and commenced ferrying supplies up the Muldrow, gaining altitude and experience as they ascended. By mid-June the team members were rested, had bolstered their strength with a diet supplemented by wild game, and were ready for a summit attempt. Parker, Browne, and Merl La Voy comprised the summit team, with the fourth expedition member, Arthur Aten, staying behind to mind the camp.

Over the next few days the three men climbed and cached, climbed and cached, and Browne kept meticulous record of the terrain they covered and the dynamic movements of the terrain on the mountain. In hindsight he reflected that what he assumed was the rumble and boom of shifting ice might, in fact, have been the eruptions of the Katmai volcano, more than three hundred miles distant. The climbers also marveled at the size of Denali: "It is reared on such a gigantic scale," Browne observed, "that ice slopes that only look a few hundred feet high may be several thousand." They camped in what Browne called the Big Basin, "the wildest and most desolate spot imaginable," and there, at 15,000 feet, they were snowbound for a time. They camped again at 16,000 feet, and finally at just above 16,600 feet.

On the summit day they topped 20,000 feet and then were stopped by a building chaos of snow and wind. "The last period of our climb on Mount McKinley is like the memory of an evil dream," Browne recalled. They knew they were close—they could tell by the easing of the slope—but they were also beginning to freeze. Recognizing their mortal peril, Browne turned to Parker and yelled, "The game's up; we've got to go down."

Their defeat still rankles even armchair mountaineers; this brave and careful party was likely within about two hundred yards of the summit. "They came within an ace of success," observed Hudson Stuck.

And still they persevered. After descending and resting for a day, and despite difficulty with consuming enough calories—they couldn't digest their pemmican, a mixture of meat and fat that was a staple for mountaineers and other backcountry travelers at the time—Browne, Parker, and La Voy tried again. They didn't make it quite as high before yet another storm drove them back. At that point, with weather, exhaustion, and a lack of supplies conspiring against them, the team decided to retreat for good.

But the vagaries of the Alaskan wild weren't quite done with these beleaguered mountaineers: A massive earthquake hit after they arrived back at base camp. The eruption of Novarupta in what is now Katmai National Park and Preserve shook the earth for hundreds of miles. In Katmai it created the Valley of Ten Thousand Smokes; in Denali it shattered rock and ice, reshaping ridges and mountainsides.

"A deep rumbling came from the Alaskan Range," Browne wrote. "It had a deep hollow quality that was unlike thunder, a sinister suggestion of overwhelming power that was terrifying." As he watched, the range "melted into mist" as it was engulfed in avalanches. The earth began to "heave and roll," a lake nearby "boiled as if it were hot," and as the faces of the hillside around the camp split, the "cracks filled with liquid mud." A few moments later the climbers watched as the western flank of Mount Brooks gave way in an avalanche of "overpowering grandeur." The "great white cloud" that rose from the collapse "billowed upward with startling rapidity, two—three—four thousand feet until it hung like a huge opaque wall against the range, and then it fell." The men scrambled to secure their tent before the cloud slammed into them at sixty miles per hour.

And then they headed home.

Browne's efforts on Denali might technically be considered defeats, but the mountain didn't inspire defeat in the man. Instead, the expedition leader became a champion of the peak and its sublime surroundings, working with Charles Sheldon and Judge Wickersham to surmount the tangled terrain of moving legislation for Alaska's first national park through Congress and onto the president's desk.

The First Ascent

> *I would rather climb that mountain than discover the richest goldmine in Alaska.*
>
> —Hudson Stuck, *The Ascent of Denali*

Hudson Stuck, Episcopal Archdeacon of the Yukon, had the experiences of Browne, Cook, and the Sourdoughs to draw from when he launched his 1913 quest for the summit of Denali. He also pulled together an exceptional team of untested but soon-to-be-proven mountaineers in Harry Karstens, Walter Harper, and Robert Tatum.

Karstens, the expedition's coleader, had a solid reputation as a backcountry traveler, having followed the lure of gold from his native Chicago to Dawson City, then down the Yukon to Fairbanks, and also from crisscrossing Alaska's Interior behind a sled dog team as a mail carrier. He had experience specific to Denali, having freighted mail to Kantishna during its boom days and having worked with hunter and naturalist Charles Sheldon, making forays into the wild from the cabin he helped build on the Toklat River in 1907–08. In *The Ascent of Denali*, the archdeacon calls the young Karstens "strong, competent, and resourceful, the real leader of the expedition in the face of difficulty and danger."

Walter Harper was another fit and resourceful young man, an Alaskan native destined to be the first to stand on the summit. Stuck refers to him as a "half-breed boy"; his mother, Jennie, was Koyukon, and his father was Irish immigrant and prospector Arthur Harper. Raised in the Koyukon tradition, Walter was twenty-one when he joined the team and, in Stuck's words, "took gleefully to high mountaineering."

The third man, twenty-one-year-old Tatum, a native of Tennessee and a "postulant" at the Episcopal mission in Nenana, was brought on as cook. He proved nearly as stalwart and hardy as the other younger men.

Finally, two Native teenagers, Johnny Fredson and Esaias George, assisted the team on the long approach, which was made with the help of dog teams pulling sleds loaded with $1,000 of supplies. Esaias was cut loose from the team once base camp was established on April 15, and Johnny was assigned to maintain the camp while the other four aimed for the top.

The team, like those that preceded them, created camps higher and higher on the mountain, using dogs and sleds to ferry supplies that included silk tents (the team built igloos around the tent camps to protect them from weather); blankets, fur robes, and down sleeping bags; a trustworthy Primus stove and fuel; flour and baking powder for making bread; sugar and tea; figs and other dried fruits; erbwurst (a survival sausage); and homemade pemmican meatballs, following a recipe that involved cooking "joints" of meat in a lard can, shredding that meat, adding a "can of butter," salt, and pepper, and rolling it into balls. "We made a couple of hundred of such balls and froze them, and they kept perfectly," Stuck recalled.

As for mountaineering gear, the team brought along willow wands to mark routes through crevasse fields on the glaciers; ice axes (but only the utilitarian axes made in Fairbanks; Stuck noted the fancier ones "were ridiculous gold-painted toys with detachable heads and broomstick handles" and points that shattered when struck with force into ice); and amber-tinted snow glasses, hailed by Stuck as "an even greater blessing to the traveller in the north than the invention of the thermos bottle." From the miners in Kantishna the climbers picked up "enough large-sized moccasins to serve the members of the party." Stuffed with as many as six pairs of socks and outfitted with crampons—"terrible heavy, clumsy rat-trap affairs they looked"—the mukluk-like boots were the only footwear the expedition used to make the ascent.

The Stuck expedition followed the route blazed by the Browne-Parker expedition the year before. The first obstacle was the crevassed Muldrow Glacier. In Stuck's words, "one of us, at least, knew something of the dangers and difficulties its apparently smooth surface concealed, yet to both of us (Stuck and Karstens) it had an infinite attractiveness, for it was the highway of desire."

Stuck's account of the ascent is agreeable in tone, but the team had serious obstacles to overcome. After having a smoke at one of the high camps, either Stuck or Karstens tossed the match they'd used to light their pipes and torched the tent, destroying socks, gloves, and their sugar, powdered milk, and baking powder. Without the powder their flour was rendered inedible and their ability to consume enough calories to fuel the climb was in jeopardy. Fortunately, the pemmican meatballs survived.

The men also suffered symptoms of altitude sickness. Fifty-year-old Stuck was most seriously affected, attributing his difficulties in thin air to his age. Smoking couldn't have helped, but Stuck observed that "Karstens, who smoked continually, and Walter, who had never smoked in his life, had the best wind of the party." Still, Karstens would confess that he felt "heavy" above 13,000 feet.

The team's biggest hurdle, however, was the ascent of what would become known as Karstens Ridge. This had been described as a smooth passage by the Browne-Parker expedition, but in the wake of the earthquake of 1912, "there was a sudden sharp cleavage, and all below was a

The Stuck expedition, first to summit Denali's North Peak in 1913, included Robert Tatum, future park superintendent Harry Karstens, Alaskan native Walter Harper, and a pair of Native Alaskan teenagers named Esaias and Johnny.
PHOTO COURTESY OF THE NATIONAL PARK SERVICE, DENALI NATIONAL PARK AND PRESERVE MUSEUM COLLECTIONS.

jumbled mass of blocks of ice and rock in all manner of positions, with here a pinnacle and there a great gap," Stuck observed. "Moreover, the floor of the glacier at its head was strewn with enormous icebergs that we could not understand at all." What had taken Parker and Browne a few days to surmount would take Karstens and Harper more than three weeks to hack a path through, hewing "a staircase three miles long in the shattered ice."

But with the exception of the ravaged ridge, Stuck admitted that "Denali is not a mountain that presents special mountaineering difficulties of a technical kind."

Summit day dawned cold—Stuck recorded the temperature at the high camp at –21 degrees Fahrenheit in the morning, warming to –4 degrees later in the day under clear skies. With the exception of Harper, "we were rather a sorry company," as Tatum and Stuck nursed headaches and Karstens suffered "internal pains." Thus it was that "Walter, who had been in the lead all day, was the first to scramble up; a native Alaskan, he is the first human being to set foot upon the top of Alaska's great mountain, and he had well-earned the lifelong distinction," Stuck wrote. Karstens was right behind. The archdeacon was last, and admitted that he "had almost to be hauled up the last few feet, and fell unconscious for a moment upon the floor of the little snow basin that occupies the top of the mountain."

On the summit the team spent more than an hour conducting scientific experiments to help determine the exact height of the peak. Stuck also hammered another nail in the coffin of Dr. Cook's first-ascent claim. Commenting on the spectacular views, particularly the appearance of Mount Foraker, also known as Denali's Wife, the archdeacon wrote, "We were all agreed that no one who had ever stood on the top of Denali in clear weather could fail to mention the sudden splendid sight of this great mountain."

As for achieving the ultimate first, Stuck wrote:

> *There was no pride of conquest, no trace of that exultation of victory some enjoy upon the first ascent of a lofty peak, no gloating over good fortune that had hoisted us a few hundred feet higher than others who had struggled and been discomfited. Rather was the feeling that a privileged communion with the high places of the earth had been granted, that not only had we been permitted to lift up eager eyes to these summits, secret and solitary since the world began, but to enter boldly upon them . . . to inhabit them, and to cast our eyes down from them, seeing all things as they spread out from the windows of heaven itself.*

A Quiet Exhale

After the Stuck expedition the slopes of Denali went quiet. For nearly two decades not a single attempt was made on the summit. While the glaciers ground down, and the winds whipped, and the jumbles left by the 1912 earthquake settled and froze into place, a national park was established around the peak. World War I raged. The National Park Service was established. Alaska settled into its long tenure as a territory of the United States. A railroad linking Seward to Fairbanks was completed, with a station established at McKinley Park. Construction began on a long road that would eventually connect the rail line with the mining town of Kantishna, where a small community of men and women chipped at the skin of the mountain, not to scale its heights but to extract its riches. A trickle of tourists began to drift north to experience the wilds surrounding North America's highest point. But none expressed a desire to scale its imposing heights.

Chapter Four

Kantishna

One forgets, sometime, on seeing the bearded faces in the old photographs, or on listening to a bent old sourdough recall the good old days, that the great majority of those who took part in the stampede were young men . . . They were young enough to see a mountain and climb it, though they had never climbed a mountain before; to see a glacier and cross it without second thought.

—Pierre Berton, *The Klondike Fever*

In American history two gold rushes stand out. The first blew open the western continental United States in 1848, when gold was discovered on the American River in the foothills of California's Sierra Nevada. Tens of thousands of hopefuls poured across the High Plains, the Rocky Mountains, and the rippling Great Basin to the mother lode; thousands more came from farther afield, pouring across the seas. Boomtowns popped up wherever the diggings were promising, populated in short order by prospectors and their attendant cooks, dry goods dealers, carpenters, saloonkeepers, dance hall proprietors, and ladies of the evening. A few of the forty-niners got lucky: William Bourn with his Empire Mine in Nevada City; George Hearst with his Ophir Mine, which delved into neighboring Nevada's Comstock Lode. Most went bust within a few years. The fortunes that endured belonged to entrepreneurs who sold miners the goods they needed to support their obsession, like the blue jeans made by Levi Strauss, the banks run by Henry Wells and William Fargo, and the enterprises of merchant turned railroad tycoon turned politician Leland Stanford.

The second gold rush blew open a new frontier in Canada's Yukon Territory, and spilled over into America's Alaska District. Sparked by the discovery of what one historian termed a "thumb-sized chunk of gold" on a tributary of the Klondike River in 1896, tens of thousands of young hopefuls stampeded into the remote, inhospitable, and sometimes deadly north country. It took most argonauts a year to reach the diggings on the Klondike from the Lower 48, a journey that involved hauling thousands of pounds of gear over infamous mountainous terrain like that traversed by the Chilkoot Trail. More than forty thousand people eventually reached the Yukon goldfields, many of them landing in Dawson City, the boomtown that burst to raucous life at the confluence of the Yukon and Klondike Rivers. Others settled in—or got stuck in—gateway burgs like Skagway, which flourished in a murderous way at the foot of the Chilkoot Trail. Both towns survive into modern time, now mining the wallets of tourists who sift the placers hoping to uncover the rogue nugget missed a hundred years before.

As the gold on the Klondike dwindled, prospectors drifted down the Yukon into Alaska, looking for the "next big thing." That turned out to be in Nome, all the way west across the Alaskan Interior, where a handful of miners had discovered riches in the sands deposited by grinding rivers and streams as they fanned out into the Pacific. As far as mining went, Nome was widely regarded as a cakewalk. You could reach the goldfields by boat, as opposed to marching for miles through storms over mountain passes, and pay dirt was on the beach, easily recovered with tools as mundane as a shovel and bucket.

Midway between the Klondike and Nome, another strike was made. When an Italian immigrant named Felix Pedro discovered gold at the confluence of the Chena and Tanana Rivers in 1902, an enterprising E. T. Barnette publicized the find. Prospectors flooded the outpost where the rivers met, and camps that sprang up in the broad river valley eventually coalesced into a town called Fairbanks. The profiteering came hard and fast: By one estimate $10 million worth of gold was panned and pummeled from the riverbeds of the "Golden Heart City" over the life of the Fairbanks rush.

The Tanana is fed by the Kantishna River, which is fed by Moose Creek and Friday Creek and Slippery Creek and other streams that bleed off the Kantishna Hills. In their gravels each of these waterways carried the promise of glittering minerals and the women, whiskey, and prosperity it could buy. As with Sutter's Mill, the Klondike, and the beachheads of Nome, it was only a matter of time before something precious was found in the foothills surrounding the High One.

The Kantishna Stampede

The rush to Kantishna predated the establishment of Mount McKinley National Park by more than a decade. Prospectors had delved into Denali's foothills in earlier years, but the Alaska Range had yet to provide stampede-caliber temptation. That changed after Judge Wickersham attempted to climb Denali in 1903. The judge was a veteran of the Klondike gold rush, and neither his passion for dispensing justice nor for mountaineering completely cured his gold fever. The judge couldn't help himself: He did a little prospecting as he headed up the mountain. He sifted color from Chitsia Creek and staked a handful of mining claims. Then he brought the news back to Fairbanks.

In 1905 a pair of prospectors following up on the Wickersham find had more significant luck in the Kantishna Hills. Joe Quigley and partner Jack Horn made a modest strike on Glacier Creek. While they were in Fairbanks recording their claims—Quigley, by one account, had in his possession a two-ounce nugget of raw gold that was impetus for the stampede that followed—another pair of prospectors, Joe Dalton and Joe Stiles, struck gold on nearby Eureka Creek.

Reports of the discoveries lit a fire in Fairbanks—not hard to do, since prospectors, like tinder, flare up with the slightest spark. Miners swarmed the Kantishna Hills. By late summer 1905 about two thousand people, by some estimates, occupied boomtowns—Glacier City, Roosevelt, Diamond, and Eureka—that sprouted up at the confluences of the promising streams, each town outfitted with the full complement of saloons, dry goods stores, roadhouses, sawmills, and other establishments

Shannon's Mine on Slippery Creek in summer 1941.
PHOTO COURTESY OF THE NATIONAL PARK SERVICE, DENALI NATIONAL PARK AND PRESERVE MUSEUM COLLECTIONS.

to support the placer miners. Any gear or foodstuffs the miners couldn't find or produce on-site was freighted more than one hundred miles from Fairbanks by river, while flows permitted, and by sled dog team come winter. Eureka became the enduring hub of the district. Once a post office was established, the camp was renamed Kantishna. Among the mail carriers traveling by dogsled in winter were Harry Karstens and Charley McGonagall.

Folks who would become integral to the park's personality and development established claims in Kantishna rush, including Tom Lloyd and McGonagall of the Sourdough expedition, Fannie and Joe Quigley, John and Polly Anderson, and Johnnie Busia. They all worked claims, but some branched into other occupations, like the Andersons, who went on to run a roadhouse and fox farm in the region following the boom.

The easiest gold to recover was in the placers—a word derived from the Spanish meaning "shoal" or "deposit." The gravel bars of the creeks and streams flowing out of the Kantishna Hills held (and hold) plenty of promise—not only for gold, but for antimony (used in the manufacture of ammunition in the Russo-Japanese War and later in World War I), zinc, lead, silver, copper (think Copper Mountain before it was renamed Mount Eielson), and coal (which was mined from an outcrop on what would become known as Coal Creek to fuel equipment used in construction of Denali Park Road, and also produced at the East Fork Mine).

But the Kantishna stampede, like so many before, was short-lived. According to historian Jane Bryant, the value of the gold wrested from Eureka Creek in the two-year-long heyday of the rush was about $150,000. Historian Tom Walker notes that Dalton and Stiles "brought in flakes and nuggets worth $86,000," and a nugget weighing forty-three ounces, dubbed "Queen of Eureka," was unearthed on the Discovery claim. But "less than a dozen men struck it big," Walker notes in his history of the rush and its aftermath. Thus, despite whatever potential riches the Kantishna still held, by the time autumn glazed the tundra with frost in 1906, most of the prospectors were moving on. They'd wrested what they could from the glacier-tossed gravel bars and virgin mountainsides, and the payout was no longer worth the time and effort. After all, Nome was still in play, and elsewhere in Alaska a bonanza of pristine rivers and streams awaited exploitation.

After the Rush

About fifty hardy, persistent souls remained in the Kantishna after the rush, still hitting modest pay dirt in the placers and enamored of the wilderness they had staked claim to. The boomtowns became ghost towns, with the miners working out of cabins scattered along creeks in steep drainages sculpted for isolation. Among them was Joe Dalton, who mined on and off on Eureka Creek until he was found dead in his Kantishna cabin at age seventy in 1943. Lloyd and McGonagall persisted as well, as did the Andersons, Busia, and the Quigleys. They and a handful of others formed a scattered community sustained by what they could dig up and translate to cash, the food they cultivated in gardens, and the game they trapped and hunted in the wild.

As was the case elsewhere in frontier Alaska, life in the post-stampede town was rough. Winter shut down most mining enterprises, and the residents resorted to trapping or hunting to sustain themselves. Not least among the hardships was cabin fever, which Walker documents vividly in his history, *Kantishna.* Unable to endure the isolation of the long, wicked winters, some men went mad ("got bushed")—especially those who responded to the cold by "hibernating" in their mean cabins. The men who fared best, the historian notes, were those who stayed active, hunting and trapping even in the dark and snow. Walker also notes an interesting potential contributor to the cabin fever problem: Miners were exposed to lead and mercury in the course of their work, both of which are toxic and linked to mental health issues.

The Quigleys had some modest success in the years following the rush, expanding into hard-rock mining on what is known as Quigley Ridge. Both Joe and wife Fannie staked claims, but Joe proved a "superb prospector," according to Walker, and was able to ferret out deposits of value time and again. His most promising hard-rock strikes came during the Kantishna's second wind, which followed World War I, the completion of the Alaska Railroad in 1923, and construction of the Denali Park Road, which worked westward from McKinley Park Station and the railroad toward the hamlet through the 1920s and into the 1930s. The Little Annie claim, leased to a developer with deeper pockets than the Quigleys', produced promising gold- and silver-bearing ore that was shipped to San Francisco for processing. But the yearlong turnaround, including recovery, shipping, and smelting, proved fiscally prohibitive, and the developer bailed out.

Quigley's Red Top claim was a bit more lucrative and long-lasting. Though the miner pried pay dirt from the claim for years, friend and park ranger Grant Pearson recalled that "he'd have made more money if there had been a smelter closer than 1,900 miles away."

The Red Top was eventually leased and, according to historian William Brown, became one of three mines that improved output from the Kantishna District in the latter half of the 1930s and early 1940s.

Three people, identified as Joe and Fannie Quigley and John Busia, stand next to hydraulic mining equipment.

PHOTO COURTESY OF THE NATIONAL PARK SERVICE, DENALI NATIONAL PARK AND PRESERVE MUSEUM COLLECTIONS.

Known in those years as the Banjo Mine, the enterprise included an "airstrip, mill, assay shop, bunkhouses, blacksmith shop, and other facilities." But work on the claim fizzled within a couple of years, shut down by costs and, with the advent of World War II, a ban on gold mining as nonessential (though mining for antimony and some placer mining did continue, according to historian Erik Johnson). The mine experienced a brief revival in the 1970s, but the Mining in the National Parks Act of 1976, which required that mining activity on parkland "be conducted so as to prevent or minimize damage to the environment and other resource values," combined with an injunction on mining instituted in 1985 after environmentalists raised concerns about impacts, "effectively ended mining operations in the Kantishna Hills," Johnson explained.

The environmental consequences of placer mining in the Kantishna, as elsewhere, were problematic. Prospectors with shovels and sluices disrupted the long-established beds of Kantishna's glacial streams, left tailings (piles of potentially toxic debris) to leach into the waterways, and harvested more than their share of the local wild game populations.

The mercury used to process gold from ore also had a deleterious effect on wildlife, as did poison set out by market hunters to keep scavenging wolves and foxes from consuming cached carcasses, according to Walker.

But that was nothing compared to the damage wreaked by hydraulic mining, which came into play during the district's resurgence in the 1920s. The technique, developed by Anthony Chabot in the Sierra Nevada during the California gold rush, involves firing pressurized water into ore bodies or creek beds, and is capable of tearing down mountains. It was outlawed in the Golden State when the runoff clogged river channels as far downstream as the San Francisco delta and caused massive floods in flatland towns.

In the Kantishna two operations, the Kantishna Hydraulic Mining Company (KHMC) and the Mount McKinley Gold Placers Company, set up shop in the 1920s. Tempted by the prospect that transportation to the district would be easier with the Alaska Railroad in place, and given that the legislation establishing the neighboring national park was friendly to mining interests, the companies believed they had the means to deliver heavy equipment to the placers. The KHMC built a dam to supply hydraulic "giants," or cannons, that were aimed at the streambed of Moose Creek near its confluence with Eureka Creek. But, according to Johnson, despite receiving money for improvements, the trail between the old boomtowns of Roosevelt and Eureka proved as frustrating for the hydraulic companies as it had been for prospectors in the stampede nearly two decades earlier. Fortunately, from an environmental standpoint at least, the returns of the operation didn't justify the outlay of capital, and the KHMC pulled out quickly. After 1924 the hydraulic works, including the dam and an associated ditch, were abandoned.

The company's bunkhouse was commandeered by miner and trapper Johnnie Busia, who spent much of his life in Kantishna, part of the core community that endured in the district into the 1940s. His contributions to the hospitality that visitors like National Park Service ranger Grant Pearson enjoyed in the mining enclave included storytelling, backwoods savvy, and a homebrew known as "Kantishna champagne." Reflecting on the brew's potency, Pearson said, "After one drink you started talking to yourself. After two drinks you answered yourself."

Once most mining in the park was shut down during World War II, Kantishna's population dwindled further. By 1944 only a handful of people remained in the former boomtown. Some small-scale mining continued in the ensuing decades, and with a spike in gold prices following its delinking from the U.S. dollar in the 1970s, mining in Kantishna saw another brief revival. But the focus, by that point, was shifting toward tourism in the national park next door.

How to Mine a Park

Preserving the rights of miners in Kantishna was built into the legislation that established Mount McKinley National Park. The men who championed preservation of the massive game refuge—hunter and naturalist Charles Sheldon, Judge Wickersham, explorer Belmore Browne, and others—recognized that Alaskans would have to back the park to win congressional approval, and to court Alaskans, mining activities in the future preserve would have to be protected. Provisions sanctioning mining activity in a national park had precedent; mining rights were recognized in the legislation that established Mount Rainier National Park in 1899 and Crater Lake National Park in 1902. There was also precedent for the conservation of mineral deposits, which was the case in Yosemite, Yellowstone, and Sequoia National Parks.

The McKinley park bill also expressly permitted miners and prospectors to hunt game within the park for subsistence, but not for commercial sale. This addressed the depredations that spurred Sheldon's campaign for a "Denali" national park in the first place; he'd witnessed the wholesale slaughter of caribou, moose, and Dall sheep by market hunters, and the ancillary damage those hunting practices wreaked on other animals within the ecosystem, including wolves, foxes, and bears. Sheldon and other park advocates knew that, as was the case for mining, without making allowances for subsistence, Alaskans would balk and the legislation would never see the presidential pen. The provision allowing miners to hunt in the park was rescinded in 1928 due to enforcement difficulties.

The Kantishna District lay outside the initial boundaries of the park, though mining activity sprawled across the hills along the borders.

To ameliorate any uneasiness between miners and the fledgling park—viewed as the long arm of an intrusive government—Superintendent Harry Karstens, a Klondike gold rush veteran, cultivated friendships and fostered good relations with his mining neighbors and encouraged his rangers to do the same. This went some distance toward softening the blow when the park's boundary was stretched northward in 1932, encompassing Wonder Lake and bucking closer to active mineral claims.

Relations with miners got stickier in 1980, when the American National Interest Lands Conservation Act (ANILCA) became law. ANILCA's multimillion-acre additions to the park encompass most of the Kantishna Hills and most of the claims therein. By the time ANILCA hit the books, the population of active miners in the Kantishna was minuscule, so few active claims were negatively affected. On the plus side the park was also now charged with protecting the remnants of Kantishna's long mining legacy, such as the cabin where Fannie Quigley lived out her days, which is being considered for National Register of Historic Places status.

Some mining still takes place within the park today—mostly placer mining on inholdings, but exploratory mining as well. The inholdings are steadily being acquired by the park, an outgrowth of a lawsuit filed by environmental groups charging that Denali was ignoring the negative impacts of continued placer mining on the park's waterways and ecosystems. This led to an injunction on mining on federal parklands throughout the state until environmental assessments could be completed, and, at least within Denali, mining's never fully kicked back into gear.

But mining is not dead in the park, either. In the years since the injunction, a couple of miners have applied to work their Denali claims—the *Fairbanks Daily News-Miner* reported on one claim being considered by the park in May 2016. The owners of other claims are, in the words of one park ranger, "holding out hoping for more money" from a government buyout. It's a reasonable gamble, given that the value of Kantishna inholdings has shifted from mineral wealth to tourist wealth. And tourism, as the ranger pointed out, is a more appropriate use of parkland.

Making a New Mint

These days Kantishna mines tourists. Instead of log shelters isolated in taiga and tundra, the mining district is outfitted with several wilderness lodges that offer what would be, for a turn-of-the-twentieth-century sourdough, luxurious accommodations: cozy cabins, comfy beds, prepared meals, optional massages, and guided nature hikes into the hills and to Wonder Lake, where visitors can enjoy spectacular views of Denali when the clouds lift.

But some things stay the same. Kantishna is still "out there." It takes time and effort to reach, via either a long bus ride up the Denali Park Road or a scenic flight from Fairbanks or Anchorage. There's no Internet connectivity and no power grid. Come wintertime the place shuts down, but for a few hardy souls content to maintain the properties in the splendid seclusion of a Denali backwater village.

The lodges are, like the remnant mining claims, located on inholdings. Doyon Corp., the Athabascan native corporation that holds a park

Fannie Quigley and Chris Edmunds, foreman of the Alaska Road Commission, stand in front of Quigley's Kantishna cabin.

PHOTO COURTESY OF THE NATIONAL PARK SERVICE, DENALI NATIONAL PARK AND PRESERVE MUSEUM COLLECTIONS.

concession in joint venture with Aramark, runs the Kantishna Roadhouse Backcountry Lodge (not to be confused with the historic Kantishna Roadhouse, which was completed in 1920 for the region's mining commissioner and served as post office and community meeting place into the 1930s). Camp Denali was built on a mining claim by bush pilots and conservationists Ginny Wood and Celia Hunter; it was purchased by Wally and Jerryne Cole in 1975, and as of 2017 was operated by the Coles' daughter Jenna and her husband, Simon.

In terms of hospitality Kantishna is like many surviving gold rush towns. At Sutter's Mill in Coloma, tourists hunker alongside the American River with pans, hoping to wash out a few flecks that miners might have missed 150 years earlier. So too in Dawson City on the Klondike, where old saloons and cathouses list in the shifting permafrost and the Yukon flows with a ferocity the American River can only aspire to. Perched on the banks of icy Moose Creek, visitors to Kantishna can also try their luck, sifting placers awash in glacial milk, and, if they are lucky, go home with a fleck of Denali gold.

Going for Gold

In the wake of its gold rush, California would be farmed and developed. With its pleasant climate and linkage to the markets of the East Coast via railroad, it became America's Golden State.

Alaska was too remote, its weather too wild, its winter season too long, to support the same kind of golden dream. Instead, it celebrated its fierceness, its wilderness, its mineral deposits, and its oil repositories by becoming America's Last Frontier.

But the independence of the prospector, whether in the sun-splashed Sierra Nevada or the frigid heights of the Alaska Range, still resonates with residents of both states. There's a kindred spirit born of the gold rush mentality, which motivates creativity and free-thinking in both the frozen North and the far West.

There's an edge to this gold rush–born spirit of independence, however. The appeal of the get-rich-quick scheme is alive and well. Dig a bigger coyote hole; get a bigger pan. Map mountains; survey wildernesses so that claims can be staked and resources exploited. It still happens, all over the world.

The problem is that gold's value is hitched to a market cornered by a cadre of wealthy investors who hold the asset as a safe haven in the event of economic collapse—as though the bar in the safe or the ring on the finger can be exchanged for food or water in the postapocalyptic world they plan for.

In *The Age of Gold*, an examination of the California gold rush, author H. W. Brands writes, "Were the benefits worth the costs? To ask the question is to imply that an alternative existed. Maybe it did, but only if human nature could have resisted the temptation to seek a shortcut to human happiness." With the pursuit of happiness a cherished and inalienable American right, "when the gold of California promised a way to find happiness all at once, [Americans] couldn't resist."

There was no resisting temptation when gold was found in the Klondike, either. And the pursuit of golden happiness was taken to another extreme in Kantishna. But Kantishna lies in a land of extremes. Finding happiness there may start with a grubstake, or a mountain climb, or a hunt, but it's built of more than a nugget, or a summit, or a trophy. It's born when the essence of the place embeds itself, generating a different kind of fever, just as persistent but not as likely to be squandered.

Chapter Five

Denali in Two Steps: Defining and Redefining a National Park

Two defining moments stand out in Denali National Park and Preserve's century-long history: its establishment in 1917 and its massive expansion in 1980. In the context of the national parks idea, what was created in both instances was huge.

Both iterations involved drawing lines on the ground that shifted control of millions of acres to the National Park Service (NPS) and out of the hands of Alaska residents. Establishing those boundaries was delicate in the first instance and rancorous in the second, requiring persuasive and powerful men to both strong-arm and sweet-talk lawmakers and presidents.

Setting the boundaries in the first place was hard enough, given the conflicting interests of conservationists versus hunters, trappers, and prospectors in the early twentieth century. Blowing those boundaries outward more than six decades later, down the slopes of the Alaska Range to the south, across the Kantishna Hills to the north, and across the lowlands stretching toward the Kuskokwim River drainage to the north and west, resulted in fiery demonstrations. The Alaska National Interest Lands Conservation Act (ANILCA) removed millions of acres from unrestricted public use in a territory where use moves across the landscape based on the seasonal advance and retreat of snow lines, on the flows of rivers, on the migrations of fish and game, on when plants flower and fruit, and on tradition. Making lines on a map conform to those ebbs

A car passes through Mount McKinley National Park's gateway arch (circa 1930).
PHOTO COURTESY OF THE NATIONAL PARK SERVICE, DENALI NATIONAL PARK AND PRESERVE MUSEUM COLLECTIONS.

and flows, as well as the conflicting interests of political, commercial, and private enterprises, has been an ongoing challenge.

Between those two pivotal events, Denali's evolution as a national park was slow and careful, centered around construction of a single scenic road stretching ninety miles from entrance to terminus and a smattering of tourist facilities built along the route. It was also guided by recognition of the assets that brought the park into being: its spectacular wilderness landscapes and its abundant wild game.

"Discovering" Denali

Bands of Athabascans have lived in the shadow of Denali for generations, their material lives revolving around the resources at its base. Explorers from Outside, creeping inland from the coast starting in the eighteenth century, defined the mountain in a different way. Rather than an object of reverence and power, Denali was an X on the map, a distant and impressive landmark. Given the vastness of Alaska as an unexplored territory, it took a while before any Outsiders reached that X.

Mapmaking in Alaska began with the exploratory expeditions of Russia's Vitus Bering. By command of Tsar Peter the Great, Bering ventured into the northern seas on two journeys of discovery—the first in 1728 and the second in 1741. The goal was expansion of the empire, a survey to find a connection between Russian Siberia and the North American continent. The Bering expeditions proved the continents weren't connected and generated maps of the Alaskan coastline that enabled colonization.

The Russian colonial movement picked up steam in the 1740s, driven by the fur trade. Russian pioneers established missions and trading posts along the Alaskan coast from Sitka to the Kenai to Nome. They didn't delve far into the Interior in those early days, but it's hard to imagine they didn't notice the massive peak that dominated the snowy range north of what would become known as Anchorage. The peak would make the Russian map in the mid-1800s, according to park historian Erik Johnson, with the name Telida. Russians also called the peak Bolshaya Gora, the "big mountain."

The next recorded sighting of the peak was made by George Vancouver, a British explorer who ranged along the Pacific coastlines of Oregon, Washington, British Columbia, and Alaska in the early 1790s. He named a number of peaks and landmarks on his journey, but of Denali, histories only record his mention of the Alaska Range as "distant stupendous mountains covered with snow" far north of Cook Inlet.

Americans on missions of Alaskan discovery didn't reach the Interior until the mid-nineteenth century. Naturalist William Dall, for whom the Dall sheep that would play a singular role in the ultimate preservation of the park are named, made note of the Alaska Range in 1866 while traveling on the Yukon River. At about the same time, a trapper named Arthur Harper—father of Walter Harper, first man to stand atop Denali—also mentioned a "great ice mountain to the south" while exploring along the Tanana River in the late 1860s. But history doesn't record whether either man gave the peak a name.

By this time William Seward, Secretary of State for Abraham Lincoln and Andrew Johnson, had negotiated the purchase of Alaska from Russia for $7.2 million—though the transaction has been called, with questionable historic veracity, "Seward's Folly," it turned out to be a fantastic deal. Though technically part of the United States starting in 1867, Alaska was remote enough that only the hardiest Americans ranged north to settle there, and government was virtually nonexistent. That changed upon the discovery of gold in the Yukon in 1896 and the subsequent population influx that numbered in the tens of thousands. Given the disorderly nature of gold rushes in general, the enforcement of law and order, however scanty, became necessary. The attention of the federal government on the law side included the installation of territorial judges. To get a grip on the topography and natural resources of the new territory, cartographers from the U.S. Geological Survey and scientists from the U.S. Biological Survey spread across the future state. These scientific and mapping expeditions eventually reached the Denali massif.

Frank Densmore was among the flood of fortune seekers; this prospector reportedly waxed so poetic over the beauty of Denali that for a time it was known as Densmore's Mountain. The name McKinley was bestowed not by a trained cartographer but by another prospector, William Dickey, in 1896. Though William McKinley was only the Republican nominee for president at the time and had no connection whatsoever to the distant peak, he backed the gold standard, a policy that Dickey favored. The name McKinley stuck.

A Stampede Begets a National Park

> *The only other region on this continent which might be included in a comparison with this region of the Alaska range for the grandeur of the scenery and the topographical interest is the Grand Canyon.*
>
> —Charles Sheldon

Neither Densmore nor Dickey established lasting prospects on the mountain; that would come when territorial judge James Wickersham attempted to climb the peak in 1903. He staked a series of claims on Chitsia Creek in the Kantishna Hills after returning from the aborted climb to Fairbanks, opening the remote and daunting terrain to miners, hunters, and trappers.

The Kantishna stampede that followed lasted about two years. In that time the flood of hopefuls took a hefty toll on the big game that roamed the flanks of Denali. With two thousand people suddenly concentrated in the prime forage of the Kantishna Hills, animals large and small were hunted not just for subsistence but also for market. The market hunters tallied staggering numbers of kills, drastically reducing the caribou, moose, and Dall sheep populations in the region. Even after the bulk of the prospectors moved on to other goldfields, park historian Frank Norris notes that "between 1913 and 1916, market hunters harvested between 1,500 and 2,000 Dall sheep each winter from the Toklat and Teklanika river basins alone."

Charles Sheldon, a conservationist and hunter cut from the same cloth as the likes of Theodore Roosevelt, witnessed firsthand the devastation wrought on the spectacular white mountain sheep that he loved (and loved to hunt). On two trips to the Alaska Range, the first in 1906 and the second over the winter of 1907-08, Sheldon indulged his passions for exploring, hunting, collecting plant and animal specimens (many ending up with the U.S. Department of Agriculture), and compiling the copious notes that would become his *Wilderness of Denali*. His companion on the Toklat River was a veteran of the Alaskan frontier, Harry Karstens, who became a close friend and, years later, Denali park's first superintendent.

The depredations of market hunting on the Dall sheep population, as well as on Denali's caribou herds, moose, grizzlies, and fur-bearing residents including wolves, foxes, and wolverines, appalled Sheldon. He returned from his sojourns with a mission: to ensure that Denali was preserved as part of America's new national parks system.

The presence of the tallest peak on the North American continent, and the stunning landscapes that surround it, might have been enough to garner national park status for the region eventually. But Sheldon and another park advocate, mountaineer Belmore Browne, had a bigger hook: the wild game. Setting Denali aside as a refuge would remove its game from the market, ensuring that herds, packs, and individuals had an opportunity not only to thrive but to support populations outside the park, and also to provide pleasure for sightseers. Whether for sport,

The park road and a cluster of buildings with Denali's northeast face as backdrop.
PHOTO COURTESY OF THE NATIONAL PARK SERVICE, DENALI NATIONAL PARK AND PRESERVE MUSEUM COLLECTIONS. PHOTO BY CHARLIE OTT.

market, or subsistence, hunting was critical to the welfare of all Alaskans, the park proponents argued, and could only be sustained if game around the mountain were protected and thoughtfully managed. If Denali's sheep, caribou, and moose were obliterated, hunters outside the region would feel the impact.

Sheldon and Browne took their proposal to the power hubs on the East Coast, including the Boone and Crockett Club, an exclusive and influential organization dedicated to hunting and conservation. The issue didn't gain urgency, however, until construction on the Alaska Railroad, connecting Seward on the coast to Fairbanks in the Interior, neared the Alaska Range. Having seen the chaos wrought by the Kantishna rush, Sheldon knew what the influx of men associated with the railroad could do to the game populations around Denali. In a letter sent to future NPS director Stephen Mather in December 1915, Sheldon, then chairman of the Boone and Crockett Club, wrote: "The region is a vast reservoir of game—sheep, moose and caribou, bears and the small animals. The building of the railroad will destroy the game for it will be killed to supply the construction camps." In considering Denali for a national park, he advised, "the idea of a game reservation should also be included."

Sheldon also enlisted the help of Judge Wickersham, by then serving in Congress as a nonvoting delegate from the Alaska Territory. Wickersham was behind the national park idea, having a deep appreciation for the mountain himself, but was keenly aware that subsistence hunting rights, as well as rights to mining claims, would need to be part of the park's enabling legislation. Another proponent was the railroad itself, which recognized the value of a national park as a draw for tourists.

Sheldon, Wickersham, and Browne helped draft legislation authorizing the park's formation in 1916, including a provision that prospectors and miners in the park "may take and kill therein so much game or birds as may be needed for their actual necessities when short of food, but in no case shall animals or birds be killed in said park for sale or removal therefrom, or wantonly."

The bill moved slowly through Congress, which had bigger things to cope with, including the world war that had enveloped Europe in the previous two years. But the legislative body had national parks on its radar: In 1916, Denali was passed by as parks were established surrounding Calfornia's Lassen Peak, which had erupted the year before in spectacular fashion, and Hawai'i Volcanoes, which oozed spectacular rivers of lava. Denali's enabling legislation was also delayed as proposed amendments were considered, and by the inevitable volleying back and forth of bills between the Senate and the House of Representatives.

But the park finally won approval in both houses, and Sheldon, who Norris noted "had moved from his Vermont home to Washington in order to help move the bill through Congress," hand-delivered the legislation to President Woodrow Wilson. Though Wilson was preoccupied with developments overseas, he found the time to put pen to paper to create something grand. On February 26, 1917, Mount McKinley became America's twelfth national park.

The Early Days

Getting the park established was step one. Step two involved getting money appropriated to manage said park.

That wouldn't happen for four years. The United States entered World War I just two months after Mount McKinley National Park was set aside. The NPS, established the year before, was minimally funded itself, and had to allocate its meager resources across all parks, including Yellowstone and Yosemite, where visitation was growing and encroachment was more pressing. McKinley was remote and easily overlooked. Meantime, railroad construction heading south from Fairbanks had reached Healy, not far north of the unmarked park boundary, and market hunting continued unabated.

The fiscal dearth ended in 1921, when survey work for the park was initiated. Also in that year, on Charles Sheldon's recommendation, Harry Karstens was installed as superintendent and chief ranger.

Karstens's appointment and tenure in the park is lauded across the historical board. He understood Alaska, he knew Denali, and he was a determined and dedicated man. He brought gusto and confidence to the position, the same qualities he'd exhibited in his previous endeavors as a prospector, mail carrier, guide, and mountaineer. He outlasted a number of subordinate rangers who came on board in the park's early days; they were turned off by the hard work, the long winters, the isolation, and the poor pay. Karstens had thrived with those impediments for most of his adult life. That's not to say he was perfect. Karstens is also remembered as volatile and uncompromising, characteristics that would eventually lead to his resignation.

But that was years down the line. Choosing a site for park headquarters was the first order of business, and Karstens settled on a parcel near Riley Creek. Building that headquarters was next up, and the superintendent did that himself, constructing the park's first residence (his "home cabin"), an office, and a ranger cabin. The site was near McKinley Park Station (aka "the Hole"), a small, rustic enclave established by miners at the turn of the twentieth century. McKinley Park Station began to blossom with construction of the Alaska Railroad's Riley Creek bridge, and again when trains began making stops at the McKinley Park depot.

The new superintendent did his share of politicking as well, lobbying with his friend Sheldon to expand the park boundary eastward, toward the Nenana River, to better facilitate visitation and also to monitor potential poachers. The expansion was approved in 1922, though it didn't extend all the way to the river.

And significantly, Karstens oversaw the survey and start of construction on the Mount McKinley Park Road (now the Denali Park Road), the sole track leading into the heart of the park. This road, he recognized, was key to meeting the second mandate of the NPS—to provide for the "enjoyment" of the scenic and wild wonders preserved within the parks. Survey and brush work on the road started in 1922, with the Alaska Road Commission providing the manpower.

In 1924, Karstens decided to move headquarters three miles up the rough park road, to a spot where the weather was warmer in winter and that was less prone to flooding in spring. By 1925 work was underway on a complex that remains the hub of administration in the park. Again, only Karstens and one or two rangers did all the work. Catering to visitors was not a major challenge and certainly not a time drain in the park's infancy, especially through the long winter months. That gave the

The Morino Roadhouse was a popular rest stop for early travelers to Mount McKinley National Park.

PHOTO COURTESY OF THE NATIONAL PARK SERVICE, DENALI NATIONAL PARK AND PRESERVE MUSEUM COLLECTIONS.

superintendent and his underlings plenty of time to dismantle and move the existing structures on Riley Creek, as well as build new structures, which involved felling trees, cutting and prepping logs, freighting the logs to the construction sites, milling lumber, and then putting it all together. The buildings, many now part of a National Historic District, conformed to the "Rustic" style that dominated park service construction of the time, and were reminiscent of the chinked log miners' and trappers' cabins that dotted Alaska's wildlands. Over the years buildings in the headquarters district would be moved, destroyed by fire, rebuilt, and repurposed. But what visitors see when they tour today's headquarters is mostly what Karstens saw: charming cabins with sloping roofs and narrow porches—functional structures built to withstand time and the elements.

Rangers also built a series of patrol cabins, again in line with what the miners and trappers used, with caches on stilts to keep supplies out of reach of wildlife. Some of the cabins were built alongside the park road as it progressed, roughly a day's travel distant from each other via dog team. Some have been maintained, while others fell into disuse and disrepair and ultimately were destroyed. In the 1930s the end of the patrol cabin line was the Kantishna ranger station, located in Big Timber. It was thoughtfully and laboriously built by rangers Fritz Nyberg and Grant Pearson; the latter spent two memorable winters stationed at the cabin while patrolling the park's northern boundary. When the park road reached Wonder Lake, a new end-of-the-line ranger station was constructed and the Kantishna station fell into disuse. A bear thrashed the place in the 1940s, but it was restored and used by hikers and mountaineers until consumed by fire in 1956.

McKinley Park Station

By the time visitors began trickling into the national park, McKinley Park Station had all the trappings of a small town. There was the Park Gate Roadhouse, run by Italian immigrant Maurice Morino, who offered both lodging and meals at his establishment. Historian Jane Bryant quotes ranger Fritz Nyberg's observations on the accommodations: "The bedding in the old Morino roadhouse was made from the hides of caribou and the menu was always beans and caribou meat." The roadhouse is also remembered as a "center for the rough and drunken element," as Morino was known to make and sell a potent "home brew."

Morino's second, larger roadhouse was, reportedly, a bit more refined, with comfortable beds and a more diverse menu. It was dubbed the Mount McKinley Park Hotel. Park service literature notes that "one visitor described the unusual, flat-roofed, two-story log building as 'Italian-Alaskan.'" The roadhouse stood long after Morino passed on; his homestead and all its associated buildings, rundown and long vacant, were acquired by the park in 1947, ten years after his death.

Other businesses popped up in McKinley Park Station as well, including Mary Thompson's trading post and Jack Donnelly's restaurant. Duke and Elizabeth Stubbs ran a fox farm nearby on Riley Creek. Morino ran the post office for a time. Bryant records this about the local schoolhouse, from the *Nenana Daily News* in December 1922: "At the present, McKinley Park has a day school, with an attendance of eight pupils, and a night school three times a week, with an attendance of six grown people. It is very gratifying to note the interest taken by these grown folks, who are desirous of improving their position in life."

When the park boundary was finally pushed east to the Nenana River in 1932, most McKinley Park Station properties became inholdings and were acquired by the park as owners died or moved on. There was talk of preserving some of them, including the old Morino roadhouse, as examples of pioneer construction. But before that could happen, in 1950, the roadhouse succumbed to a fire started by a cigarette-smoking "drifter" who planned to spend the night in the building. Other structures on the old Morino homestead, along with adjacent properties in McKinley Park Station, were eventually demolished by the park service.

In the meantime, a new McKinley Park Hotel was built, just uphill from the railroad station. The hotel's façade was painfully utilitarian from a modern point of view. What's captured in historic photographs is essentially a block of concrete with a flat roof; there is no hint of the charm that prevailed at park headquarters. Completed in 1939, the hotel was built by the Works Progress Administration, an agency created as part of Franklin Delano Roosevelt's New Deal. Its appearance

A crowd of visitors is pictured outside the McKinley Park Hotel in 1939.
PHOTO COURTESY OF THE NATIONAL PARK SERVICE, DENALI NATIONAL PARK AND PRESERVE MUSEUM COLLECTIONS.

was described as "an atrocious sight" by Jane Ickes, wife of Secretary of the Interior Harold Ickes. Park historian Frank Norris documents her description of an "elongated pile of bastard-modern, dun-colored boards, pierced by niggardly slits of windows . . . Without exception, it is an appalling monstrosity."

When park visitation was curtailed during World War II, the hotel was used by the military as a "recreation site," which seems appropriate given its resemblance to army barracks. After the original structure burned in 1972, a new McKinley Park Hotel was cobbled together using railroad cars. The hotel operated in that configuration until 2001, when accommodations being built outside the park, in what is known as Glitter Gulch on the banks of the Nenana, were able to more adequately fill the needs of visitors. Denali's visitor center now stands on the hotel site.

Another New Deal agency, the Civilian Conservation Corps (CCC), also left its mark on the park, as it did in a number of national parks in the Lower 48. C Camp, located just downhill from park headquarters, was the CCC camp from 1938 to 1939, and the young men who made up the corps were employed building the park's machine shop and residences for park employees, installing water lines, and in fire control and landscaping activities. The CCC also built the Wonder Lake Ranger Station, which was completed in 1939.

Concessioners, Visitors, and a Second World War

As is the case throughout the national parks system, Denali contracts with concessioners to provide services to visitors. The first concession was granted in 1923, to Dan Kennedy, and consisted of guided horseback excursions to a rustic camp—tents for sleeping, tents for cooking and dining—near the Savage River. Kennedy quickly fell out of favor; the park wanted tourism to expand, and Kennedy, arguing that there weren't yet enough tourists to make it worth his while, didn't comply. After a couple of years of wrangling, the park and Kennedy parted ways and the concession was granted to the Mount McKinley Tourist & Transportation Company (MMT&T Co.).

Under the MMT&T Co. banner, Savage Camp evolved into tourist central. After disembarking from the train at McKinley Park Station, visitors were ushered into automobiles (later buses) and driven up the rough park road to what was still mostly a cluster of tent cabins, along with a dance hall and a dining hall. The stay was typically short—one night or two—and meals were provided. Tourists could take guided hikes and horseback trips farther into the park, where they might see big game or, weather permitting, more of the big mountain. Interpretive programs were offered when ranger-power permitted, and Karstens was known to visit the camp on occasion, sharing stories about the first ascent of Denali around the campfire.

Bobby Sheldon was a popular fixture during his tenure as general manager at Savage Camp, telling stories about his gold rush adventures and attending to every detail of a visitor's stay. Sheldon arrived in Alaska as a teenager, part of the 1896 stampede to the Klondike goldfields. He started out in Skagway, where he witnessed the shooting of Soapy Smith, one of the most notorious figures from the rush. A skilled mechanic, Sheldon built the first car in Alaska using only "sketches" as a guide, telling ranger Grant Pearson he'd done it to impress a girl. After settling in Fairbanks, Sheldon and several passengers made the first automobile crossing of what would become the Richardson Highway: The group "jolted over washouts, plowed through slides and forded streams, covering 370 miles in 59 hours of driving time," historian Jane Bryant recounts in *Snapshots from the Past.* When he arrived in Valdez, Sheldon sold the auto and rode home on a bicycle, "becoming the first person to ride a bike from Valdez to Fairbanks."

The MMT&T Co. faced a number of challenges as concessioner. It survived a slump in park visitation in the 1930s, when the number of tourists sagged due to the Great Depression. Fewer than four hundred people made it to Denali in 1932 and 1933, a significant hit considering that about a thousand people had made the long journey to the park in more prosperous times. The abbreviated summer visitor seasons also curtailed business; no one visited when Denali was dark and cold. Once the McKinley Park Hotel was completed in 1939, the MMT&T Co. phased out Savage Camp at the behest of the NPS and phased in Camp Eielson at Mile 66 on the park road, hoping to take advantage of the views and access to the roadway to boost profits. But it remained difficult to make money in the park, and with the new hotel also sucking on the revenue stream, both enterprises suffered. The MMT&T Co. was rolled into the Alaska Railroad Company in the early 1940s, a move that consolidated the flow of tourists both getting to and traveling within the park.

The fiscal trials of concessioners weren't limited to the MMT&T Co. Until tourism began to gain steam in the latter half of the twentieth century—visitation doubled in the mid-1950s, when the Denali Highway opened, and doubled again in the early 1970s, after the George Parks Highway was completed—concessioners struggled financially. The hardships of the Great Depression were compounded by the advent of World War II, which slammed visitation even harder: A total of thirty-six tourists were officially logged between 1942 and 1945.

But World War II did something unexpected: It focused strategic attention on Alaska, and by extension on Mount McKinley National Park. While tourism was quashed in the park, the American military tested winter equipment—clothing, shelter, eyewear, supplies—on summit expeditions, a practice that continues into modern times. The Alaska

Highway (aka the Alcan Highway) was conceived and built in a rush in the early 1940s, opening vehicle access to the state from Canada and, by extension, the Lower 48. The long, then-unpaved road started from a hub in Dawson Creek, British Columbia, and ended in Delta Junction, not far south of Fairbanks. It was built so that matériel—tanks, planes, and personnel—could be transferred from America to its allies, in this case the Soviet Union. Construction peaked in 1942, with four hundred officers and nearly eleven thousand enlisted men plowing fifteen hundred miles of roadway through muskeg and permafrost in eight months, aided by more than fifty civilian contractors employing about seventy-five hundred men. The rough road opened in November 1942.

With the highway's completion, the Last Frontier cracked wide open. In the years after the war, as visitation at Denali spiked, companies found it easier to operate successful flightseeing, guiding, lodging, food, interpretative, and educational service concessions in the park. These days Doyon Corp., in joint venture with Aramark, holds a concession to provide transportation, food, lodging, and camping services to visitors out of the park's Wilderness Access Center. Other concessioners include Alaska Geographic (a park partner for half a century), which runs interpretive and education programs through the Murie Science and Learning Center, and the nonprofit Denali Education Center, which also offers interpretive programs.

Mission 66

Development of a hotel at Wonder Lake was long on the national park agenda. Superintendent Karstens first identified the scenic region as a possible site in the 1920s. Wonder Lake's allure—the water, the sprawling tundra, the iconic Denali views—was undeniable, and this was the impetus for its inclusion within the national park when the boundaries were expanded in 1932.

Though interest waned after the McKinley Park Hotel was up and running, plans stayed in the potential development mix for years, despite objections from more conservation-minded park supporters and administrators who felt that intensive development deep within the park was inappropriate. The Wonder Lake campground was built in the meantime, and when Camp Denali, a private enterprise run by the conservation-minded Celia Hunter and Ginny Wood, opened for business in 1951, interest waned again.

But with the advent of Mission 66, a ten-year, system-wide program intended to modernize aging infrastructure within the national parks, development proposed at the lake included not only a hotel, but also administrative and maintenance buildings, a service station, and housing.

Mission 66 sparked conflict throughout national parks, and Denali was not immune. Environmentalists and conservationists, including the Sierra Club and park champion Adolph Murie, lobbied hard to protect the wilderness setting at Wonder Lake and elsewhere. At the lake the conservationists eventually won; once Mission 66 was put to bed, plans

The west face of the Eielson Visitor Center in 1967; the building underwent a complete renovation in 2008.

PHOTO COURTESY OF THE NATIONAL PARK SERVICE, DENALI NATIONAL PARK AND PRESERVE MUSEUM COLLECTIONS.

for intensive development at Wonder Lake were put on ice. The ranger station and the campground are the man-made structures that survive. Though the ranger station is plagued by foundation problems—it turns out it was built on an "ice lens"—it is eligible for inclusion on the National Register of Historic Places.

But other Mission 66 developments in the park were completed, including a new visitor center at Mile 66 on the site of Camp Eielson. Though it boasted impressive views of Denali through massive picture windows, the visitor center drew scorn from conservationists like Murie, who derided its design as reminiscent of a fast-food restaurant.

Improvements to the Denali Park Road were also part of Mission 66. The vision was to widen and pave the roadway for its entire length. Some of this work occurred before conservationists quashed the effort, which is why the road is paved for fifteen miles, to Savage River. The park's shuttle bus system was initiated in the early 1970s, to enhance safety on the narrow, unpaved section of the roadway; reduce visitor interaction with wildlife; and improve the sightseeing experience. It's much easier to enjoy the views, after all, when someone else is behind the wheel.

ANILCA

Alaska is huge. Its people, Native and immigrant, are fiercely independent. It is detached from the nearest state by a thousand miles as the raven flies. For all these reasons and more, Alaska pretty much governed itself for decades after its purchase. In the wake of the Klondike gold rush, some federal legislative order was imposed, but the territory's population was self-regulating; only those with the toughest constitutions chose to live there, and they took care of themselves. Alaska was admitted to the union as the forty-ninth state in 1959, but even then, it was mostly left alone.

That all changed in the late 1960s when vast reservoirs of oil were discovered on the North Slope and offshore in Prudhoe Bay. Starting in 1967, America's largest oil companies headed north in a rush to claim the newfound black gold. Within six years the Alaska pipeline was approved and under construction, and by 1977 hundreds of thousands of barrels of oil were flowing eight hundred miles across the state from Deadhorse on the Beaufort Sea to Valdez on the Gulf of Alaska, where the bounty was shipped to refineries in the Lower 48.

Plans to extract the oil and build the pipeline brought conflict. Corporate efforts to control—to own—the land that underlay the resource and its sprawling supporting infrastructure kicked into high gear. The heaviest impacts fell, once again, on Alaska's Native peoples. Long victimized by the get-rich-quick schemes of Outsiders—fur trappers, market hunters, and gold diggers—they found their ability to abide in their ancestral homelands threatened once again by development of the oil fields.

This time, however, the world was changed. When Inuits, Athabascans, and others took a stand to defend their birthright, they found allies in the blossoming conservation and civil rights movements. While that stand didn't win them complete sovereignty, it did result in passage of the Alaska Native Claims Settlement Act (ANCSA), signed into law in 1971. The act created Alaska's Native corporations—for-profit entities that give tribes some control over their economic destinies, as well as the right to live in traditional fashion on their traditional homelands. These corporations were deeded forty-four million acres, which they hold in trust for the benefit of their Native shareholders. ANCSA also cleared the way for construction of the Trans-Alaska Pipeline System, and it included a provision backed by the conservation lobby that would eventually redefine land use in Alaska, including the use of national parkland.

ANCSA stipulated that, in addition to the forty-four million acres reserved as tribal lands, another eighty million acres of wildland be set aside as "conservation units" within the next eight years. Then–Secretary of the Interior Rogers Morton didn't waste any time: He designated those eighty million acres for withdrawal, and then some. Another eighty-eight million acres were targeted for study as additional conservation units and as buffers around the tribal reserves. The action infuriated many Alaskans; it was denounced by politicians and the press as a "massive land grab," a "sellout," and a "dirty deed." Lawsuits and negotiations ensued, and when the proposal reemerged, it had been whittled back to eighty-three million acres in total.

And then Washington imploded with the Watergate scandal. The proposition fell off the radar and wasn't revived until Jimmy Carter was elected president in 1976. When Morris Udall, a conservation-minded congressional representative from Arizona, introduced legislation to move the ANCSA provision along in 1977, he upped the ante again. To protect what he called Alaska's "crown jewels," his bill, H.R. 89, reserved 115 million acres.

Another round of political kickball followed. The bill was debated and modified and filibustered, batted between House and Senate, and nearly died in the delay. Congressional inaction lit a fire under the Carter administration as the deadline neared. It also fired up the state of Alaska, which attempted to leverage its own claims to the lands. Using the Antiquities Act and other legislation, Carter and his Interior Secretary, Cecil Andrus, withdrew more than 150 million acres from the public domain—and thus out of reach of mining and other commercial uses—in late 1978, setting aside study areas and seventeen new national monuments, including Denali National Monument. As an article by the Alaska Humanities Forum relates, this was without doubt "the most dramatic and sweeping withdrawal of public lands in the history of the nation, and it left Alaskans in a state of confusion."

Confusion and outrage, actually. President Carter was burned in effigy in Fairbanks, residents of Eagle made it clear they wouldn't abide by NPS rules, and protestors staged the Great Denali-McKinley Trespass. At least a thousand people, and maybe as many as three thousand by one report, gathered in Cantwell to protest the new Denali monument "with the goal of trying to violate 27 national monument regulations in two days, everything from using a public address system to skydiving and taking target practice," recalled an *Alaska Dispatch News* reporter.

When Congress took up the Alaskan land issue again after the Carter coup, two bills wound through the separate houses: Udall's bill in the House and a trimmed-back bill proposed by Alaskan Ted Stevens in the Senate. Another kickball game followed: more delay, more negotiations. After Jimmy Carter lost to Ronald Reagan in November 1980, and recognizing that the Alaska lands legislation would be dead on Reagan's desk,

Udall capitulated and persuaded the House to approve the Senate bill. Carter, the lame duck, signed ANILCA into law on December 2, 1980.

Denali in ANILCA's Wake

The numbers are impressive. With the passage of ANILCA, the acreage under federal management as conservation units in Alaska doubled to 222 million. According to the Alaska Humanities Forum, the federal government now owns about 60 percent of all land in Alaska, with the bulk of that property "off limits to most economic development." The reserves created by ANILCA fall under the auspices of the NPS, the U.S. Forest Service, the U.S. Fish and Wildlife Service, and the Bureau of Land Management. Ten new national parks and preserves were created, along with two national monuments and nine wildlife reserves, including the Arctic National Wildlife Refuge on the oil-rich North Slope.

The upshot for Denali: It became the Denali National Park and Preserve. Four million acres were added to the original Mount McKinley National Park, and the old park, renamed Denali National Park, was designated Wilderness, receiving extra protections. In the preserve and park outside the Wilderness, subsistence activities are permitted, and in the preserve sport hunting is allowed.

What's telling about ANILCA is that, while its provisions caused a huge uproar when they were enacted, most people touring Denali on any given summer's day thirty-five years later have probably never heard of the law. But the legislation is integral to the Denali experience. For example, a visitor can ride a bike up the Denali Park Road but can't take that bike into the Wilderness, which begins 150 feet from the road's centerline. A climber can take a plane to reach base camp on the Kahiltna Glacier, but that plane must land outside the Wilderness boundary. And in the preserve, far removed from the centers of activity near the peak and along the park road, people could shoot and trap the wildlife that most tourists travel to the park to take pictures of.

For the park service, passage of ANILCA required adaptation to a new set of rules and presented new challenges in terms of administering a park suddenly tripled in size. Given that ANILCA took nearly nine years to become law, the NPS had some time to prepare. But the process was hampered initially by inadequate funding, and required the careful rebuilding of relationships with neighboring communities, some of which had been badly damaged as the political wrangling unfolded.

Now, decades later, adjustments have been made and provisions integrated. Unlike visitors, however, park rangers are keenly aware of how important ANILCA was, and continues to be, to the administration and conservation of Denali National Park and Preserve. There are inherent contradictions to mediate—for example, attracting tourism with the lure of seeing big game while at the same time permitting the hunting of that game. With visitation growing every year, the park also grapples with ensuring access to its wonders while complying with both NPS mandates and provisions of the lands act to ensure that those wonders are preserved intact for posterity.

The trick: instilling an understanding that though Denali is vast, it is limited. There are boundaries to wilderness, and they change with the times. In the beginning two million acres was enough. In 1980 six million acres became enough. The story of how people use this place, like the story of the national park idea, continues to evolve.

Chapter Six

Of Sheep, Wolves, and Men: Charles Sheldon, Adolph Murie, and Gordon Haber

Iconic landscapes are the stuff of America's national parks, from Yosemite's waterfalls and monoliths to the Grand Canyon of the Colorado River and Yellowstone's simmering volcanics. Denali, the highest peak in North America, certainly qualifies as park material using that metric. But in the end, preservation of the mountain wasn't the prime motivation for inclusion in the national park family. Rather, it was the dynamic wildlife that ranged low on its folded flanks.

Most of Denali's "megafauna" are extraordinary, imposing creatures that stop the buses on Denali Park Road. The grizzly, the caribou, the wolf, and the moose are undeniably charismatic. But the quietest of the large mammals that comprise Denali's Big Five initiated the preservation movement—the Dall sheep, peacefully munching on tundra, looking down from on high. Dall sheep captured the imagination of Charles Sheldon, a wealthy young naturalist from back East who would dedicate roughly a decade of his life to ensuring that the landscape that nourished these animals was set aside for all time.

Adolph Murie assumed Sheldon's mantle as park wildlife champion in the 1930s. Enchanted by wolves, Murie, through his long-term, on-the-ground observations of Denali's packs, challenged the common perception of wolves as villains, showcasing the prominent role these predators play in the ecosystems they inhabit and helping reshape management policy toward predators not only in Denali but throughout the national parks. The work and advocacy of a more strident wildlife biologist, Gordon Haber, dovetailed with Murie's, though Haber's legacy has yet to be fully defined.

A ram strikes a pose in Denali National Park and Preserve.
PHOTO COURTESY OF THE NATIONAL PARK SERVICE, DENALI NATIONAL PARK AND PRESERVE MUSEUM COLLECTIONS.

Denali's preservation as a "game reserve" in Alaska—a territory defined by a tradition of hunting and fishing dating back millennia—has proven difficult to reconcile. The animals have no concept of the legislative battles won and lost on their behalf over a century. Boundaries drawn by politicians and bureaucrats are meaningless to the wild ones. For the people who hunt them, those boundaries and laws range from sacrosanct to disdained, and those conflicting views helped define, and then redefine, the park.

Sheldon and His Sheep

Naturalist and big-game hunter Charles Sheldon was a young retiree from Vermont who'd made a fortune in railroading and mining concerns. He was also fascinated by sheep. He'd already studied them in the Rocky Mountains and in northern Mexico, where his railroad had been located. Now it was time to challenge his inquiring mind with study of Alaska's fabled white mountain sheep. Sheldon undertook two Alaskan expeditions to study the creatures, and they, more than the scenery that surrounded them, inspired the conservationist to champion Denali for protection as a national park.

Sheldon first traveled to Denali in 1906, just as miners sifting the gravels of Kantishna creek beds began to realize that the gold had played out. He hired a packer named Jack Haydon as he passed through Dawson City, and in Fairbanks he hired Harry Karstens, another gold rush veteran, to help out as well. The three approached Denali via the Tanana and Kantishna Rivers, catching sight of the mountain as they crested a hill near Wonder Lake. Sheldon was smitten.

He'd fall ever more deeply under Denali's siren call as he observed, wrote about, and hunted its big game. The small expedition camped near the Toklat River, where hundreds of sheep roamed the hills. In *The Wilderness of Denali*, Sheldon compiled a hefty and detailed record of his time among the sheep, as well as the grizzlies, the caribou, the moose, and even the gray jay. From discussion with Karstens about the wonders of the place during their time together in the wilderness, Sheldon's national park idea was born. He was forced to leave in early September, as he needed to catch a steamboat homeward before winter froze the rivers, but he vowed to return. Because he and Karstens had become fast friends over the course of the summer, he asked the experienced packer and musher to join him on the Toklat the following year.

Sheldon and Karstens arrived back on the river in August 1907 and immediately set about building a cabin and preparing for the long winter. This involved hunting, and Sheldon wrote about that too, with the same detail that he did his other observations. For the conservationist-hunter, like so many others in that day, tracking, killing, and dressing a sheep (or any other creature) offered just as much opportunity for learning more about their lifeways as watching the sheep interact with each other and with their environment unmolested. Even more, specimens could be collected, and could then be studied in greater detail at institutions of higher learning. Plus, there were meals involved.

On one occasion Sheldon spent hours carefully, patiently stalking a small band of sheep. Finally, he shot and killed four adults, but only wounded a lamb. Dark was descending by the time he'd dressed the kills, and he went off in search of the wounded lamb. "While searching for it, it suddenly jumped up and staggered on. Upon my approach it would drop in an attitude of hiding, lying flat with its head and neck stretched forward against the ground. When I was very close it would jump up, stagger ahead, and attempt to hide. This was repeated several times before I

Naturalist Charles Sheldon feeds a gray jay on the slopes below Denali in 1908.
PHOTO COURTESY OF THE NATIONAL PARK SERVICE, DENALI NATIONAL PARK AND PRESERVE MUSEUM COLLECTIONS.

caught it—clearly illustrating the hiding instinct of lambs. I walked back to camp through the darkness as the mists settled on the mountains."

On this second trip Sheldon became convinced that Denali's preservation as part of the fledgling national park system was the only way its wildlife would survive. He had witnessed firsthand the damage done by market hunters, who slaughtered vast numbers of sheep, caribou, moose, and smaller fur-bearing animals for sale to miners and in Fairbanks. If the populations weren't protected from commercial interests, Sheldon recognized that they could be hunted to near extinction. It had happened before, in the American West, where vast buffalo herds were now only memories.

When Sheldon returned to civilization, he began his crusade. The wealthy Easterner had the connections. He was a member of the Boone and Crockett Club, a conservation-minded hunting club founded by President Teddy Roosevelt, proof that ardent conservationist and sport hunter could coexist. If game were properly conserved and managed,

Roosevelt, Sheldon, and their cohorts understood that it could thrive in numbers healthy enough to support hunting in a responsible manner. That was the linchpin for the Denali proposal: the idea of the park's preservation as a game reserve.

It took a long time for the legislation establishing Mount McKinley National Park to wend its way through the halls of Washington. Having secured the backing of the Boone and Crockett Club, Sheldon went after the approval of Judge James Wickersham, former mountaineer and now congressional representative for the territory of Alaska. Belmore Browne, another Denali mountaineer, also threw his voice and pen behind the proposal. When the bill was finally ready for the presidential signature, on February 19, Sheldon himself delivered it to Woodrow Wilson. The legislation languished on the president's desk for days while he dealt with other, more pressing matters (for one, the United States would enter World War I less than two months later). On February 26, 1917, Wilson found time to sign the act, and Mount McKinley National Park was established. According to historian William Brown, Sheldon was given the pen.

Brown adds this anecdote to his account of Sheldon's legislative efforts, an unfortunate twist in a winning effort: "Sheldon had moved from Vermont to Washington to shepherd the park bill through. During the climax of the legislative process he had haunted the halls of the Capitol and mobilized his cohorts for the final push. Finally, he took a day off, and that was the day the bill passed. Next day, [Horace] Albright, acting as Park Service director at the time, saw Sheldon approaching his office, jumped up, grabbed his hand, and congratulated him for leading the creation of this great park. For his part, Sheldon stood aghast. Unaware of the bill's passage he had dropped by simply to check progress. His day off made him miss the vote."

Sheldon never went back to Denali, his attention diverted by business concerns back east and by marriage. But he forged a lasting legacy in his crusade for the park, ensuring that conservation of Denali's wildlife was on equal footing with preservation of its monumental landforms, and establishing a tradition of study that endures into modern times.

Murie and His Wolves

Wilderness is adventure, discovery, science, inspiration, restoration, humility, and restraint.

—Quote from the Alaska Public Lands Center in Fairbanks

Adolph Murie wrote about Denali's wolves with the clipped efficiency of a scientist. In *The Wolves of Mount McKinley*, he meticulously describes den sites and destinations, tasks, feeding habits, parenting techniques, and which wolf led and the order of the wolves that followed when the pack went hunting. He reveals his affection for the objects of his study in quiet ways. Most of the wolves in the East Fork family, for example, are described dispassionately, as the "black female" or the "mantled male," but one he named "Grandpa." And though the manner in which the wolves greeted each other is factually recorded, the tail wagging and romping clearly delighted him.

When it came to defending the integrity of Denali's wilderness, Murie's language got a bit more colorful. National Park Service (NPS) plans to widen the Denali Park Road as part of its Mission 66 initiative prompted the ardent conservationist and his colleagues to decry the construction of a "speedway" in the park. The design of the Eielson Visitor Center, another Mission 66 improvement, was called a "monstrosity" and likened to a "Dairy Queen."

Murie's lifelong passion for wilderness, and specifically for Denali, was a family affair. In 1922 his half-brother, Olaus, was working on a caribou study in Alaska's Brooks Range, and young Adolph traveled north to assist him. He spent five transformative weeks on the tundra among the herds. A project intended to "enhance" reindeer by breeding them with caribou brought the brothers to Mount McKinley National Park in 1922 and 1923. This work inspired both Muries, and later their wives—Adolph married Louise Gillette, of Fairbanks, and Olaus married her half-sister Margaret Thomas—to dedicate their lives to the causes of wildlife and wilderness.

After his first Denali sojourn, Adolph returned to the Lower 48 to complete his education, earning a doctorate from University of Michigan. In 1934 he was recruited by George Melendez Wright, the visionary naturalist who pioneered the park service's Wildlife Division, and was hired as one of three biologists for the NPS. He returned to Denali to work in that role in 1939. In spirit he'd never leave.

Over the next five years, Murie logged more than seventeen hundred miles on foot studying Denali's wolves in the wild. He spent hundreds of hours, day and night, observing the comings and goings at a single wolf den. Because the animals were considered "master killers of wildlife," were depicted as vicious and conniving in fairy tales, and had been extirpated without regrets in America's national parks with the exception of Mount McKinley, Murie faced considerable resistance when it came to proving wolves had value beyond their pelts. To overcome generations of antipathy, the biologist meticulously described packs that were equally meticulous in selecting prey, culling the weakest, sickest, and oldest from herds of caribou and sheep and serving as ecosystem-cleansing scavengers when the circumstance presented itself. He also documented the lifelong relationships that developed among the family groups.

His observations were published in 1944, and his conclusions were groundbreaking: Predators, including wolves, played a critical role in the health of the wildlife populations that sustained them and were as worthy of conservation as the caribou and sheep they hunted. The predator-prey relationships documented in *The Wolves of Mount McKinley* became a cornerstone of the then-revolutionary argument that "predator control," standard practice within the NPS, should be abandoned in favor of resource management practices that protected the hunters as well as the hunted. Wolves, in the Murie paradigm, were integral to the overall stability of ecosystems, from the tiniest flora to the most impressive megafauna. He affirmed John Muir's declaration: "When we try to pick out anything by itself, we find it hitched to everything else in the Universe."

That's not to say Murie's methods were orthodox. He also appropriated a wolf pup from a den as part of his research and ended up raising her as a pet, a move contrary to the modern conservation ethic. Though Murie's regret isn't expressed directly, he wrote about watching the young

Adolph Murie stands in front of a trapper's cabin near the Toklat River.
PHOTO COURTESY OF THE NATIONAL PARK SERVICE, DENALI NATIONAL PARK AND PRESERVE MUSEUM COLLECTIONS.

wolf's mother approach while the pup was chained up outside his cabin, making note of the pup's whining and attempts to follow: "If the pup had been loose, it surely would have gone off with the band." Rather than roaming the tundra with her sisters, brothers, and cousins, Wags the tame wolf made friends with a Denali sled dog and a picture in the park archives shows her in the arms of Murie's daughter, Gail. Wags remained in the park after Murie and his family moved on.

Murie secured a permanent job in Mount McKinley National Park in 1947. He was hired to continue studying the park's predator-prey relationships, including the grizzly bear. As he found his voice as a conservationist, he also created controversy. He advocated for the reintroduction of wolves to Olympic National Park in Washington State, and to Isle Royale National Park in Michigan to help control its moose populations. Both proposals met opposition; the idea that predators were a danger to people and livestock was hard to overcome. He also argued for the preservation of coyotes in Yellowstone National Park, speaking up for a creature as vilified by ranchers and big-game hunters as wolves. He even protested mosquito control, as these pests played a role in a healthy ecosystem.

Murie voiced vehement opposition to the park service's Mission 66 plans for Denali. If, for example, the park road was widened and paved, an infrastructure improvement the NPS believed would improve the flow of tourist traffic, motorists would be inclined to blast through the park at speed rather than at a pace that invited observation and contemplation. Murie also argued against interpretive signs along the roadway, likening them to billboards as examples of visual litter. There was no need to build trails, since visitors could hike where they wanted without them. In a letter to the superintendent in 1956, Murie calls Denali an "outstanding wildlife park, even outstanding by Alaska standards." The mountain, the glaciers, the tundra ponds, and river bars were all important components of Denali as a "veritable fairy land," but more than that, the "wilderness spirit" of the place needed preservation, Murie wrote. Blowing it open to hotels, interpretive signs, camps, and smooth pavement was a threat to that spirit, unique among national parks at the time. Murie's voice, added to a chorus raised by fellow conservationists, limited Mission 66 development in the park.

The collective Muries had profound impacts on wildlife science and conservation in Alaska and beyond. Olaus and Margaret Murie, like Adolph and Louise, were proponents of the concept of Wilderness, where a landscape could retain "its primeval character and influence" such that "the earth and its community of life are untrammeled by man, where man himself is a visitor who does not remain." Olaus served as president of the Wilderness Society from 1945 to 1962 and advocated for the passage of the 1964 Wilderness Act. The Muries also helped wage the successful campaign for preservation of the Arctic National Wildlife Range, established in 1960; with the passage of the Alaska National Interest Lands Conservation Act (ANILCA) in 1980, this became the Arctic National Wildlife Refuge.

Adolph Murie's work in the park earned him the title "Denali's Wilderness Conscience," and the Murie Science and Learning Center is named in his memory. His legacy, like Sheldon's, reaches beyond his beloved wolves; he generated a new way of thinking about, and conserving, the wilderness they inhabit.

A Thorn in the Side

Gordon Haber, the independent wildlife biologist who, like Murie, built his career on the study of Denali's wolves, brandished his advocacy like a warrior. Haber dedicated his life to the animals, but he clashed with everyone he needed to work with in pursuit of their protection: the park's resource managers, who were constrained by systems and protocols Haber disdained; Alaska's Department of Fish and Game, which sanctioned wolf hunts; and the hunters and trappers who opposed any policy restricting their ability to kill wolves that strayed outside the park.

But wolves don't play by the rules of men; they don't recognize the same boundaries. Moreover, as Haber pointed out with vigor, crossing lines drawn on a map was a matter of life and death not just for a single wolf, but possibly for all the animals in that wolf's pack. One of his solutions—creating buffer zones along the park's boundaries—needed the backing of the park, the state, and neighbors. He had the data and he'd done the footwork, but his contentious nature made him what former chief of Denali's Division of Research and Resource Preservation Gordon Olson, and others, termed a "thorn in the side."

Haber's infatuation with wolves originated in Michigan in the early 1960s. He received his first degree in wildlife biology from Michigan Technological University, south of Isle Royale National Park, and would later earn a doctorate from the University of British Columbia. He became a seasonal ranger in Denali in 1966 and launched into the long-range study of the park's wolves that would become his life's work. One of the groups he followed was Adolph Murie's Toklat pack: Cumulative study of the generations of wolves that comprise the Toklat group, from Murie through Haber, would encompass nearly seven decades and reveal intimate details of how the animals interacted not only with the environment and their prey but also with each other.

Haber's studies were complementary to the park service's. The NPS focus was on monitoring populations, predation, and causes of death (among other things), while Haber's was on behavior. He championed the idea of the wolf pack as a "family group," which he argued more accurately described the complex relationships he'd studied and documented in the wild. This understanding fed his crusade for a buffer zone covering what's known as the Wolf Townships, a conspicuous rectangle of land along the Stampede Trail that juts into the northeastern corner of the national park. By protecting the lone wolf who strayed into the Wolf Townships from extermination, Haber maintained, the survival of Denali's wolf family groups could be better guaranteed.

Haber was able to document in detail the impact of trapping in the Wolf Townships. Wandering out of the park and into a trap claimed the life of the Toklat group's alpha female in 2005. With her loss the young wolves in the pack also lost her institutional knowledge of hunting strategies, particularly for larger game, which older wolves pass on to younger. Haber noted that the remaining young wolves were able to sustain themselves on a booming population of snowshoe hares in the park, and with age and experience the Toklats were able to move on to bigger game. But the group took another hit. In *Among Wolves*, a collection of Haber's writings edited by Marybeth Holleman, the biologist wrote: "Toklat consisted of seventeen wolves at the beginning of the 2007–2008 winter and nine at the end, with a high likelihood that most of the missing wolves were trapped during an extraterritorial foray into the northeast park boundary trapping area in February 2008."

The decimation of the Toklat group was Haber's latest crusade; he'd had many others. He had observed the disappearance of the entire Savage River pack in the winter of 1982-83, which he contended was the result of illegal hunting. In 1994 he filmed the destruction of four snared wolves: The footage and subsequent publicity resulted in the removal of about seven hundred snares, "wire nooses designed to catch wolves around the neck and kill them quickly," in a large area of the Alaska Range, according to a *New York Times* article. The trapping was part of a state-run three-year program intended "to increase moose and caribou herds for the benefit of hunters," the article stated.

Despite his reputation for confrontation, Haber's work was influential and he forced people to pay attention. Though he didn't conform to resource management requirements that his studies be shared with the park, park officials never forbade him from working within Denali. NPS wildlife biologist Tom Meier is quoted in *Among Wolves* as saying, "Gordon had a real history with the park. I admired him getting out there so much, doing really tough and grueling work." Haber was appointed to an NPS advisory panel exploring the reintroduction of wolves in Yellowstone National Park; those packs also suffer losses when they stray outside park boundaries. Additionally, Haber worked among the wolves in Yukon–Charley Rivers National Preserve and Wrangell–St. Elias National Park. He was a lecturer and photographer, wrote articles and op-eds for newspapers, and was featured in profile articles. Just as the word "controversial" appears in association with Haber's name, so does the word "revered."

Haber died in a plane crash in Denali in 2009 while studying his beloved wolves. Reports attribute the crash to the region's erratic winds, but some speculate about the pilot's inexperience, and others suggest that perhaps Haber pushed the pilot to take chances in conditions that were unsafe. "So many times, he'd say, just one more turn, again and again, sometimes literally twenty times," recalled pilot Troy Dunn in *Among Wolves*. "He had such a difficult time pulling himself away from those wolves." And there's this, from Priscilla Feral, president of Friends of Animals, which provided financial support for Haber's independent studies: "The way he wanted to die was to be flying in a plane and hit a mountain at 100 mph."

Balance and Persuasion

How Haber's work will shape the future of Denali's wolves over the long term is not yet known. The buffers he fought for have yet to be permanently instituted. Even in the wake of all his groundbreaking work—and that of Adolph Murie—the animals battle stigma.

But Haber followed Murie's lead, as well as Sheldon's, by shining a spotlight on the perils endangering Denali's wolf packs. The balance is there to be struck, like the compromise on subsistence hunting that permitted Denali to be preserved as a game refuge, and like the recognition that wilderness is healthiest when both predator and prey are present.

Acquiring the data is one thing. Making sure everyone understands what that data implies is another. Even in modern times wolves in Alaska, Yellowstone, and elsewhere are embattled. For the sheep it's a bit less complicated . . . for now. The impacts of growing numbers of visitors, and of climate change, could bring about changes that will threaten Sheldon's favorites, as well as the Toklat grizzly, the wolverine, and the Arctic ground squirrel.

The saving grace of all is what happens on the bus in summer, or on the dogsled in winter, as visitors and rangers scan the distance hoping not only to catch sight of the big mountain but also to catch sight of the big game. The spark that lit up Sheldon, Murie, and Haber still kindles fascination among those who wander the tundra.

Chapter Seven

Mountaineering: The Second Wave

The second half of Denali's mountaineering story begins in 1932, as does the story of death on the mountain. But exponential growth in the number of summit attempts didn't begin until the 1970s. By then the nature of the climb had pivoted dramatically. The advent of air taxis had reduced an approach that, for the pioneering climbers, had involved weeks of travel over difficult terrain, laboriously hauling supplies on dog-sleds, to mere hours spent in a cockpit with gear stowed in cargo holds. This opened Denali to a population that might otherwise have been deterred. With easy access the numbers spiked. By the 1990s more than one thousand climbers were attempting to reach the summit each year.

The number of climbers who died on the mountain spiked as well. To reiterate a point made by climber, former seasonal ranger, and writer Jon Waterman, prior to 1967 only three people had died on Denali. From 1967 forward that number has mushroomed to about 120, with annual death tallies that, in the worst years, reach into double digits. The culprits? Falls, bad weather, and altitude sickness top the list.

What draws climbers to a mountain where the climbing can be so dangerous? Ego, most certainly. The lure of the "first" is compelling: the first ski ascent; the first solo ascent; the first winter ascent; the first female ascent; the first ascents by teams from Mexico, Japan, South Korea, and Italy. And there were, and remain, other cherries to pick: the fastest ascents, the first ascents on new and different routes; the youngest person to summit, the oldest person to summit. Then there are the firsts that never make the books, personal aspirations born on backyard mountains, desert crags, and hidden icefalls, in dorm rooms and barrooms and living rooms.

Denali's summit is not the only mountaineering prize wreathed, on occasion, in bad luck and bad outcomes. Ego and the lure of the first result in death and disaster on many peaks. When climber Joe Wilcox inquired about whether his party could claim a first during its 1967 expedition, the famed summiter Bradford Washburn pointed out the prickly nature of ego-driven quests: "McKinley has not yet been climbed blindfolded or backward, nor has any party of nine persons yet fallen into the same crevasse." Then he added sarcastically, but with some degree of prescience, "We hope that you may wish to rise to one of these compelling challenges."

The Lindley-Liek and Cosmic Ray Expeditions

I'd come suddenly around a turn and there, through the trees, would be that snow-capped peak brushing against the sky. I'd think, "You are a mighty mountain, Denali, but I've been on top of you, with all the world at my feet."

—Grant Pearson, *My Life of High Adventure*

The long mountaineering drought on Denali—no one had attempted a climb since the Stuck expedition claimed the summit in 1913—broke in the spring of 1932. Two expeditions set sights on the mountaintop that April, venturing onto the slopes at the same time and following essentially the same route. The goal of the Lindley-Liek expedition was to make the first ascent and descent on skis; the team would fail in that regard but would notch a different first by summiting the North and South Peaks on consecutive days. Spearheaded by Alfred Lindley, the team included Mount McKinley National Park's superintendent, Harry Liek, and a future superintendent, Grant Pearson, as well as Norwegian skier and mountaineer Erling Strom.

What would become known as the Cosmic Ray expedition was on the mountain to study just that: the effects and behavior of cosmic rays, also known as gamma rays, at high latitudes and high elevations. This expedition notched two firsts, and both, in very different ways, helped define how the mountain would be climbed in the future. The Cosmic Ray team was the first to employ aircraft to ferry climbers and their gear to a base camp on the mountain's flanks. The second first is sobering: The expedition leader and another young scientist became the first men to lose their lives climbing Denali.

With the assistance of the park's dogsled teams, the Lindley-Liek expedition made an overland approach to the mountain via the Muldrow Glacier. Aside from the use of skis, the Lindley-Liek team followed the pattern set by earlier expeditions, establishing a base camp and caching supplies higher and higher on the mountain as they ascended. The climbers successfully reached both Denali summits but were not able to travel entirely on skis given ice and snow conditions high on the mountain. Still, Strom and the others were able to set an altitude record for skiers, reaching about 17,000 feet, before abandoning the sticks to continue on foot. (Tsuyoshi Ueki and Kazuo Hoshikawa are credited with the first ski descent from summit to base in 1970.)

Team member Grant Pearson was no newcomer to travel in Denali, having been a park ranger for more than five years, but his adventures on the expedition epitomize the strengths and folly of youth and exuberance in the wildlands. He joined the party with next to no experience on skis and suffered miserably for the lack at first. It took some instruction from Strom, who demonstrated how to execute both a functional stem christie and a graceful telemark, before Pearson began to resemble a skier and not "a snowman on a bender," as Strom termed it. As for Pearson: "'These things,' I thought, falling over backwards, 'are just a fad,'" he wrote.

The young ranger also survived a pair of falls that would have shut down a lesser mountaineer. The first was a skittering ride down a high ridge as the team began its descent from the South Peak; to arrest his slide, Pearson attempted to set his ice ax into the snow, but it rebounded off a patch of ice and impaled his other hand. "I knew if I didn't get myself stopped, I was likely to have a cliff a quarter mile below named after me," he recalled. Despite his injuries he made it to the top of the North Peak on the following day.

Harry Liek, Grant Pearson, Erling Strom, and Al Lindley pose for a photo after climbing both the North and South Peaks of Denali in 1932.
PHOTO COURTESY OF THE NATIONAL PARK SERVICE, DENALI NATIONAL PARK AND PRESERVE MUSEUM COLLECTIONS.

The second fall came farther down, when he plunged into a crevasse—an ominous event given what transpired for the Cosmic Ray team.

The leader of the Cosmic Ray expedition was Allen Carpé, an electrical engineer and experienced mountaineer. The team also included a pair of scientists, Edward Beckwith and Theodore Koven, as well as Percy Olton and Nicholas Spadavecchia. The experiences of these five men demonstrate how quickly luck can turn on Denali, and how devastating a turn of luck can be.

The expedition got off to a historic start. Pilot Joe Crosson made the first successful landing on a glacier in support of an expedition when he delivered gear to the team's base camp at 5,700 feet on the Muldrow (the park service's sled dogs also hauled some of the Cosmic Ray team's gear to the Muldrow Glacier camp). Successive flights by Crosson and another pilot deposited the rest of the climbers and more equipment at the camp and made an aerial drop of supplies to Carpé and Koven, who had climbed above to scout a route and set up a higher camp.

A storm halted all progress on the mountain for both teams for a couple of days following the Lindley-Liek team summit on May 8. When the successful party reached the Cosmic Ray high camp on the Muldrow, the climbers encountered a disturbing scene: Koven and Carpé were nowhere to be found, but their sleeping bags and packs were still inside their tent. Descending farther, the Lindley-Liek climbers discovered the body of Theodore Koven, who had fallen into a crevasse and been badly injured, but had somehow climbed out and then perished on the glacier. Carpé disappeared completely; the Lindley-Liek team found evidence that he too had fallen into the crevasse. Pearson, reflecting on both his own plunge into the void and the fates of Carpé and Koven, wrote: "The story was plainly written in the snow, a stark tragedy of two men, supposedly experienced mountaineers, betrayed by their eagerness to greet their friends. They had gone down the glacier unroped, over a trail they thought they knew, and one of the mountain's oldest traps had sprung shut on them as it almost had on me."

The Lindley-Liek team continued down to the Cosmic Ray base camp, where they found Beckwith incapacitated by illness and tended by Olton; these two would be retrieved by aircraft. Spadavecchia, who'd been dispatched to get help for the sick Beckwith, got lost on his way down the mountain and ended up having to be rescued as well.

A Better Way: Bradford Washburn and the West Buttress Route

My but this is a magnificently spectacular route . . . the views of the Kahiltna Glacier, of Mount Foraker and Mount Hunter, are stunning in every conceivable combination of light and shadow.

—Bradford Washburn,
from Michael Sfraga's biography

In his lifetime Bradford Washburn would distinguish himself as a photographer, a geographer, and a scientist, winning the respect of colleagues and students worldwide.

But he was a mountaineer as well, possessing the temperament, physical strength, wilderness smarts, and keen eye needed to pick a line, prepare an attempt, and descending. He cultivated an intimate knowledge of Denali, and his willingness to share his insights made him a guru of sorts for the climbers of the generation that followed.

His lasting contribution to the park, and to the sport of mountaineering, is Denali's West Buttress route. The key to success on the West Buttress, accessed via the south side of the Alaska Range, is air support. The difficulties that pioneering climbers like Frederick Cook and Belmore Browne encountered on the south side—long slogs through mosquito-infested country, treacherous river crossings, and uncertain route-finding—could now be simply flown over.

Washburn first traveled to Denali when he was dispatched to Alaska on a photo shoot for *National Geographic* in 1936. His spectacular aerial images of the mountain, some taken on that trip, some taken on subsequent trips, were fundamental to the detailed maps he created and to the lifelong association he would have with the mountain. The images—each face and ridge and glacier in crisp focus, blacks and whites in explicit contrast—were also integral to his discovery of, and aspirations for, the West Buttress route.

Washburn was a two-time summiter when he ventured onto the mountain to take on its unclimbed West Buttress in 1951. In 1942, as part of a team conducting cold-weather field tests of military gear—tents, lip balms, overcoats, ropes—the geographer and photographer was dispatched to Mount McKinley National Park. Unable to resist the lure of the High One, Washburn was part of the third successful attempt on Denali's summit in that year. In 1947, Washburn was a member of an expedition with a triple billing—part summit attempt, part entertainment, part science—dubbed Operation White Tower. The entertainment focus was on getting footage for a short film intended to pique interest in a feature-length movie based on a popular book of the day. Washburn's wife, Barbara, was urged to join the expedition by the filmmaker, RKO Pictures, which believed a feminine touch would add value to the movie. Barbara Washburn did much more than add value; she became the first woman to stand on both the South Peak and the North Peak, with her husband by her side.

Bradford Washburn in 1944: The explorer, photographer, and cartographer had a profound love for Denali.

PHOTO COURTESY OF THE NATIONAL PARK SERVICE, DENALI NATIONAL PARK AND PRESERVE MUSEUM COLLECTIONS. PHOTO BY J. M. GREANY.

Washburn had climbed the mountain via the Muldrow Glacier in 1942 and 1947; by 1951 he was more interested in the south side, where the Kahiltna presented itself as a second glacial highway to the summit. Air support was critical to any attempt on the south side, given the difficulty and length of the approach. But by the 1950s air support on Denali had more than demonstrated its viability.

The goal of the 1951 expedition was, again, not only about pioneering a new route; science was in play, with the party also conducting mapping surveys, studying the mountain's geology, and scouting possibilities for a high-altitude station to study cosmic rays.

The climb started a bit higher on the Kahiltna Glacier than the site of today's base camp, at about 7,700 feet (versus 7,200 feet). Once the team and its gear were deposited on the glacier, the men commenced moving supplies and equipment upward from camp to camp, enduring the challenges of weather and altitude the massive mountain is famous for. Some alpinists have called the West Buttress route a "slog," referencing a lack of technical terrain. But for many climbers, including members of the Washburn team, it was what some Denali guides term a "final exam." As seems inevitable, a storm pinned the climbers down at what Washburn named Windy Corner. They had to chop steps in rotten snow and ice to gain the buttress proper; freezing temperatures and thin air whittled away at their strength and endurance. But all eight members of the party reached the summit.

And with that success the West Buttress vaulted ahead of the Muldrow Glacier as the route of choice. Today, an estimated 80 percent of climbers attempt to reach Denali's summit via Washburn's route.

1967

If the mountain wants to throw the book at you it can.

—Bradford Washburn
in conversation with Dave Krupa

With the West Buttress route open and base camp on the Kahiltna Glacier accessible by air, the number of teams attempting to climb Denali rose steadily. In 1967, a pivotal year in the climbing history of the park, eighty-three people tried to reach the summit and sixty-seven succeeded. Nothing remarkable in that. But two teams made the record books that year, one by design and one by accident. The experiences of both epitomize the seriousness of any Denali summit attempt.

The First Winter Ascent

In 1967 one major "first" had yet to be claimed. Denali had never been climbed in winter. The reasons were obvious. The formidable cold, wind, and snow encountered on the mountain in summer was ominously magnified when the earth tilted away from the sun. Endless dark, inhumane weather, and misery were guaranteed.

But the plum was there to be picked, and an accomplished young mountaineer named Art Davidson set about pulling together an expedition to do just that. It took him a while—understandably many of those he approached thought the idea was mad—but eventually he assembled a roster of experienced teammates: Dave Johnston, Gregg Blomberg, Shiro Nishimae, George Wichman, and John Edwards. This core was joined by a Frenchman, Jacques "Farine" Batkin, and a relative novice from Switzerland, Ray Genet, who went on to become a formidable and memorable alpinist. It was during this epic winter ascent that Genet earned the nickname "Pirate"; he acquired it by marking his colorful gear with the skull and crossbones, but the renegade title would prove a perfect fit for life.

Despite experience and careful planning, members of the winter team were slammed at the outset by disaster. On the first day of the expedition, Farine, traveling unroped on the Kahiltna, plunged into a crevasse and was killed, throwing the party into disarray and delay. In the days of soul-searching and waiting that followed—Genet escorted Farine's body off the mountain, and the rest of the team mulled the circumstances while they waited for him to return—the dynamics of the group were tested. With reservations they decided to continue. When Edwards later fell into another crevasse and was injured, his rescue forced the teammates to pull together. Driven by necessity and ambition, the winter expedition coalesced, albeit raggedly.

After coming to the half-hearted decision to carry on, the climbers endured unnerving and sometimes brutal conditions as they continued the ascent. Genet also plunged into a crevasse. The blizzards came and went. The party constructed elaborate snow shelters to protect themselves from the elements, one dubbed the Kahiltna Hilton, and a second, known as the "iglooplex," at 10,200 feet.

The members of the winter team were well provisioned, and their cumulative mountaineering experience served them well; when one man or another became incapacitated by frostbite or altitude sickness, a teammate would step up. No one else wanted to die on the peak, and cooperation, patience, and good luck were all needed to ensure survival.

Creeping up the West Buttress route camp by hard-fought camp, the team finally reached 17,200 feet and was in position to summit. The first chance came on February 27, but the climbers would be turned back by a whiteout at about 19,000 feet. They'd all try again the next day, but four members of the team retreated, leaving only Davidson, Genet, and Johnston to claim the summit. The three reached the apex in wind and darkness, the views that had inspired other summiters hidden by the Arctic night, save the greenish glow of lights from Anchorage, which struck Davidson as an "unfair" reward for their effort. The summit celebration was brief, and then the climbers began the descent.

They only made it as far as Denali Pass, at 18,200 feet, before the weather took a devastating turn. The violent storm lasted more than a week, trapping the men in a snow cave scratched from the ice almost single-handedly by Johnston. The men had summited carrying minimal gear, and little food and fuel. Davidson's hands were frostbitten, as were Genet's feet; in his account of the climb, *Minus 148°*, Davidson describes withholding his booties from Genet to protect his own feet from the cold, and then finally giving them up to ease the other man's suffering. When the fuel ran out, Genet plunged into the blizzard and returned from an old cache congealed in snow and ice nearby with a full bottle. When the last of their meager food stash proved inedible, Davidson pillaged the cache yet again, wielding an ice ax with his frozen hands and, miraculously, coming up with enough sustenance to keep them all alive until a window of good weather allowed them to attempt a descent.

When the storm diminished, Davidson, Johnston, and Genet crept down toward the relative shelter of the camps below. Their four teammates had bailed from the highest camps, beset with their own altitude- and storm-borne hardships, as well as the crushing certainty that the three above had perished. Two would make it back to base camp, and two would be rescued from a higher camp. The three men given up for dead were airlifted by helicopter from Windy Corner, at 13,500 feet, on March 7.

The Wilcox Expedition

The 1967 winter expedition had climbed in anticipation of wicked weather. But the "perfect storm" that converged on Denali that summer, just as seven members of the Wilcox expedition descended from its summit, could not have been anticipated. Two weather systems collided on the mountain in the last weeks of July, creating a vortex of cold, snow, and wind that immobilized every expedition for days. Given the technology available at the time, there was no way to forecast the ferocity or duration of the storm, nor was there a reliable way to relay a forecast to the men on the mountain. The climbers who were forced to bivouac near the summit, in subzero temperatures and pummeled by winds in excess of one hundred miles per hour, had no idea what they were in for.

The seven men did not survive. It remains the worst mountaineering disaster in the history of climbing on Denali, and one of the worst in North American mountaineering.

As such, it's only natural that the tragedy is the subject of ongoing scrutiny and controversy. What exactly happened to the seven who perished? Who, if anyone, is to blame for their deaths? Bad luck, bad choices, bad weather—all have been considered in the memoirs, articles, and reports written by survivors, observers, and students of the sport. There is agreement on this: The perfect storm that engulfed the Wilcox party is about more than just weather. If cohesion was a challenge for the Davidson team, it was a nonstarter for the Wilcox expedition. The expedition was a mash-up of two separate groups—a nine-man team Joe Wilcox pulled together consisting of young, arguably inexperienced climbers, and a three-man team from Colorado led by Howard Snyder, composed of men a little older and with more impressive summits under their belts. Merging the teams was a park service solution intended to serve two ends. First, the combination allowed Snyder's team to continue, since one man had had to pull out after breaking his hand, bringing the number below the National Park Service–mandated minimum of four. Second, with the addition of the more experienced Colorado climbers to Wilcox's team, the park service believed it improved the odds of a safe, successful ascent. But the two groups would never mesh, leading to discord on the mountain and to lingering speculation about how this friction played into the disaster.

A number of decisions made by the party have been questioned in the aftermath, including abandoning equipment necessary for building adequate snow shelters at high camps and a disputed attempt to refuel a stove that resulted in a fire that destroyed a tent and some gear. The team was also fractured when Wilcox, Snyder, and the two other Colorado climbers set off for the summit on July 15, while the other climbers rested in camp at 15,000 feet or made a final supply run to the high camp at 17,900 feet.

Wilcox, Snyder, Jerry Lewis, and Paul Schlichter had reached the top and descended to the high camp just as their teammates arrived from the lower camp. All of the men tucked in when a storm—a more typical summer storm, not *the storm*—descended. When the weather broke a couple of days later, the four who had summited and one other teammate opted to continue the descent to the 15,000-foot camp. Seven remained at the high camp, prepping for their summit bid. Five of the seven who stayed reached the apex of the South Peak on July 18; two opted out and remained at 17,900 feet, reportedly nursing altitude sickness.

Then the monster storm arrived and refused to relent. Rescue attempts, including flyovers and aerial supply drops, were aborted due to the weather. When a short-lived and relative window of calm settled over the high ridges, the men at the 15,000-foot camp, including team leader Wilcox, attempted to rally and climb to their teammates' aid. The group ended up descending instead. This was not a unanimous decision, by some accounts. Some of the men were truly ill and needed to go down; those who tried to go up were forced to turn back almost as soon as they set out due to weather and exhaustion.

The Wilcox climbers met a team from the Mountaineering Club of Alaska (MCA) as they descended; this group helped get the worn men safely down to camp at 12,000 feet. The MCA team, though also blasted by the storm, then continued to climb. They would be the first to encounter what remained of the Wilcox expedition high camp: two abandoned tents, an ice ax, a sleeping bag wrapped around one climber's summit flagpole, and a decomposing corpse. The next day, after aerial reconnaissance, two other bodies were found, sitting on a steep slope at 19,000 feet and frozen in place. The bodies of the other climbers were never found.

Examinations of the Wilcox expedition, including postmortems by the climbers themselves (both Wilcox and Snyder wrote books, as have others; one ranger describes them as "rebuttals to rebuttals"), chronicle the disaster in painstaking detail. All of the following has been found lacking: experience, effective leadership, teamwork, the right equipment, the time to acclimate to altitude, the ability to communicate with the park service and potential rescuers, and delays in rescue attempts. And, most important, adequate weather forecasting. By all accounts this was no ordinary storm, and there was no way, in those days, to predict the deadly bloom of the two systems when they slammed into the mountain.

Remove the weather wild card, and expeditions through the previous decades had all suffered some degree of inadequacy. The Sourdoughs certainly lacked most of the prerequisites, but they survived. The popular West Buttress route enticed more climbers onto the mountain, and by definition not all of them would be prepared, either in terms of experience or equipment, for what lay ahead. What happened to the Wilcox expedition honed climbers' awareness of the difficulties of even the least technical way, and has colored how mountaineers, and rangers, have looked at an ascent of Denali ever since.

In the wake of the 1967 deaths, the park service backed away from trying to regulate climbers. Imposing rules had been a thorny issue for decades, and enforcement was difficult, given the independent nature of mountaineers in general. The four-person minimum was dropped after the Wilcox disaster, and seasonal camps to support climbers on the Kahiltna Glacier were established at 14,200 feet and 17,200 feet.

But climbers gamble with their lives every time they step onto the mountain. Despite regulation, education, improvements in equipment, advances in medical technology, better techniques for weather forecasting, and high-tech communications, mountaineers are subject to random acts of nature: avalanche, storm, altitude sickness, bad judgment, and bad luck.

Another Kind of Kahiltna Hilton

Let's start with the numbers. Despite the tragedy of 1967 and the mountain's reputation for fierceness and difficulty, Denali continues to reel

An aerial view of the Kahiltna Glacier in 1977; this is the jumping-off point for most modern mountaineers.
PHOTO COURTESY OF THE NATIONAL PARK SERVICE, DENALI NATIONAL PARK AND PRESERVE MUSEUM COLLECTIONS. PHOTO BY BOB BUTTS.

climbers in. Through the latter half of the twentieth century the number grew steadily: In 1970 there were 124 attempts and 72 summits; in 1980 there were 659 attempts and 283 summits; after 1992 no fewer than 1,000 climbers each year set the summit in their sights. By the end of 2016, more than 43,000 recorded attempts had been made, with about 20,600 completions; a success rate hovering around 50 percent has been fairly consistent for nearly half a century.

The number of attempts has plateaued at about 1,200 per year. Denali's mountaineering rangers attribute this to the same factors that likely caused the lull after the Stuck expedition in 1913: cost, time, and accessibility. Sure, a climber can fly to base camp on the Kahiltna now, but that flight is expensive. So is the gear, and the supplies needed to support an expedition. Climbers typically set aside a month or more for traveling to and from base camp, for acclimating, for moving caches up the mountain . . . not to mention the time they spend at home—wherever home is—to make arrangements, pull a team together, and train. And then there's just getting to Alaska: It's a long way from anywhere to Fairbanks or Anchorage, and then a long way from those cities to Denali.

The steadiness of the summit success rate is also relatively flat. Two factors play major roles in why about half of Denali's climbers don't get to the top: weather and altitude. The big storms get all the attention, but nearly every summit story includes a quieter reckoning with altitude sickness. Acclimatizing—the process of building the body up to function at extreme altitude—takes two to three weeks. This effectively makes every Denali climb an expedition. Headache, vomiting, and loss of appetite are the relatively minor effects of exertion in thin air and can be severe enough to render the summit unreachable. More devastating altitude-related conditions, like high-altitude pulmonary edema, require immediate descent or evacuation.

The focus on firsts has persisted unabated into modern times. No one has yet climbed Denali blindfolded or backward, but some climbers still seek the unique. The verifiable firsts are documented in hefty binders at the mountaineering ranger station in Talkeetna, as well as in park databases. Some of the stories stand out: Consider Ricardo Cassin and his team, which pioneered a route on Denali's south face (now called the Cassin Ridge) in 1961. The face, like the formidable Wickersham Wall on the north side, had been considered unclimbable, but Bradford Washburn's camera and eye saw a way. Cassin, a well-respected European alpinist with a number of impressive ascents under his belt, came to see if it would go. The expedition chipped bivouacs onto icy shelves, was pinned down by the Arctic winds and snow, and committed to dangerous pitches of rock and ice climbing. Several climbers, including Cassin, suffered from frostbite, which slowed progress on the descent and, in one instance, precipitated a fall that Cassin was narrowly able to arrest. In 1976 veteran Yosemite climber Charlie Porter soloed the same route in what has been called a "sprint" and a "blitz"; the two-day ascent was hailed as "one of the greatest individual climbing achievements in North America" by *Rock and Ice* magazine. Super-alpinist Mugs Stump set another record in 1991 when he climbed the Cassin in fifteen hours.

While some firsts make the book, others can't be documented. People checking in at the Talkeetna station sometimes tell rangers they are the first from their country to attempt an ascent or make other claims rangers have no way to confirm. But they also don't discourage: Regardless of whether a first is in the making, rangers do everything in their power to ensure that climbers make it on and off the mountain successfully, mostly in the form of recommendations. Climbers must adhere to a few hard-and-fast park rules. For example, they must check in and check out so the park knows whether someone has gone missing (if a mother, father, or other family member hasn't already made a worried call). Climbers are required to preregister sixty days in advance of their expeditions. There's also a mandatory ranger briefing, an interactive, route-specific, slide-by-slide trip up the desired route that includes conversation, cautionary advice, and resource–related messages, such as how to dispose of human waste and garbage, and how to properly bury caches of supplies.

But no one is prohibited from heading up, even if rangers suspect an aspiring summiteer doesn't have a clue. Fortunately, the unprepared often check themselves. Desiring Denali from afar is one thing; sucking air, nursing a screaming headache, and struggling to warm hands and feet at 14,000 feet is quite another.

On the mountain itself the park dispatches a patrol team every eight to ten days throughout the climbing season. These month-long patrols, which include at least one paid ranger and three or four volunteer rangers, are there to help deal with medical emergencies and trauma, as educators, and to help keep Denali clean. The focus is the West Buttress route, pursued by the bulk of aspiring summiters, as well as the West Rib and Cassin Ridge. Base camp is at 7,200 feet on the Kahiltna Glacier, and a full-time base camp coordinator is on-site throughout the climbing season (April through July). Additional camps are established annually at 14,200 feet and 17,200 feet. A medical tent is staffed at the 14,200 camp; the higher camp is generally the launching pad on a summit day.

Rescues are another big concern on the mountain. They are dangerous and expensive to mount, and Denali's backcountry and mountaineering rangers are adamant about climbers and hikers being prepared to self-rescue. When that can't happen, however, the park mobilizes. Denali's high-altitude helicopter is a pivotal piece of equipment in case of emergency, able to reach the highest camp for evacuations if needed. The focus on education is also key: When climbers from South Korea began to die on the mountain in the 1990s, the park service dispatched rangers to the country to give programs on preparing for a summit attempt, with positive results. In Talkeetna the resources needed to set a rescue in motion exist, but foremost are the resources needed to ensure that climbers are educated well enough to not require that rescue.

The Era of the Guide

> *Trampling the summit regularly seems part sacrilege, part conquest, and more to do with business than climbing.*
>
> —Jon Waterman, *In the Shadow of Denali*

While the number of climbers on Denali has remained relatively stable in recent decades, the makeup of that population has changed. Where once most teams on the mountain in any given season were independent, now most make the trek under the wing of professional guide services. Today, rangers estimate that one-third of the climbers on Denali each year are members of guided expeditions.

Guide-led climbing got its start in the 1960s. Swiss-born Ray Genet, the Pirate, who first reached the summit with the Davidson winter expedition of 1967, became the mountain's first commercial guide and reached the top repeatedly in his long career: twenty-six times by one count, more than thirty by several others. His techniques are legendary: To get climbers to the top, he would "cajole" them, "haul" them, holler at them, carry them "as if they were bundles of firewood." He is remembered as a joyous, driven, physically fit individual with a love for Denali that never waned. In a memorial published in the *American Alpine Journal* after his death—he lost his life descending from the top of Mount Everest in 1979—Richard Loren Doege wrote: "By specializing on McKinley, he developed an intimate knowledge of its terrain and weather. Genet understood McKinley, and with this understanding he attained an extra margin of aptness as a guide."

Genet's legacy on Denali is not without controversy. Explorer and journalist Jon Waterman lamented that, in leading "huge groups" to the summit, Pirate "left an indelible imprint of feces, trash, and overcrowding." On the flip side, Genet was a fearless rescuer, remembered for making a heroic effort with another guide, Brian Okonek, to save three South Korean climbers who'd fallen on their descent. Pirate tales are full of bombast and arrogance, and also of remarkable skill, strength, endurance, and an indomitable love for Denali. "Genet really believed it was his mountain," Waterman wrote.

The advent of guided climbs has highlighted significant changes in the nature of mountaineering on Denali. The all-encompassing solitude and spirit of complete self-reliance that characterized the early expeditions has evaporated. By 1980 the park service was issuing permits to guide companies in an effort to get a handle on the environmental, logistical, and safety issues posed by large groups concentrated on a focused area—the West Buttress—in a short season. How to dispose of trash and human waste were significant concerns. The guides themselves faced additional challenges, trying to fuse discordant clients into cohesive climbing teams and dealing with clients determined to summit but not remotely prepared for the physical or emotional challenges.

And that wasn't all, as Waterman, a one-time guide, attests to in his book, *In the Shadow of Denali.* "If a rescue breaks somewhere on the mountain, it is the guide who evacuates a stranger all night," Waterman wrote, "then turns around to take his clients another thousand feet up the mountain."

Despite the difficulties the work of park service mountaineering rangers and trained guides has paid off in terms of mitigating the potential death toll: Fewer people died on Denali in the 1980s than in the previous two decades. According to Waterman, 2,284 guided clients attempted to reach the summit during the decade, with 1 fatality; among the 5,247 unguided climbers who made the attempt, 33 died.

That said, the worst year for deaths was 1992, when eleven people died on the peak (and two more climbers lost their lives on Mount Foraker, bringing the park total to thirteen that year). Many of those fatalities came during yet another epic storm. According to the park's annual mountaineering report, more than sixty inches of snow fell at base camp and the winds at 14,000 feet clocked in at 110 miles per hour. Seven people died during the ten-day onslaught, and another six were rescued. In that unfortunate year, twenty-two climbers would be rescued; the cost of those rescues was more than $430,000. One of 1992's casualties was veteran alpinist and Denali champion Mugs Stump, who disappeared into a crevasse.

These days six authorized guide services hold concessions, renewed every ten years, to operate on the mountain.

Impact

The number of climbers permitted on Denali has an annual limit of fifteen hundred, set in place by the park's 2006 backcountry management plan. But that may change in the future, as aspects of the plan are open for review after ten years. To date, the number of climbers on Denali has never exceeded 1,340 in a season.

The driver will be mitigating impacts. Denali's backcountry and mountaineering rangers are keenly aware of the precarious balance that must be maintained to protect the wilderness while also ensuring that climbers have access to that wilderness. On the Kahiltna, with as many as sixty climbers heading for the summit on any given day in the four-month climbing season, the glacier, and the fourteen-mile "trail" leading to the summit, take a beating. Base camp is "like a little town." It can get crowded, not just with people but with their tents, their bulky packs, and their sleds loaded with gear. Planes land and take off (outside the wilderness boundary, of course), and, if needed, rescues are staged on the glacier. Higher up, anchors are fixed into the headwall that leads from the camp at 14,200 feet onto the West Buttress itself. It's impossible to imagine the Kahiltna as a "wilderness" in the height of the season, but that doesn't mean the ideals of stewardship should be forgotten or abandoned.

Addressing at least one major impact has gained traction in recent decades. Trash accumulates rapidly on Denali's summit routes, and proper disposal of human waste is an ongoing problem. To mitigate these impacts, the park has instituted a clean climbing policy—a version of "pack it in, pack it out" that includes packing out poop. Longtime mountaineering ranger Roger Robinson has spearheaded a clean climbing drive from 1980 through the present, pioneering use of the Clean Mountain Can, a sanitary system climbers use to cart their personal waste off the mountain.

The Legacy of the First

Interpretive ranger Laura Wright wanted to climb Denali because she'd been staring at it and talking about it for years. Since she was stationed in Talkeetna, the mountain was in her face all day, every day. She felt she was prepared: She trained for the climb; she had backcountry experience; she went with a guide; and because of her job, she had a good secondhand understanding of what she would face up there.

She made it to about 16,000 feet before time and weather forced her to turn around. But she doesn't express disappointment, nor does she feel a need to go back and try again. She got what she wanted: She can speak to others headed out on their first attempts from firsthand experience now.

"It scares me that this mountain, without its protections, would be friendlier, with trams, cabins, Sherpas, storage areas, which is what people are used to on higher mountains," she says thoughtfully. "I'm thankful that you must pull your own weight on this mountain. I'm thankful that the mountain looks much the way it did when it was first climbed."

There's no denying the power of the first. The firsts go down in history, indelible on the human psyche. First steps, first day of school, first kiss, first love . . . first backpacking trip, first ski trip, first summit. For those who climb mountains, that first is the highest, the hardest, the sweetest. The views from the top are the most spectacular.

And that first summit begets the next: a higher peak, a different route, a longer trip. And the next. And then, for some, comes the challenge of the highest peak. Because of where it is, because of what it is, a climb on Denali, whether to the summit or not, is forever that first.

Chapter Eight

Supermen: Harry Karstens and Grant Pearson

In the Who's Who of Denali National Park and Preserve, the names of two park superintendents stand out. The legacy of Harry Karstens is overarching; his tenure as the park's first administrative head is nearly a century old, but his vision still resonates. Grant Pearson's history in Denali goes back almost as long—Karstens was his boss for a short time—and his passion, too, still informs the park experience.

These two share certain personality traits: They were daring, driven, and not intimidated by hard work. Their love of Denali was as enormous as the park itself, and their tolerance for remoteness played into their successes. They fostered the park's development, navigating the confused seas created by the oppositional mandates of the National Park Service (NPS): to open the wilderness to exploration by visitors and to ensure that wilderness remained as unmarked by humankind as possible for posterity.

They were also very different men, with unique backgrounds and divergent styles. Karstens is remembered for fierce, combative competence; he had no patience for slackers. Pearson's wit overflows in his memoir, enhancing rather than detracting from the serious challenges he faced.

In national parks, superintendents come and superintendents go. They oversee the construction and maintenance of infrastructure; shape policy; handle paperwork; deal with the press; entertain visiting dignitaries; and

Harry Karstens stands alongside his mail carrier's dogsled in 1905, near Birch Lake on what would become the Richardson Highway.
PHOTO COURTESY OF THE NATIONAL PARK SERVICE, DENALI NATIONAL PARK AND PRESERVE MUSEUM COLLECTIONS.

hire and fire the rangers who enforce law and order, protect resources, develop interpretive programs, and interface with visitors. Karstens and Pearson tackled these ordinary administrative tasks with competence and a compelling sense of duty. But because they worked in a park built around America's grandest, most illustrious peak, it makes sense that their stories are extraordinary.

Harry Karstens

Denali's first superintendent was dubbed "the Seventymile Kid" when he was a very young man. It was one way friends and acquaintances on the Alaskan frontier could wrap a name around the adventure Harry Karstens personified. Even in his early twenties, he demonstrated an almost superhuman affinity for meeting the challenges that the Far North mustered . . . and he hadn't even seen Denali yet.

Born in 1878 in Chicago, Karstens left home when he was seventeen. Historian Tom Walker recounts "family lore" that attributes the young man's flight to a bloody (but not lethal) altercation with an older brother. Karstens wandered the northern states for a time, picking up odd jobs and a good sense of independence, until word of the gold strike in the Canadian Yukon drifted south in 1896. Along with thousands of others, Karstens and a friend headed to Seattle, boarded a steamer, and rushed to the Klondike.

He first set foot in Alaska in the rowdy boomtown of Skagway, where he and the other fever-struck hopefuls outfitted themselves for a crash course in endurance and survival. Getting from Skagway, at the head of Alaska's Chilkoot Inlet, to Dawson City, hub of the gold rush, required humping more than a thousand pounds of gear hundreds of miles through a frozen, empty wilderness. Accounts of the epic trek are peppered with death and failure, many already fixed in the lore by the time Karstens arrived. He chose to travel the notorious Chilkoot Trail, a thirty-three-mile slog through the coastal mountains that included a staircase chipped into steep rock and ice, because the alternative route, the White Pass Trail, was reportedly paved in the carcasses of miners' packhorses.

Karstens and his partner beat the odds by making it to Dawson City: A third of those who started the journey didn't complete it, either turning back or dying along the way. He didn't beat the odds in terms of striking it rich, which was the outcome for most who rushed to the Yukon's goldfields. But one claim he staked was in good company, with writer Jack London's claim located upstream, according to Walker.

Looking for the "next best thing," Karstens continued down the Yukon River into Alaska, prospecting briefly on the Seventymile River, where he picked up his nickname. The Seventymile didn't pan out either, so the young man moved on, downstream, into the heart of Interior Alaska, where he'd fall into the occupation that built the foundation for his future.

Being a mail carrier in Alaska at the turn of the twentieth century puts a new spin on the classic tagline "Neither snow nor rain nor heat nor gloom of night. . . ." Karstens and his dog team braved obscenely cold temperatures—Walker writes that though the Canadian Yukon prohibited travel when temperatures dropped below –45 degrees Fahrenheit, "no such regulation curtailed travel on the Alaska side of the border . . . reluctant mail carriers were forced out even at –65°F or colder." Karstens and his team were on the trail (if one existed) for weeks at a time, traveling five hundred miles round-trip on a route that linked Eagle on the Canadian border, to Tanana Crossing near present-day Fairbanks, to Circle City on the Yukon River. Later, Karstens moved the mail from Valdez, on the Gulf of Alaska, to Fort Gibbon near Tanana, also via Fairbanks, with the Valdez-to-Fairbanks leg following the Richardson Trail, an old prospecting route nearly four hundred miles long. Karstens also ran mail between Fairbanks and the Kantishna mining district, which would, many years later, be incorporated into Denali National Park.

If surviving the Chilkoot Trail was a crash course in sub-Arctic survival, then being a mail carrier earned Karstens an advanced degree in the subject, with a second major in dog mushing. "The frigid, demanding wilderness transformed the inexperienced young Karstens into one of the toughest of the tough," Walker wrote. Karstens had a small dog team when he undertook his first mail route; by the time his career as a mail carrier was over, he was an expert when it came to handling both sleds and dogs. He also demonstrated an unmatched resilience to wicked wind, epic cold, and unforgiving terrain. The harrowing journeys and narrow escapes described by Walker in *The Seventymile Kid* are testament to the man's physical strength and indomitable spirit.

His reputation as a seasoned and savvy musher, packer, and trail guide brought Karstens to the attention of Charles Sheldon, the wealthy hunter and naturalist outfitting an expedition to study Denali's big game in 1906. Sheldon's three-man party spent two months on the flanks of the High One that summer, a sojourn that made a huge impression on the "millionaire hunter" and whetted his appetite for more. Sheldon was also impressed by Karstens—in *The Wilderness of Denali*, Sheldon described Karstens as "a tall, stalwart man, well poised, frank, and strictly honorable. One of the best dog drivers in the north, and peculiarly fitted by youth and experience for explorations in little-known regions, he proved a most efficient and congenial companion."

Sheldon recruited Karstens for a second season of research and observation, during which the two overwintered on the Toklat River in 1907-08, forging a lifelong friendship and setting in motion the movement that would secure preservation of Denali and its big game as a national park.

The friendship altered the course of Harry Karstens's life. Once the park was established, Sheldon went on to campaign for and secure Karstens's installment as the park's first superintendent. But Denali wouldn't be preserved until 1917, and Karstens would not be hired on until Congress appropriated money for the position in 1921. In the meantime, Karstens's backcountry reputation earned him yet another opportunity.

In 1913, Episcopal Archdeacon Hudson Stuck headlined the team that would finally claim the coveted first ascent of Denali. Karstens was recruited for the expedition and was second to stand on the summit. Historian Walker asserts that, though Stuck garnered the glory as the party's leader, without the skill, experience, and strength of Karstens the team wouldn't have completed the ascent. The climb of Karstens Ridge, named in his honor, is testament to his stamina: He and partner Walter Harper spent weeks cutting steps in an earthquake-shattered jumble of ice along the route, excavating a staircase that opened up the highest ridges and the prize.

In 1921, when Karstens finally arrived in Mount McKinley National Park as its first superintendent, he confronted a clean slate. By this time eleven parks, including Yellowstone, Yosemite, Glacier, Rocky Mountain, Mesa Verde, Lassen Volcanic, Crater Lake, and Mount Rainier, had been outfitted, to varying degrees and with variable success, to meet one of the NPS's mandates as set forth in the 1916 Organic Act: to provide for the enjoyment of their cultural, wildlife, and scenic resources "in such manner and by such means as will leave them unimpaired for the enjoyment of future generations." These parks could be reached with some degree of ease by road or rail, concessions were in place, and rangers provided order and interpretation for visitors.

Mount McKinley National Park, by contrast, was virtually inaccessible. Not only was there no road within the park; there was no road leading to it, let alone accommodations for overnight stays or guidance for wildlife viewing or recreation. It had a solid start on the first Organic Act mandate: "to conserve the scenery and the natural and historic objects and the wild life therein." The rest, not so much. For its first four years, the park was nothing more than a name and lines drawn on paper. Karstens's challenge, then, was both to protect the park's wildlife and natural resources from miners and hunters already working in the big land, and to make sure the park was accessible to a new breed—tourists.

In those first years he labored alone or with a single ranger to assist. Karstens's temperament proved well suited for the solitary, physical tasks of the early days of his superintendency, such as cabin building, maintenance, and mushing. He was not as well suited for some of the administrative challenges. He was a daunting supervisor, quick to dismiss rangers who didn't pass muster. Walker summarizes his imperfections this way: "By nature he was combative and possessed of a volcanic temper. He suffered fools badly. He was a proud man, a self-made man, a man who did not like to be second-guessed once he took a course of action. He had supreme confidence in his own judgment. Notoriously thin-skinned, he took criticism personally."

Karstens at the Helm

In Denali, as in other national parks, the day-to-day operations documented in superintendent's reports open doors to history. By 1924, Karstens had settled into the superintendent's position, and his reports from that year provide insight not only into his temperament but also into what it took to wrangle an institution from an Alaskan wilderness.

The 1924 reports document time spent on the mundane, including stacking firewood, feeding the sled dogs, and office work—"readjusting filing system and compiling liability record" . . . "working on correspondence and filing system" . . . "working on correspondence and expense account." He developed a budget projection for 1926 of $20,000, and arranged for the shipment of caribou to the Alaska Agricultural College and School of Mines, forerunner to the University of Alaska in Fairbanks.

Keeping warm in winter was a priority. In an entry from January 20, with the temperature at –45 degrees Fahrenheit, Karstens notes "consid-

Superintendent Harry Karstens and Stephen Mather, first director of the National Park Service, are seated in front of what appears to be the cabin Karstens and naturalist Charles Sheldon built on the Toklat River in 1907.
HPC-000200; NATIONAL PARK SERVICE HISTORIC PHOTOGRAPH COLLECTION.

erable time consumed in keeping fires going and fixing barn to keep stock warm." The cold also discouraged visitors. When a pair of "distinguished Texans" arrived in the park to view "a real dog team," Karstens wrote they were so put off by the weather—it was –55 degrees Fahrenheit—that they left before he could get their names.

The park's first visitors arrived in April that year; Karstens would be able to count the tourists arriving daily through the summer months on one hand. Thirty-five people attended the Fourth of July dance in McKinley Park Station, then site of the park's headquarters as well as its gateway. The next day Karstens noted that the "good time was somewhat marred by some of the men being full of Moonshine."

Construction work on the Denali Park Road was under way by May, and the superintendent helped the Alaska Road Commission crews deal with cutting a track in the frozen ground, bridging streams, and draining water from the "bottomless mire that takes the place of frozen muck" along the route as the summer season progressed. Other work in the park proceeded at a quick clip, with rangers stringing telephone line along the roadway as it progressed, cutting and storing hay, working with stock, hauling off brush for fire suppression, and putting up food for winter. By August, Ranger Way was gathering moss to chink the park headquarters buildings, and the tent that Olaus Murie had been using for his caribou studies on the Savage River had been retrieved.

Poaching occupied much time and thought. Karstens was mindful of the conundrum he confronted, in that "such hunting as is going on in the Park is being done illegally or by prospectors who are permitted, under the law, to kill game when short of food." It was hard to differentiate between the two at times.

In one instance, considering the case for potential poaching put forward by Rufus Nichols, the Alaska Railroad's station agent and telegraph operator in McKinley Park Station, Karstens concluded that Nichols "had had a quarrel" with some of the people he was ratting out, and that the evidence Nichols passed along was, in the superintendent's opinion, "not worth the paper it was written on. It consisted o' surmises and guesses."

But Karstens was more confident of crimes being committed by a poacher named Jack Donnelly, who was seen on several occasions outside the park pulling sleds loaded with kills. Karstens confronted the man when he encountered him hauling a dead caribou out of the park, reminding him that hunting within the boundaries was illegal and that the kill should be reported. "What in hell would I do that for?" the prospector replied, asserting that it was the park's business to find out about the kill, not his to report.

Karstens was disappointed when prosecution of Donnelly failed in court, in part because sympathies among witnesses and judges leaned toward the hunters. "Our only hope for adequate conservation lies in the obtaining of whole-hearted support by the people," Karstens wrote. "The process of swinging the attitude of these people to the point of recognizing the importance and value of conservation of wild life, as practiced by the national parks, promises to be a slow and tedious one, requiring much missionary work."

An incident in August illustrates the superintendent's prickly temperament. The scene was a dinner party, hosted by Karstens and his wife, with two ladies and Ranger Way as guests. Way "was rather morose and quiet," Karstens wrote, and when the ladies attempted to include him in the conversation, the ranger "took advantage of this kindness in what I considered an insulting way." The superintendent, noting that "what followed I can hardly be responsible for," dismissed the rude ranger from the event and then followed him "over to the barn and there gave him a trouncing and ordered him off park lands paying his salary due him." Way levied charges, which Karstens pled guilty to. The former ranger then went to work for the park concessioner.

Karstens discharged a second ranger a month later. In early September, Karstens felt that Ranger McFarland had been derelict in his duties on patrol, and he also had received a report that McFarland had shot and killed a park dog the previous fall. "His methods are not in accordance with my ideas of honest administration of the park," Karstens wrote in his report for September 11.

In October, as winter settled in, Karstens prepared a roundup of the tourist season: 128 people had ventured to McKinley Park Station but not come into the park proper. Sixty-six ventured in, including twenty on foot, two by airplane, and thirty-five escorted by the concessioner. He also tallied game—1,540 caribou were seen in the park, but only 50 sheep—and recapped progress on construction at park headquarters. And as was his habit, he dutifully recorded the steadily dropping temperature. . . .

The End of the Karstens Era

Harry Karstens's time was almost up when Grant Pearson was hired on as a temporary ranger in 1926. He'd accomplished a lot in a few short years. The Denali Park Road had been advanced well into the park. Patrol cabins had been built along the route. Park headquarters had been relocated from McKinley Park Station to its present site. Karstens had acquired a contingent of sled dogs to help with park patrols. And he'd spread the welcome mat for the national park's first visitors, which had been growing in numbers since the completion of the Alaska Railroad line in 1923.

But his volatility finally translated into a conflict that would end his career with the NPS. According to Pearson, an argument about where to build a cabin had flared between Karstens and his chief ranger, Fritz Nyberg, which culminated with Nyberg's dismissal. Nyberg fired off a letter to the park service, "citing the civil service regulation that a man cannot be fired without just and due cause." When Nyberg won, Karstens walked. He resigned from the park service in 1928.

Karstens was fifty years old at the time of his retirement. He settled quietly into business in Fairbanks with his wife, Louise, and son, Eugene. He lived the rest of his life in that northern town, which boasts views of Denali and the expanse of the Alaska Range on clear days, and was laid to rest there in 1955.

Grant Pearson

It's as if your spirits are lifted up as the mountain goes up. When a man has that feeling, he'd better hit for the high places because, let's face it, he's a sucker for perpendicular real estate.

—Grant Pearson, *My Life of High Adventure*

There's simply no way to dislike this man.

Grant Pearson arrived in Alaska young, inexperienced, full of good will and good humor, and completely open to freedom, opportunity, and adventure. His path north was very different from Karstens's, but like the man he'd idolized as a boy, Pearson would never leave. His autobiography, *My Life of High Adventure*, is a joyful account of his life and times in Denali National Park.

Pearson was born in Minnesota in 1900. When his mother was forced to break up the family after Pearson's father abandoned them, the teenager ended up on an uncle's farm. Unable to complete high school, Pearson educated himself by reading the books in his uncle's library, including stories about Alaska and the Yukon by Jack London and Robert Service, and tales of a young adventurer called the Seventymile

Park superintendent Grant Pearson at the Toklat patrol cabin in 1954.
PHOTO COURTESY OF THE NATIONAL PARK SERVICE, DENALI NATIONAL PARK AND PRESERVE MUSEUM COLLECTIONS.

Kid. A passion for the place and a desire to meet the Kid was sparked by those books, but it would be a few years before Pearson could manage a journey north. After leaving home he served briefly in the army, and then headed west to Washington State to work as a logger. Both were satisfying occupations, but when a friend proposed they go to Alaska, telling Pearson, "They're building roads and they're crazy for men," the young man didn't hesitate.

Pearson and friend arrived in the port town of Cordova on the Gulf of Alaska with empty pockets. Unable to pay for rail tickets to the Alaska Road Commission jobsite, the two stocked up on "bread and bologna" and walked the railroad line north toward Fairbanks and the promise of a paycheck. Pearson spent a season in the employ of the road commission, building in the shadow of the Alaska Range and the Wrangell

Mountains, eyes drawn to the distance whenever they didn't have to focus on the work. When winter shut down the roadwork, Pearson continued north to Fairbanks and found employment there.

Word that Mount McKinley National Park was looking for a seasonal ranger materialized in the spring, and Pearson took the train to McKinley Park Station to see if he might land the position. "I found myself applying for a job from the one man I'd never thought I'd meet, Harry Karstens, the Seventymile Kid," he recalled. After assuring Karstens he could handle himself in "wild country," he was hired.

A Ranger Is Born

Settling in on that first night as a ranger, Pearson reviewed the paper Karstens had given him describing what he'd be doing in Mount McKinley National Park. He was introduced to a concept he wasn't familiar with: conservation.

"I was one of the custodians of the place, it was up to me, not to civilize this place, but actually to defend it against the encroachments of civilization. This was a new idea. The more I thought about it, the more I thought it was a good one," he wrote. Buying into the national park idea from the start shaped Pearson's career—he spent the next three decades with the NPS and became a devoted conservationist.

But his tenure in Denali got off to a rough start. He begins his autobiography with a harrowing tale of being lost in the woods of the Alaska Range, trying to find a patrol cabin in the dark and cold. Not long after that Pearson and a fellow ranger were dispatched to patrol a stretch of parkland between the Savage and Sanctuary Rivers. This was a test of their mettle, according to Karstens. The patrol was peppered with difficulties. There wasn't enough snow to maneuver a sled, so they had to cover many miles on foot, backtracking when they encountered dangerous terrain. One of the two dogs they outfitted with packs to carry supplies went on a rabbit hunt and destroyed his load. They spent one night in a cabin rank with animal droppings. But they made it back alive, handling themselves well enough to earn Karstens's spare praise. After a day off Pearson was dispatched alone on a snowshoe patrol. In those first few months he'd count sheep, rabbits, and caribou; cut trails; build and repair patrol cabins; track poachers; learn to handle dogs and sleds; and be asked to stay on permanently. He was green—a cheechako—but he was thriving.

And then it happened. As he was heading up to Big Timber, near Kantishna, where he and ranger Fritz Nyberg were charged with building a patrol cabin, Denali unveiled itself to Pearson for the first time.

"Directly across the river rose the highest mountain, from its base to its summit, in the whole world. You can't imagine the impact of that sheer rock-and-ice upthrust . . . Why, if that mountain had been any steeper I felt it would be leaning over dripping glacier water onto my hat," he wrote.

After building the Big Timber cabin, Pearson was stationed there for several long winter seasons, conducting solo patrols and learning, then polishing, a set of impressive backcountry skills—"tricks of the trade," as he called them. He befriended the miners and trappers in the fading mining town of Kantishna, enjoying the hospitality of Fannie and Joe Quigley, Polly and John Anderson, and Little Johnnie Busia, whose ingenuity in bush living both entertained and educated the young ranger.

In 1928, the same year Karstens resigned, Pearson took a hiatus from the park so that he could learn to fly. He met McKinley's new superintendent, and his future supervisor, Henry Liek, in Seward as he was headed Outside. Liek assured him that if he chose to return, he'd be hired back.

Pearson took Liek up on the offer a year later and returned to the park service and Denali. Not long after that Liek asked the young man to join him and two other adventurers, Alfred Lindley and Erling Strom, on an ascent of Denali. The trip tested every fiber of the ranger's being—physical strength, endurance, willingness to learn, capacity to overcome fear, and, ultimately, his ability to carry on in the face of tragedy and disaster. On the climb he'd learn to ski (a sport he was convinced was a fad), reach the top of the continent (the team was the first to summit both Denali's South and North Peaks), fall into a crevasse (he'd extricate himself, climbing a rope hand over hand), and help evacuate the members of the Cosmic Ray team after two of their party lost their lives in a crevasse accident. It was a triumph he'd dreamed of since boyhood, and now it was part of him.

Rising to the Top, Again

The ascent behind him, Pearson settled back into the business of rangering. He met Margaret Wolf while vacationing in Seattle in 1937. After the two were married in 1938, Margaret joined him in Denali. In 1939 he put in for a transfer to a park with more tourist traffic, recognizing that the skills he'd developed working alone in the backcountry weren't adequate when it came to dealing with the increasing numbers of tourists expected in the park. He got that experience in spades when he accepted a position in Yosemite National Park, where lines of cars formed at entrance stations and you couldn't set foot on a trail that didn't have another hiker on it. "In one day, looking out the ticket window in the little shack at the Arch Rock gate, I saw more people drive by than had visited McKinley in an entire year," he wrote. He and Margaret adopted a daughter, Shirley, during their time in Yosemite. But by 1942, Pearson had learned enough. When the chief ranger position opened at Mount McKinley, he and Margaret headed home.

By then Harry Liek had moved on to a new appointment at Wind Cave National Park in South Dakota, and a new superintendent, Frank Been, was in charge. The dogs that had been part of his patrols in earlier days had been replaced by snow machines. Pearson's autobiography is brutally honest about what the ranger thought of the new superintendent and the new regime—and it wasn't good. Fortunately, Been was called up for military duty, and Pearson received news that he had been appointed acting superintendent in Been's absence. When Been informed his chief ranger of the new assignments, he let Pearson know he didn't think he'd be "capable of the job" and that he'd recommended Pearson be replaced as quickly as possible.

"I don't know why or how I held my temper," Pearson wrote. "Must have been years of training as a ranger. I didn't wring his neck, even though I felt sure such action would have improved it greatly."

Pearson proved he was more than capable in the years that followed. With the McKinley Park Hotel closed to tourists but open to enlisted men who needed some R&R, Pearson oversaw the installation of a ski run, toboggan slide, and skating rink for their enjoyment. He joined Brad and Barbara Washburn on their historic 1947 Operation White Tower summit expedition, though he'd stop short of the top, recognizing the toll the altitude was taking. "Nothing doing," he told Washburn when his friend tried to coax him along. "The mountain has just spoken to me and he's ordered me off his front porch."

And when an Army transport plane crashed in a remote mountainous area of the park in 1944, he oversaw the expedition that attempted to recover the bodies of the men lost in the accident. The team spent six weeks in the effort, which earned the acting superintendent a Medal of Freedom, but weather and terrain stymied the recovery.

The park's chief ranger, Grant Pearson, is pictured in 1944 during a rescue mission to Mount Deception.

PHOTO COURTESY OF THE NATIONAL PARK SERVICE, DENALI NATIONAL PARK AND PRESERVE MUSEUM COLLECTIONS. PHOTO BY J. M. GREANY.

"As for bringing those bodies out," Pearson wrote, "what finer resting place could they have, cradled in that beautiful, rugged, virgin country, deep under a perpetual blanket of clean white snow, guarded by the northern lights in winter and the midnight sun in summer?"

Pearson was appointed Denali's superintendent in 1949. In his tenure he'd oversee the installation of campgrounds at Wonder Lake, Teklanika, and Savage River, as well as modern plumbing and electrical systems at park headquarters; establish the park's museum; and lay plans for the Eielson Visitor Center. His official reports, like Karstens's, reflect on the weather (there were twenty-five days of rain in August 1955); the administrative business of running the park (think paperwork); preparing to shut operations down in winter and open them up in summer; and ensuring facilities were built and maintained adequately for park visitors. In one report he noted that the Horseshoe Lake Trail had to be closed for three days because of its wet condition and because a troublesome grizzly bear was frequenting the area. Pearson also ensured that Denali's tradition of scientific inquiry was supported, including the cartographic work of friend and fellow mountaineer Brad Washburn and the long-term studies of wildlife biologist Adolph Murie.

The focus on Denali's natural wonders, common as well as uncommon, crop up often in Pearson's reports. In October 1954 the superintendent noted that an "albino bull moose has been reported several times in the vicinity of the Pilgrim mine, near the Park boundary on Lower Toklat. The animal was reported by a competent observer." Then he noted that "two ptarmigan rested on the Chief Ranger's front porch after being chased by two goshawks. The chase continued after a few minutes, with all four birds disappearing [into] the dense spruce forest across Rock Creek." This was a man who watched, and considered carefully, every aspect of the park he loved.

End of the Pearson Era

By 1956, Grant Pearson had logged more than thirty years in the park service. Recognizing that it was time to move on, he resigned and split his time for the next couple of years between a home in California and a cabin he had built on a homestake claim just outside the park boundary near Wonder Lake. After Alaska was admitted to the Union in 1959, Pearson moved back to the state full-time and won election to the state legislature, representing the district that included his beloved Denali.

As with all his endeavors, Pearson plunged into political life with vigor and humor. But life in Denali informed even this endeavor: Studying up on *Robert's Rules of Order*, he observed, "there are more devious legal meanderings in that book than there are caribou trails on the Toklat Flats." After years of public service, Pearson passed away in Anchorage at the age of seventy-eight.

> *One day last summer I was sitting on the chopping block outside my tundra cabin, getting the tangle out of a fish line. Occasionally I'd glance up at the white crest of McKinley. Out there, I finally got things kind of straightened around in my mind.*
>
> —Grant Pearson, *My Life of High Adventure*

Chapter Nine

On Denali's Skirts: Superwomen

When Mount McKinley National Park was established in 1917, women hadn't yet won the right to vote. But suffrage was ascendant, and women were beginning to stand on their own as teachers and scientists, in literature, politics, and business. As adventurers on the western frontier before the turn of the century, a handful had earned lasting and widely celebrated reputations distinct from those of their husbands or male contemporaries. But by choice and by circumstance, most were wives, mothers, and homemakers who quietly wove their voices into the fabric of their families and communities. In the historical record, their words are scanty compared to those of their male contemporaries, but women's stories are slowly gaining ground in the lore of the mining camps, small towns, and neighborhoods where they lived.

The case is no different when it comes to women on the Alaskan frontier, and in Denali. As the region's appeal spread and men—miners, hunters, mountaineers, rangers, scholars, and scientists—began to cultivate their passion for the place, women did the same. Their images, more than their words, are part of the record; they stand just outside the limelight that illuminated their husbands as they were appointed superintendent, championed the park's wildlife, or pioneered a new route to the summit of Denali.

But a number of women made significant and lasting contributions to the park. What stands out is their fitness for whatever it was they endeavored, whether killing, dressing, and preserving game; working placer mines in Kantishna; flying air taxis; running roadhouses; catering

Three women stand in front of the McKinley Park post office in this photo from 1939.
PHOTO COURTESY OF THE NATIONAL PARK SERVICE, DENALI NATIONAL PARK AND PRESERVE MUSEUM COLLECTIONS.

to the park's growing number of visitors; making a first ascent; or establishing a conservation foundation. Their stories should be told as well.

Lost in Translation

It's difficult to uncover the singular contributions of the Athabascan women who called Denali home before the arrival of white men. Their legacies and culture are difficult to fully appreciate, their stories largely ignored due to colonial prejudice, overlooked in rushes for fur and gold, literally lost in translation from the oral to the written word. Sometimes Athabascan women crop up in written histories as footnotes, with mentions as fleeting as a name and whom they married or whom they bore. Consider Jennie, Koyukon mother of Walter Harper, the first man to stand atop Denali. The details are obscure, but Jennie raised Walter in the

Athabascan tradition after his white father, prospector Arthur Harper, abandoned the family shortly after his son's birth. Walter Harper's remarkable accomplishment reflects well on his mother, but the specifics of how she reared her son and his siblings, of any words of caution or motivation, of lessons taught and hardships endured, are not readily found.

Some insight into the lives of Denali's Athabascan women is contained in oral histories. In one such history Abbie Joseph recalls the subsistence lifestyle she and her family cultivated at the foot of the High One near the turn of the twentieth century. They called Birch Creek home, but her extended family reached from the creek to "Toklat, Cos Jacket, Nenana, and Telida," traveling between these places and seasonal hunting grounds in canoes, with sleds, and on foot. The band moved with the game from lowland to highland; they harvested fish and caribou, berries and birds, and willow and spruce to build traps, shelters, boats, and sleds.

"Along the way to the mountains there was an overhanging ledge, like a porch on a house," Abbie told ethno-historian Dianne Gudgel-Holmes and linguist Eliza Jones in the early 1980s. "Willows grow around it, so it is sheltered from the rain. There, we would always camp . . . We made a smokehouse too, and dried caribou, sheep—everything we caught. We made dry meat, just like drying fish."

Abbie was married, then widowed, then married again, bearing six children and adopting another two. Her story—a modest portrait of a woman who, like others, played a critical role in the lives of those who knew her—would be lost to all but sons and daughters, grandchildren, and perhaps great-grandchildren but for the curiosity of academics and the recognition that, even if only on a single-page record prepared by Denali National Park and Preserve, Abbie's experience matters.

Fannie Quigley

Ask a ranger about women in Denali, and the first name that pops to mind is Fannie Quigley. And if there's one story that captures her essence—and the essence of many an Alaskan frontierswoman—it's one told by Grant Pearson, then a young ranger in a young national park, about Fannie and the caribou.

One day, late in the 1920s, Pearson checked in on Fannie and discovered her sopping wet. He asked why; Fannie responded by describing how she'd encountered a couple of caribou in the willow near Moose Creek and taken shots at both, intent on adding them to her winter cache of meat. The two animals bolted into the creek after the shots, and "when they got in the middle the darned fools fell dead," Fannie explained. "A nice fix to be in! Two caribou in the middle of a stream running slush ice." Undeterred, the petite hunter waded out into the stream, roped the caribou up, hauled them ashore, and then dressed and cached them, all before changing her clothes.

Born in Nebraska in 1870, Fannie Sedlacek left a hardscrabble life on the family farm when she was sixteen and headed west, following the railroad and working as a waitress and cook. Her path turned north with

Fannie Quigley holds a rifle on her lap on the porch of her Kantishna home circa 1940.

PHOTO COURTESY OF THE NATIONAL PARK SERVICE, DENALI NATIONAL PARK AND PRESERVE MUSEUM COLLECTIONS.

the stampede to the Klondike in 1896, and she landed in the boomtown of Dawson City, where women could make a good living simply by dancing with lonely miners. But in time Fannie found a better way to make a buck: She set up business offering meals to hungry men working claims outside of Dawson who hadn't the time or energy to prepare their own.

"I planned it to be first on the scene at a new strike, because that's the way you made the big money selling meals," she told Pearson, who recorded the story in *My Life of High Adventure*. "In winter I went by dog team, in summer by boat or any other way that would get me there with my tent, Yukon stove, bacon, beans, flour and other stuff. I reckon I've hung out my 'Meals For Sale' sign at most every strike in the north." Her ability to follow the miners, according to a story in the *Fairbanks Daily News-Miner*, earned her the nickname of "Fannie the Hike." She also staked her first mining claim while in the Klondike; for all that she made money using her practical skills, she'd also contracted gold fever and would never be cured.

A brief marriage to a miner named Angus McKenzie, called "mutually bad" by one interpretive ranger, ended with Fannie taking a sled dog team and fleeing the Klondike. She was known for using foul language, wearing men's clothing, and possessing a formidable ability to put away liquor, which reportedly contributed to the marital strife. Fannie eventually landed in Fairbanks, having followed the color west from strike to strike. In 1906, when gold was discovered in Kantishna, then called Eureka, Fannie headed for Denali's hills. She set up shop as a cook to the miners but also staked, and later worked, a number of placer claims in the region. The Kantishna rush flamed out quickly, but Fannie did not; she remained in the fading tundra town for the remainder of her days.

She met Joe Quigley in Kantishna—Quigley's discovery on Glacier Creek had been part of the impetus for the Kantishna rush—and they built a life together there. The *News-Miner* story hints that their relations did not get off to a conventional start—Fannie apparently didn't secure a proper divorce from her first husband, and so couldn't marry her second until Angus McKenzie met his maker. The consensus is that Joe and Fannie were properly wedded in 1918. In the meantime, Fannie set up both house and shop with Joe, a "little 100-pound bundle of energy [who

Miner and pioneer Fannie Quigley leads a sled dog team.
PHOTO COURTESY OF THE NATIONAL PARK SERVICE, DENALI NATIONAL PARK AND PRESERVE MUSEUM COLLECTIONS.

settled] down to a quiet life as a big-game hunter, trapper, dog musher, prospector, wood cutter and gardener," wrote Pearson.

By the time Pearson met Fannie in the 1920s, when he built and staffed the Kantishna ranger cabin, she and Joe were firmly ensconced as core members of the tiny, tight-knit bush community. She cooked and entertained the new ranger, preparing lavish meals featuring ingredients she grew in her spectacular garden, harvested from the land, or killed and butchered herself. "Fannie was liberal with her food," Pearson recalled, "but she would not allow anyone to waste a morsel." When a visitor left a pat of butter on his plate, Fannie advised him that it would be waiting for him in the morning; the visitor ended up finishing the butter with his pie.

She was as fearless as she was generous. She and Joe went their separate ways to conduct business—she mostly worked the placers, and he delved into hard-rock mining, with some success. She was proficient in rigging splints or setting stitches. She was there to patch him up when he got hurt, not uncommon given the nature of the work. Though Pearson says she wasn't formally educated, "she was alert and widely read, and could hold her own." She was also comfortable heading off into the wilds to hunt and trap. When Pearson found Fannie missing during another of his visits, Joe explained, "She's been gone for five days, over to Bear Creek. She took the dog team and will bring back a load of moose meat we cached there. She also put out some trap lines on her last trip and is doing some trapping."

Joe Quigley was seriously injured in an accident at one of his mines in 1930, which ended both his Kantishna career and his marriage. By one account, he met a young nurse during his rehabilitation and married her after divorcing Fannie in 1937. He moved Outside, to Seattle, with his new bride. But Fannie, enamored of Denali, stayed on in Kantishna until her death in 1944, taking up residence in a little cabin preserved within the park, presently a candidate for designation on the National Register of Historic Places.

The Backbeat

The pictures flesh out the story, because the words are skeletal. Flip through the images stored in the park's archives and the wives are there. They stand alongside, they are pictured in the wagon with the children, and they sit on the porches of cabins in the backcountry. That their husbands are beside them is testament to how integral they were to the accomplishments those husbands are remembered for, even if their contributions aren't as easy to articulate.

In the annals of the women who stood beside Denali's most celebrated men, two stand out, and remarkably, they were both called Louise. But other superintendents' wives and scientists' wives are captured in photographs and mentioned in passing as well, representing a wealth of stories that have yet to be told.

Louise Karstens

Frieda Louise Gaerisch married Harry Karstens in 1914, a year after he'd become one of the first men to stand on Denali's summit, seven years before he became the first superintendent of Mount McKinley National Park, and five years after she'd moved to Alaska and become a nurse in Fairbanks. Karstens started courting Louise the year before the climb, according to historian Tom Walker, so she must have had some idea of (and tolerance for) the independence and adventure that would follow her marriage. If not, her honeymoon would have been a wake-up call: Karstens took off on a months-long hunting expedition up the Toklat right after the wedding. He termed it "tough luck"; Walker doesn't note what Louise thought of the situation.

But in *The Seventymile Kid*, his biography of Karstens, Walker does recount these illuminating thoughts from the husband, made by Karstens to friend and fellow adventurer Charles Sheldon: "[My] wife is trying to civilize me but it is a hard job. Every once in a while I take a trip for a month or so and when I get back she is glad to see me . . . but she says she hasn't lost hope yet."

The two started their married life in Fairbanks, their first home made in that small, isolated boomtown at the confluence of the Chena and Tanana Rivers. Son Eugene was born in 1917, the same year the park was established, in an even smaller town, Nenana. The move to the new national park took place a couple of years later, after Karstens was appointed superintendent and the park's chief—and only—ranger.

Karstens's first order of business after his appointment was to build a home cabin in the new park headquarters near Riley Creek, but this was incomplete when Louise and Eugene moved to McKinley Park Station in November 1921, so the family lived in a tent. In her roadside history of Denali, historian Jane Bryant includes Louise's recollection of their arrival: "It was 15 below zero the day I arrived there. When we arrived at the park we were all loaded on a double-ender [sled] with one horse on one end and a couple of men on the other end, as we had to go down a steep hill. It was very dark and I guess the old horse must have stumbled over a stump for we all rolled off the sled and halfway down the hill before we stopped, where we picked ourselves up." A no-nonsense recollection from a woman who clearly was not only understanding of Alaska's hardships but amenable to them.

She was also amenable to whatever auxiliary duties were required in terms of park administration. Bryant notes that "like many NPS spouses during the early years, Louise was an ad hoc part of the park work force." In 1925 she earned a small wage as a "third ranger" to assist her husband in an official status; she also worked as "community nurse." When visitors or dignitaries arrived, she and her husband took charge of their care and entertainment, which included serving meals and attending special events. This was not without its perks; Karstens noted that his wife and two other guests were the first visitors to travel into the park in an automobile after the superintendent drove them to the Savage River to take in the sights.

After Karstens left the park service in 1928, the family settled in Fairbanks. The Kartenses' rustic log cabin, built by Harry and completed just before his death in 1955, still stands in Pioneer Park, according to an article in the *Fairbanks Daily News-Miner*. Louise lived there in the years after her husband's death and passed away in 1974.

Louise Murie

Louise Murie was part of a four-part conservation harmony. Her husband, Adolph Murie, is well known for his books about Denali's wolves and grizzlies, and for his outspoken defense of Denali's wilderness. Her half-sister and brother-in-law, Margaret (Mardy) and Olaus Murie, were leaders in the Wilderness Society and at the forefront of the movement that resulted in preservation of the Arctic National Wildlife Refuge.

Louise's efforts on behalf of wilderness are less celebrated, but were integral to the conservation legacy that endures in the Murie name and in conservation and learning centers in both Denali and Grand Teton National Parks. Though she was less visible, as writer Craig Medred observed in an article written shortly after her death, she, Adolph, Olaus, and Mardy were "arguably the most important figures in Alaska's early wilderness and conservation movement."

Born Louise Gillette in Fairbanks in 1912, she met Adolph when she was ten years old, according to an article in the *Jackson Hole News & Times*. "When he had to leave, he said, 'Aren't you going to kiss me goodbye?'" she told the newspaper. "He kissed me on the cheek, and the place where he kissed me burned for a long time." They married in 1932 in Jackson Hole, Wyoming, and then traveled together to the University of Michigan, where she studied botany while he worked in zoology.

Louise Murie sits with her husband, Adolph, at the East Fork cabin in 1965.
PHOTO COURTESY OF THE NATIONAL PARK SERVICE, DENALI NATIONAL PARK AND PRESERVE MUSEUM COLLECTIONS. PHOTO BY VERDE WATSON.

The couple returned to Alaska in 1939, when Murie was hired to study wolves in Mount McKinley National Park. By then they had two young children, son Jan and daughter Gail. The family took up residence in a backcountry ranger cabin in the summer season, and, as Louise recounted in the *News & Times* article, she took care of "domestic life" while, famously, her husband trekked nearly two thousand miles doing his field research.

Louise had her own querying mind, and while walking with her children, she studied Denali's flora. During the many summers the family spent in the park, Louise carefully documented its variety of plant life, researching Latin names, describing the plants in detail, and collecting about a hundred specimens that were later shipped to the University of Alaska. An article in the *Fairbanks Daily News-Miner* records the introduction to the *McKinley Flora* manuscript Louise produced:

> *For a period of 30 years my husband and I were in Mount McKinley National Park every summer while he was engaged in wildlife studies for the National Park Service. Naturally, these also led to study of habitats and their vegetation, and it was inevitable that we should learn to know the many alpine flowers. Together we became acquainted with their characteristics and with the places where they were usually found, and he took many color pictures. This booklet is an outgrowth of that joint interest and love for the delicate beauty, and hardiness, of the tundra flora.*

Louise remarried after Adolph's death in 1974, settling in Jackson, Wyoming, with second husband Donald MacLeod (who died in 1983), and was one hundred years old when she passed away in Jackson in 2012.

Women on the Mountain

The star of Barbara Washburn's talented spouse, Bradford Washburn, outshines hers in many ways. But on at least one count the wife trumps the husband. When he ascended to the summit of Denali, he was following in the footsteps of other men. When she summited Denali, she was the first of her gender to stand atop the continent. The women who've followed walk in her footsteps.

Barbara Polk was born and raised in the Boston area, and met her husband after becoming his executive secretary at the Boston Museum of Science's Institute of Geography. She didn't want to work for a "crazy mountain climber," she told interviewer Dave Krupa in an oral history for the University of Alaska's Project Jukebox. But she took the job anyway. They were married in 1940, and their mountain adventures together began on their honeymoon, when they climbed Mount Bertha near Glacier Bay.

In 1947, Barbara was asked to be part of Operation White Tower, an expedition that combined filmmaking with science and mountaineering on the slopes of Denali. Footage shot on the expedition would be used in a short film accompanying a feature film called *The White Tower*; the thinking was that having a woman on screen would add to the movie's appeal.

Barbara had three small children at home, and in her oral history she confessed to feeling guilty about leaving them for such a long time to be part of such a dangerous undertaking. She was both mother and adventurer, and she sought to strike a balance. In the end, and after much soul-searching, she and her husband arranged for grandparents and a nurse to take care of the kids, and she joined the expedition. But her stories from Operation White Tower are peppered with her desire to return home safely to her children. Dying on Denali was not an option.

The tales she relates reflect her determination, confidence, and a sense of humor that buoyed her and her companions. The expedition, which took about three months, included an epic Denali storm that trapped Barbara in a tent with two fellow climbers for nine days. Such close quarters could have been painfully uncomfortable, but the three emerged friends. She mused about the significance of her climb in context, referencing the fact that George Browne, son of pioneering Denali mountaineer Belmore Browne, was part of her summit team, and that even though he had a terrible headache, it was just as important that he make it to the top as it was for her.

Perhaps most telling is the story she relates about the final approach to the summit. She was roped in with several other mountaineers, and the man leading moved aside to let her step on top first. Her reaction: What difference would that make? His response: You are making history.

"I said, oh fiddle dee dee. I had no sense of what was happening," she recalled. She was sure no one would "make a fuss." Her first thought once on top, she said, was that she had to "get home to my kids safely." But before that could happen, she had to pass the time on the summit while her husband worked, stomping around to keep warm at –20 degrees in "a big wind." Finally, she paused to take it all in. It was just like Hudson Stuck of the first ascent party had written decades before, she said—like "looking out the windows of heaven."

She reached the summit on June 6; a photograph shows her and her husband sporting glorious smiles. The next day she and Brad climbed the North Peak; as of 2016 she remains the only woman to have climbed both peaks on consecutive days. On the final descent she and

Brad had their only (recorded) tiff. They were headed down Karstens Ridge, roped together, and she had to find the steps that had been cut into the slope on the way up, which had filled in with snow and were too long for her shorter legs. She shouted up to Brad, "Goddamn the son of a bitch who cut these steps." When he responded that he'd done it, she replied, "Well, that goes for you too!" She added that she had kids to get home to; he pointed out that they were his children too . . .

Her obituary—she died in 2014 at the age of ninety-nine—includes a quote from Lew Freedman, who collaborated with Barbara on her memoir, *The Accidental Adventurer*. "In the vernacular of the time, people referred to her as a 'game gal.' She never complained. She just sort of did it."

"I had no real feeling about being a pioneering woman on a serious Alaskan expedition," she mused in her University of Alaska interview. "I only knew that as the only woman, I had to measure up." She'd measured up on Denali, and she'd measure up throughout her career. She went on to help her husband map the Grand Canyon, New Hampshire's White Mountains, and Mount Everest. Her accomplishments would earn her the Centennial Award from the National Geographic Society in 1988, which she received along with her husband; Sir Edmund Hillary, who first summited Everest; sea explorer and filmmaker Jacques Cousteau; pioneering primatologist Jane Goodall; and astronaut John Glenn.

Many other women have followed Washburn to the summit of Denali. In recent years, according to park records, an average of 11 percent of the 1,200 climbers who take on the challenge of Denali are women—about 130 annually. The first all-female ascent was made in 1970. Betty Menard was the first female Native American to reach the top. Susan Butcher, four-time winner of the Iditarod sled dog race, was part of the first dog-team ascent of Denali in 1979. Joan Phelps was the first blind person to reach the summit in 1993. The youngest female summiter is Merrick Johnston, who made the climb in 1995 at the age of twelve; at the other end of the age spectrum, seventy-year-old Toshiko Uchida reached the top in 2001. Italian mountaineer Miri Ercolani is widely acknowledged as the first woman to make a solo ascent, in 1982. Her accomplishment was contested by Norma Jean Saunders, who soloed in 1990 and claimed the title on the grounds that Ercolani's ascent was not sufficiently documented. Such is the nature of a solo climb: No one is watching. But the accomplishments of both climbers are remarkable, no matter the first.

Denali's female mountaineers, regardless of age, background, or era, are formidable, thoughtful women who have had much more to prove in what is traditionally the domain of men. Barbara Washburn opened the door to that wonderful, dangerous, competitive world on Denali. And while some women may still feel they have something to prove in the airy heights, they also want to experience what Barbara Washburn and Hudson Stuck experienced: the view out the windows of heaven.

Business in the Backcountry

Denali is a national park, but it is also a business. From the earliest days of the park, the careers of hoteliers, cooks, fliers, packers, guides, and others were hitched to the growth in popularity of the preserve. A handful of women stand out in this regard, flourishing as entrepreneurs as well as conservationists, citizen scientists, and good neighbors.

Ginny Wood and Celia Hunter are powerful examples of how conservation can be compatible with good business. Their wilderness lodge overlooking Denali was eventually folded into the park, but before that happened, these two women folded the park into their business ethic.

The Fliers

Wood (née Hill) and Hunter became friends through work and war. Both were Women Airforce Service Pilots (WASPs) during World War II, trained to ferry military aircraft of all kinds to various bases stateside since male pilots were in short supply. Their lifelong friendship was built on a love for adventure born in the air and a strong conservation ethic built on the tundra and taiga below Denali.

The two first came to Alaska after the war, when they ferried small Stinson aircraft from Seattle to Fairbanks in the winter of 1947. The fliers decided to stay awhile and explore, working a season as bush pilots doing a different kind of ferrying—taking tourists flightseeing between Fairbanks and Kotzebue.

After Ginny's marriage to Morton "Woody" Wood, an Alaskan park ranger, the three explored the state together and eventually decided to look for a place to set up a wilderness camp, where they could introduce visitors to the landscapes they loved and the conservation ethics that would help preserve them. They settled on a homestead just outside the boundary of Mount McKinley National Park, on a ridge with a pond in the Kantishna District. Camp Denali, which opened in 1952, not only boasted uncompromised views of the mountain (when the clouds cleared) but was built using local spruce and "reclaimed materials from the National Park Service, often with the serendipitous help of friends and plucky visitors," according to a history published on the camp's website.

After a quarter of a century of hospitality, Wood and Hunter sold Camp Denali to a couple who, like so many others, had come north for a season and decided to stay. Jerryne and Wally Cole not only took over operation of Camp Denali but also acquired a lodge built on former park superintendent Grant Pearson's homestead. Both the camp and lodge, now private inholdings within Denali National Park and Preserve, have since passed into the care of the Coles' daughter Jenna and her family.

Once free of the constraints of running a business, Wood and Hunter were able to focus on their conservation efforts. They were among the founders of the Alaska Conservation Society. Wood was a vocal and effective proponent of the Arctic National Wildlife Refuge. Both advocated for passage of the Alaska National Interest Lands Conservation Act (ANILCA), which protected millions of acres as wilderness within Denali and elsewhere in the state. They received a number of awards for their conservation efforts, including the Sierra Club's John Muir Award and the Alaska Conservation Foundation's first-ever Lifetime Achievement Award. Reflecting on their conservation legacy, the then-head of the Foundation said, "Each of these women epitomizes, in their own way, the best of Alaska's conservation movement. They overcame substantial challenges to create a life in Alaska that is respectful of the natural environment. They've dedicated their lives to environmental justice and protecting Alaska's wild places. Their unique contributions of activism and stewardship are an inspiration for us all."

Florence Rucker Collins, called Ru, was another flier turned conservationist in Denali. She and a friend became pilots just after the end of World War II; it was the only way Ru and Florence Robinson, called Ro, could easily travel, since gas for cars was still rationed and fuel for planes was not. Ru and Ro, who met at the University of Chicago, learned to drive a couple of years later, and with the world open to them now on the ground and in the air, the women took to the new Alaska Highway on a road trip that would determine the trajectories of their lives.

Both landed jobs working for the U.S. Geological Survey in Fairbanks, became enthralled, and spent the next years exploring the state by air, which was really the only way given the limited number of roads. In a recollection of her mother's life published in the *Fairbanks Daily News-Miner*, Ru's daughter Julie Collins lists a number of her mother's adventures, including flights to Nome, Kotzebue, the North Slope, Canada, and Denali. Ru floated the Yukon from Whitehorse to Circle, traversing "700 miles of wilderness only 55 years after the great Klondike stampede opened the country." She also kayaked the Porcupine River with Ro from Old Crow to Fort Yukon. After a brief sojourn back in the Lower 48, confined to the offices of the USGS in Washington, DC, Ru and Ro purchased a Super Cub, one of the workhorses of backcountry fliers, and traveled back to Alaska to resume work and adventure in the bush.

A trained geologist, Ru began studying vegetated sand dunes on Lake Minchumina just outside what would become Denali National Preserve. She met her husband, Dick Collins, there; the two married and raised three children in the remote community, immersing themselves in the ancient subsistence lifestyle that had sustained Athabascans of the area for generations.

Ru brought her firsthand experience of bush living to Denali's Subsistence Resource Commission, which she led for more than twenty years. Her advocacy work with the commission, as well as other conservation work, earned her the NPS Summit Award for Lifetime Achievement, as well as other recognitions. She died in 2015 at ninety-four. In a note published after her death, a park service colleague remembered Florence Rucker as "a champion for promoting cooperation between subsistence users and Denali National Park and Preserve."

Hospitality

Paula (Polly) Anderson was what might now be called a "serial entrepreneur." Like so many others, she and her husband, John, had followed the gold to Alaska at the turn of the twentieth century. In 1918, after hitching up a dogsled and traversing the Alaska Range, the couple landed in the Kantishna mining district. John and Polly started out working mining claims. According to historian Jane Bryant, superintendent Harry Karstens called John Anderson a "bona fide prospector," and one visitor reported receiving a "gold nugget scarf pin" that Polly "personally had washed out [from] her grubstake."

Adding hospitality to their resume, the Andersons built a roadhouse, providing meals prepared by Polly, which became popular with rangers, tourists, and fellow prospectors. The couple had a fox farm where they produced furs for sale, raised sled dogs, and, like all those living in the bush, trapped, hunted, fished, gathered, and gardened to support themselves. When someone needed caretaking, like ranger Grant Pearson after he pulled his own infected tooth, Polly was there to patch them up. She and John also contributed to the scientific understanding of the region by recording their observations of weather and wildlife throughout their years in residence, collecting ornithological data for deposit with the U.S. Biological Survey.

Polly was known for providing hearty fare at the roadhouse, but like her compatriots in the wilderness, she was also ingenious and thrifty. Nothing went to waste. The roadhouse furniture exemplified this thriftiness. "From chairs to bookshelves, [Polly and John's] home was outfitted with abundant furnishings crafted from caribou antlers," park service literature recounts, adding that visitors had mixed reviews ranging "from fascination to complaint that the antlers made for pointy respite."

Lena Howard was another transplant whose work in the hospitality arena earned her a lasting place in written recollections of Denali. She first came to Alaska in 1922 as a tourist. Intrigued by the idea of experiencing an Alaska winter, she returned to Fairbanks in 1926 and then traveled the state with a friend in an attempt to "have Alaska out of our system."

That didn't happen.

Having been entranced, Lena went to work for the Mount McKinley Tourist & Transportation Company as a cook and housekeeper at the rustic Savage Camp, starting in 1928 and staying on for twelve years. Perhaps her special affinity for tourists stemmed from her having been one herself; she reportedly did everything she could to create an ideal experience for park visitors, from helping them fend off mosquitoes to keeping a "night watch" on the mountain so that she and colleagues could alert visitors when Denali shrugged off its mantle of clouds.

Lena met Johnny Howard, another Mount McKinley Tourist & Transportation Company employee, while at work, and the two explored the park on their off-hours. Married in 1937, the couple made their home in Healy, just north of the park boundary, residing there for decades. With her "pioneering and adventurous character," a park history notes, "Lena embodies the spirit of early tourism in Alaska."

Equality

Sit around a boardroom with Denali's backcountry rangers in the shoulder season, and you'll be struck by how many are women. The same holds true at the mountaineering ranger station in Talkeetna. Hang out in the visitor center for any length of time, and you'll notice the tourists are equally divided in gender. Among mountaineers men still outnumber women, but the proportions are in flux. There's no difference between the passion rangers or visitors feel for the park based on gender. Within the park women curate history, uncover artifacts, manage the historic kennels, lead interpretive programs and overnight field trips for schoolchildren, educate mountaineers, and staff the base camp and higher camps on the Kahiltna Glacier. Denali has yet to boast a female superintendent, but chances are that historic step will be taken in short order. As of December 2016 the park's deputy superintendent is Denice Swanke.

Denali is a woman's world too.

Chapter Ten

Let the Big Dogs Run

I figure I've mushed more than twenty thousand miles of snowy trail, and I'm convinced there's nothing to compare with careering along behind a dog team sled, creaking and crunching over drifts, snow flying up from padded feet, every ear alert and every tail curled proudly over a sleek, rippling back.

—Grant Pearson, *My Life of High Adventure*

We should all love our work as much as a sled dog does. To hear Denali's kennels manager Jennifer Raffaeli tell it, it's all any musher can do to keep the huskies from running. It's what they are built for. It's what they want.

They are also built for adoration. The kennels are a short walk from the park's headquarters, and on any day, at any time, a ranger, an administrator, or a visitor can be found there, slowly walking the loop around the dog houses, chatting with the huskies, petting them if the opportunity arises. Among the dogs avalanches of stress roll off human shoulders. And if there are puppies—oh, if there are puppies!

When it's time to eat, train, participate in one of the park's popular sled dog demonstrations, or go out on patrol, the sled dogs light up the Hines Creek drainage with noise, their yips and yowls rising above the trees to the mountaintops, lighting the sky and the soul with excitement. The sound turns heads, piques curiosity, and brings smiles to the faces of all who hear it. For those lucky enough to experience it, ranger

Sled dogs at rest in the winter of 1939–40.

PHOTO COURTESY OF THE NATIONAL PARK SERVICE, DENALI NATIONAL PARK AND PRESERVE MUSEUM COLLECTIONS.

Sarah Hayes describes the counterpoint, "the silence that follows the excitement as you take off on a winter run—just the swish of the [sled's] runners, the panting of the dogs, the pattering of paws on snow, and your own heartbeat echoing in your ears."

What Is a Husky?

Alaskan huskies are not technically a breed. Unlike the malamute, the Siberian husky, or other working dogs such as the Australian shepherd, the Alaskan husky doesn't have specific physical attributes that can be judged by a kennel club, and thus isn't formally recognized. The emphasis in breeding is on performance rather than appearance. Thus, while all of Denali's sled dogs are lean, strong, alert, and very healthy, they are otherwise a mash-up: Their fur ranges in color from black to red to white;

some have longer coats than others; their ears and muzzles are distinctive and individual.

But breeding takes place in the park regardless. Denali is the only national park in the system with a working sled dog kennel, and the filing cabinets in the historic kennel building contain records of each husky's bloodlines. Breeding pairs are matched specifically to produce pups that exhibit both the personality traits and the requisite physical attributes to perform the job at hand. Raffaeli, like the kennels managers who came before, follows Denali's huskies from conception, selecting the parents, supervising the whelping, raising and training the pups, overseeing their working years, and finally, after about nine years of service, finding just the right family for a sled dog's retirement years. "It's much different from how we handle other government employees," Raffaeli notes with a smile.

The continuity found in the bloodlines is important, Raffaeli explains, because sled dogs have become attuned to conditions in the Far North. They are "both physically and mentally tuned in to the place," and are able to read ice and terrain in ways a person never could. Trust and training play into the equation as well, as does the ability for a musher and a lead dog to "have a conversation" about conditions and progress over the eighty feet that separates the back of the sled from the front of the line. The best sled dogs are confident, smart, and capable of problem solving, traits that don't evolve if an animal is bred, and then trained, to strictly obey.

The observations of former park superintendent Grant Pearson illustrate this point: In *My Life of High Adventure*, the then–park ranger tells a number of stories about how his dogs' instinctual understanding of Denali's snow and weather, coupled with their confidence, saved his skin. His lead dogs, on different occasions, shied away from dangerous river crossings, stopped to avoid plunging over a cliff that was hidden in a whiteout, and refused to leave the kennels for a patrol in weather that, as it turned out, plunged to –73 degrees Fahrenheit.

And the experience of longtime park ranger John Rumohr showcases the value of a dog that can have a "conversation" not only with the musher but also with other dogs on the team. After Rumohr, his dogs, and his sled broke through ice on the Toklat River in 1940, the lead dog, Tige, roused the rest to pull everybody, and everything, free of the freezing water. The dog received the Dog World International Diploma of Honor for bravery.

What a Husky Does

The work of Denali's huskies varies with the season. Since the park's inception—with the exception of two interludes in the mid-twentieth century—dogsled teams have been employed in winter to patrol the park. Their aptitude for this job is tied to more than just their desire, fitness, and instinctive ability to read and negotiate changing snow and weather conditions. They also enable rangers to comply with provisions of the Wilderness Act of 1964, specifically the wilderness ethic of "using the minimum tool" to accomplish a job. And they don't have motors, which are prohibited in designated wilderness.

The park estimates that Denali's sled dogs log three thousand miles on patrol each winter season, both in their home park and sometimes while on loan to other Alaskan wildernesses, such as Gates of the Arctic National Park. In the park's early days sled dogs helped track down poachers; in modern times they make up what is termed a "freight hauling kennel." Sometimes the work is prosaic: The huskies help with utilitarian tasks like hauling out trash from remote corners of the park, where helicopters might otherwise have to be employed. Park literature notes that sled dogs have hauled out "fifty-five-gallon drums, two-hundred-pound bridge timbers, a coal car, Model A parts, culverts, discarded climbing gear, and metal roofing" over the years.

But some of the work defines the park in profound ways. The dogs help rangers and researchers explore and monitor Denali's wildlife, soundscape, and plant life; they assist in glacier monitoring projects and the repair and restoration of historic cabins; they haul mountaineering equipment for rangers on north-side patrols of the mountain; they break trail for other visitors and concessioner use.

In summer the huskies combine training with performance. Denali's first sled dog demonstrations took place in 1939 and were as popular then as they are now. Park officials estimate that more than fifty thousand visitors have taken in a sled dog demonstration in recent years, and as many

Pups begin their careers as Denali sled dogs (1953).
PHOTO COURTESY OF THE NATIONAL PARK SERVICE, DENALI NATIONAL PARK AND PRESERVE MUSEUM COLLECTIONS. PHOTO BY GEORGE PETERS.

as seventy-five thousand people watched in 2017. The demonstrations take place three times a day in high season, with more than 250 people watching each day. The exhibitions also help keep the dogs fit in the "off-season" and enable them to develop and nurture relationships with their mushers and with other dogs on the teams.

Given what could be construed as a grueling schedule, Raffaeli is sometimes asked whether the dogs are bothered by the daily routine. That's just not the case, she says; the huskies love it. In fact, sometimes a musher must employ tools to keep an enthusiastic team from taking off with a sled without permission. There are multiple braking devices, including steel snow hooks that can be deployed to keep a team in place. And if all else fails, the sled can be tipped on its side. Going for a good run is going for a good run, whether you're pulling a sled on runners or a sled on wheels, but even the strongest team, composed of nine bundles of muscle and willpower, find it difficult to "pop" and haul a sled that's been tipped.

A Brief History of Dogs in (and on) Denali

Griffith would shout, "Mush!" Sixty-eight furry feet would tear madly at the snow and the sled would lurch upward, to an accompaniment of gasps and flying snow. In this way with our tendons cracking in the mad rush we won to the top.

—Belmore Browne, *The Conquest of Mount McKinley*

The use of sled dogs predates Denali National Park and Preserve by generations, with a long tradition of use among the Athabascan bands of Alaska's Interior. But using dogs on Denali itself is a relatively recent phenomenon. They worked just about every early summit expedition on the mountain—a natural extension of their traditional native use and their employment in the Yukon and Alaska gold rushes. Dogs and sleds had a long, successful history transporting people and supplies over snow and ice in all but the worst weather a sub-Arctic winter could conjure, making them a perfect fit when it came to the fierce conditions encountered regularly on Denali's approaches and glaciers.

But dogs weren't the first transportation choice for early expeditions. Belmore Browne tried to climb Denali three times. The first team he was part of used horses to approach, swimming them across glacially charged rivers and dragging them through dense forest toward the foot of the distant peak. That attempt failed, though through no fault of the beleaguered horses. On the second attempt Browne and his team employed a boat, the *Explorer*. The mountaineer and his companions plowed the vessel upstream, grinding through propellers as they motored across sandbars and ferried from eddy to eddy on the Chulitna and Susitna Rivers. That second attempt failed as well.

The third time, dogs and sleds carried the mountaineers and their goods to the base of the peak. The expedition members traveled farther than they had in the first two attempts, aiming to make the climb from the north side of Denali rather than the south. The trail to, and then through, the Alaska Range was soggy, then icy, then buried in soft powder, then icy again—a challenge in every respect. But what's telling in Browne's description of this third approach, recounted in *The Conquest of*

Mount McKinley, is that there were times when the journey was roller-coaster fun . . . and that was largely because of the dogs. Ultimately Browne and his team would fail again, but the admiration he felt for the huskies was genuine, and he devoted long passages to their praise.

His stories are charming and enlightening. Recounting how his musher once selected a dog to lead a team, Browne wrote, "Now among Griffith's seventeen dogs there was one puppy, a splendid intelligent animal whose fine head and big bones promised well for the days to come. He ran loose a good part of the time, frisking along in the soft snow beside the dignified working dogs" and learning the tricks of the trade. When it came time to pick the lead dog, Browne continued, "the puppy at that moment happened to be sitting near by gazing at our activities with the vacuous stare peculiar to puppies, so Griffith, laughing, hitched him at the head of the long line. If we could have understood canine talk we would undoubtedly have heard some indelicate and sarcastic remarks from the old dogs, but the puppy was already leading up the steep slope, and we were engrossed with the task that confronted us."

Browne wasn't entirely starstruck when it came to the dogs, however. Though he thought them "splendid animals—hard working, faithful, affectionate, and lovable," he also determined that "among themselves they were savage brutes. Each team was held together by the frail bond of daily companionship and when a fight started each team would back its favourite to the death."

Members of the Stuck expedition, including Denali's future superintendent Harry Karstens, also rained praise on the dogs that helped ferry caches from camp to camp on their successful first ascent in 1913. In his memoir of the climb, *The Ascent of Denali*, Stuck writes about Snowball, "the faithful team leader of four years past, who has helped to haul my sled nearly ten thousand miles." As the team made its way up the Muldrow Glacier, Snowball broke through a snow bridge and "the belly band parting, slipped out of his collar and fell some twenty feet below to a ledge in a crevasse." The expedition came to a halt so that Walter Harper could rescue the husky; there wasn't a man in the party who questioned that decision, or Snowball's value. To this day, dogs are used to haul mountaineering gear up the Muldrow.

When Karstens became superintendent in 1921, he brought with him a long history as a musher. He worked as a mail carrier for years before the park was established, using dogs and sleds to travel thousands of miles over inhospitable terrain and through ferocious storms. He'd delivered freight and mail to Kantishna, climbed Denali, and worked with naturalist Charles Sheldon, all with the help of his dogs. He knew he'd need huskies to patrol the new Mount McKinley National Park, so he purchased his first team in 1922, a year after he'd been installed as superintendent.

When Karstens relocated the new park's headquarters from McKinley Park Station on Riley Creek to its current site on the Denali Park Road in 1925, building dog kennels, as well as a cache and cookhouse, was high on his list of priorities. The kennel building that rangers constructed in 1929 is still in use today, though on a different site from its original location—the oldest building in park headquarters still used for its original purpose, according to Hayes.

Karstens also took the dogs into consideration as he laid out ranger patrol cabins along the park's perimeter and the developing Denali Park Road. Much like the Catholic missions along California's El Camino Real, which are located a day's ride from one another, Denali's patrol cabins are spaced roughly a day's mush apart. Grant Pearson was one of the rangers who made frequent winter patrols via sled dog team in those early days. "In the winter working season, sled dogs are like a winning football team. They are keyed up, eager and full of excess energy," he observed. However, "every so often that extra steam has to blow off, which it does when those vibrant bundles of fur and muscle get into one of their fang-slashing free-for-alls, or when the whole team goes off headlong on a wild, gleeful chase after anything from a rabbit to a caribou."

The park's sled dog teams were famously employed by the Lindley-Liek and Cosmic Ray expeditions in 1932, but this kind of assistance for mountaineers would not become park policy. Though the dogs displayed good sense, they could also fall victim to the same dangers people faced when crossing a glacier. Ranger and experienced musher John Rumohr, who was driving a sled from a Lindley-Liek camp low on the Muldrow

Ranger John Rumohr and a team head out on a patrol in the winter of 1940-41.
PHOTO COURTESY OF THE NATIONAL PARK SERVICE, DENALI NATIONAL PARK AND PRESERVE MUSEUM COLLECTIONS.

Glacier to another camp higher up, nearly lost his team when a snow bridge collapsed. Pearson, then a park ranger, described how "two of the dogs were dangling in the air over a crevasse, held only by their neck lines." While Rumohr leaned on the sled's brake, Pearson reached over the lip of the crevasse and "managed to snag the two pooches out by hooking my ski pole into their harness and snaking them back to safety." Rumohr betrayed his nerves in the aftermath: according to Pearson, he'd had "his pipe in his mouth, and he bit right through the stem."

Dogs were mostly absent from the park for two brief periods. The first came as the nation geared up for World War II, when Superintendent Frank Been decided sled dogs were uneconomical; historian Frank Norris records Been commenting that "the money and time given to dog care may thereby be devoted to foot patrolling." Denali's huskies were deployed to the military, including, by one account, the famed Tenth Mountain Division. This meant, according to Raffaeli, that the bloodlines and instinctive memory of place that had been carefully bred into Denali's huskies starting in the era of Harry Karstens were lost.

The second hiatus came with the advent of the snow machine. In the 1950s and '60s, an era in which the creations of human ingenuity were often considered superior to whatever was provided by nature, the park cut back on its use of dog teams and invested in snowcats and snowmobiles. While vehicles driven by internal combustion engines have uses within the park, a picture on display in the kennel office depicts why Denali still has dogs: a snow machine tipped on its side, its treads tilted uselessly into the air. That just doesn't happen to a team of huskies.

Rumohr was a fierce advocate for the dogs. In a quote from the superintendent's monthly reports, the chief ranger voices his preference for dog teams over motor vehicles in freezing conditions: "The distance traveled in a day over unbroken trail [by a motorized vehicle] exceeds the best a dog team could perform. But . . . dogs have less trouble with their carburetors." He adds that cussing out dogs for bad performance is more satisfactory than cussing out a snow tractor, which "just sits there." Cuss out the dogs, and "they would at least raise their ears."

Grant Pearson echoed Rumohr's carburetor analogy, noting that a husky "will not freeze up." Pearson also asserted that sleds and dogs were better suited to maneuvering the steep slopes and narrow canyons rangers were required to traverse on patrol. Finally, Pearson wrote that with regard to fuel, the dried fish needed to keep the dogs humming along was considerably less expensive than gasoline.

Since 1980 snow machines—or any mechanized vehicles, for that matter—have been prohibited in the two-million-acre core of the park, which was designated Wilderness with the massive expansion instituted in that year. While snow machines may still be used elsewhere in the park, the wilderness is the sled dogs' domain.

In the 1970s, Sandy Kogl became Denali's kennels manager. Her dedication and abilities as a breeder, trainer, and administrator resulted in a new focus and investment in Denali's sled dog program. Kogl brought back the Alaskan husky; her predecessor, Roy Sanborn, had brought malamutes into the park, and while they were splendid dogs, park staff came to understand that the dogs best suited to the long-haul task of patrolling Denali were the smaller, "not particularly handsome" Alaskan huskies. Kogl built the bloodlines that Jennifer Raffaeli now fosters. Raffaeli's first priority, as was Kogl's, is the health and safety of the dogs: making sure they get the care and training they deserve. The park may have other demands, Raffaeli says, "but dogs drive what I do . . . the dogs were born into this, so I hold myself to a high standard."

The Legacy of Dogs in Denali

> *Things like porcupine chases, I suppose, help a team driver not to get too exaggerated an opinion of the wisdom of his dogs. Nevertheless, a man can easily acquire an inflated estimate of their intelligence, living and working with them in the wilderness of the park, which in winter is a 3,000-square-mile snowfield brooded over by the highest mountain in North America.*
>
> —Superintendent Grant Pearson

Famously, sled dogs have summited Denali. In 1979, Joe Redington Sr., creator of the famed Iditarod dogsled race, and Susan Butcher, four-time Iditarod champion, reached the top of the High One along with a small team of dogs, guided by Ray Genet, the famed veteran Denali climber. Another Iditarod veteran, Jacques Philip, also used dogs in his Denali summit climb in 1990.

Those feats are remarkable. But Denali's sled dogs are not remarkable for that reason. Intead, their legacy is one of tradition and practicality. Dogs, as Jennifer Raffaeli explains, help preserve the wilderness character of the place. They enable people to connect to a past that reaches farther back than the origins of the park. And perhaps most important, Raffaeli says, the dogs "help people see the joyful place that Denali is in winter. They can become captivated by what the dogs know, which is a landscape covered by ice."

Chapter Eleven

Planes, Trains, and Automobiles

In America's national parks the idea is not only to preserve the natural resources and landscapes for posterity but also "to provide for the enjoyment of the same in such manner and by such means as will leave them unimpaired for the enjoyment of future generations." Such is the mandate laid out in the 1916 Organic Act that established the National Park Service (NPS).

For Denali, located in middle-of-nowhere Alaska, meeting that mandate would be no small feat. Getting from point A to point B in what was now a national park had always presented a challenge, no matter the season, whether visitors were traveling on foot, on horseback, by boat, or via dogsled. The routes forged by early mountain climbers, surveyors, and explorers would not suffice: Few tourists would entertain the idea of a vacation that involved slogging for weeks through mosquito-infested swamps, camping on rough ground in tents they carried on their backs, and munching on pemmican balls washed down with tepid tea.

The initial problem—getting potential tourists close to the new park—was solved in relatively short order with the completion of the Alaska Railroad, which linked Seward, on the Gulf of Alaska, to Fairbanks, and passed close to the park's eastern boundary. Later in the twentieth century, a pair of highways would augment access by rail.

Then there was the problem of getting around within the park. As the age of the automobile was in its ascendency, the logical answer was a road. Since its completion, the slender ribbon of pavement and gravel that now stretches nearly a hundred miles from the Nenana River canyon

A car crosses the old wooden Igloo Creek bridge.
PHOTO COURTESY OF THE NATIONAL PARK SERVICE, DENALI NATIONAL PARK AND PRESERVE MUSEUM COLLECTIONS.

into Denali's imposing wilderness has come to define the experience of most every visitor to Denali National Park and Preserve.

Mountaineers, a separate breed from tourists, had a specialized set of needs when it came to travel within the park. Even with the road in place, it was still difficult to get them and their gear to a base camp suitable for a summit attempt. They needed to be deposited within striking distance of the summit on one of the peak's glaciers, and the best way was by air. A small, talented, gutsy group of aviators would rise to meet that challenge, creating a new industry as they innovated.

The Denali Park Road

In a nation elsewhere defined by interstates and intersections, the Denali Park Road is one of a kind. The road is mostly unpaved, and it actually doesn't reach the mountain proper. It climbs through taiga, wanders through tundra, slips across rivers on fragile bridges made of concrete and steel, and dead-ends in a tiny mining town near the toes of the mighty glaciers that flow off Denali's flanks.

For all but a handful of days each year, visitors can't drive on the park road. The pavement, and the traffic, stops at a gate at Mile 15, the Savage River. If travelers want to venture farther, they must walk, ride a bike, or travel by tour or shuttle bus. Even on the few days when private vehicles are permitted, numbers are limited and passes are issued by lottery.

Road construction began almost as soon as the park received funding, four years after it was established. It took nearly twenty years to complete the project, but the entire route, under the watchful eye of Superintendent Harry Karstens, was reconnoitered and brushed out by 1922. The number of miles built varied from year to year depending on terrain: Construction focused on the Sanctuary River bridge in 1926, and the road progressed only ten miles between 1928 and 1930, inching from Sable Pass to Polychrome Pass. But by 1938 the narrow, fragile roadway was in place, at a cost of about $1.3 million.

The Alaska Road Commission (ARC) was in charge of construction, but the NPS had plenty of input. The NPS's charge was to minimize the impact of the project on the scenic values and natural resources of the park, which conflicted, at times, with what the ARC considered convenient or expeditious. Migration paths and vista points played into the layout, the roadway sweeping and curving to accommodate both. Layout was also guided by providing access to future development, like possible hotel or camp sites at Wonder Lake and near Mount Eielson.

But as with any major construction project, there were bound to be impacts. Pictures in park histories, most notably Jane Bryant's *Snapshots from the Past*, capture crews using arguably minimalist tactics, such as hewing at rocky slopes with hand tools and plowing up tundra behind teams of horses. But the ARC utilized whatever means necessary to get the job done: Crews also employed explosives to blast rock from mountainsides and heavy machinery to force earthworks into place.

The extreme tactics had spectacular payoffs. Construction on the "highline" at Polychrome Pass, for example, required extensive blasting but resulted in a roadway with views and exposures that thrill travelers to

A tour bus heads up the park road at Polychrome Pass in 1967.
PHOTO COURTESY OF THE NATIONAL PARK SERVICE, DENALI NATIONAL PARK AND PRESERVE MUSEUM COLLECTIONS. PHOTO BY W. V. WATSON.

this day. Bryant describes early bus passengers so unnerved by the stretch that they disembarked and walked, rather than ride. She also quotes NPS director Horace Albright, who traversed Polychrome Pass in 1931 with then-Superintendent Harry Liek: "This road is one splendid location and is one of the most scenic highways in the National Park system."

The hurdles impeding quick and steady progress on the road were significant. The construction season was short, and inclement weather could stop the work for days, crimping the season even more. Bridging rivers and streams was technical, and also subject to the vagaries of nature: Floods, ice, and unpredictable hydraulics all jammed up the works at times.

Then there was the earth itself. Permafrost, the perpetually frozen soil that underlies much of the road (as it does most roadways in northern latitudes), is a challenging substrate. As it melts and refreezes, highways heave and subside. When the permafrost in Denali warmed in the summer months, it devolved into a morass more difficult to work through in some places than others. At Stony Hill, for example, workers encountered an apparently bottomless "black gumbo," sticky, claylike, and difficult to cut switchbacks through.

Securing equipment was also difficult. The heavy machinery needed for road construction wasn't manufactured in Alaska, so everything had to be shipped from Outside. Construction hit a significant roadblock due to equipment "failure" in 1935, when the SS *Denali*, a freighter carrying dump trucks and other heavy machinery destined for the park, "plowed into rocks" off Zayas Island, south of Ketchikan, and was lost.

And sometimes moving forward required the ARC to move backward as well. Accounts of construction make note of some crews being dispatched to survey and break ground ahead while others were dispatched to maintain or complete roadwork laid down in previous seasons.

A significant portion of the park road underwent a major overhaul as part of the NPS's Mission 66 program, a system-wide, decade-long initiative intended to improve infrastructure throughout the national parks. The initiative called for both widening and paving the road; the administrative argument was that the existing narrow, winding gravel track wasn't safe for travelers. The counterargument, made by conservationists and longtime park advocates like brothers Olaus and Adolph Murie, was that the proposed improvements would essentially convert the road into a "speedway." In a letter from December 1959, Olaus Murie declared that the park "will not serve its purpose if we encourage the visitor to hurry as fast as possible for a mere glimpse of scenery from a car, and a few snapshots." Adolph Murie wrote articles for national magazines that argued along the same lines, decrying not only the desecration of slow and purposeful exploration of the park but also the degradation of the environment caused by the construction.

The arguments of conservationists resulted in an aborted mission: The Denali Park Road was only paved as far as the Savage River and was only widened to the Teklanika River. Other Mission 66 mandates associated with the highway went ahead, however, including construction of the Eielson Visitor Center at Mile 66 and campground facilities at Teklanika and at Wonder Lake.

A curve in the Denali Park Road at Polychrome Pass.
PHOTO COURTESY OF THE NATIONAL PARK SERVICE, DENALI NATIONAL PARK AND PRESERVE MUSEUM COLLECTIONS.

The three levels of development on the Denali Park Road reflect "a three-part, telescoping degree of access and use," according to park literature. The paved portion is open to all vehicle traffic, limited camping traffic is permitted on the wider roadway to Teklanika, and the remainder of the 20-foot wide, gravel road is the domain of the shuttle and tour bus, with very few private vehicles allowed. Tourist travel in private vehicles on the Denali Park Road was restricted starting in 1972, after completion of the new George Parks Highway (AK 3). As predicted, traffic to the park doubled the year after the highway was finished, and park officials understood that the influx of automobiles on the park road would not only be a logistical nightmare but also impact wildlife, driving it away from the thoroughfare and out of sight of visitors. More vehicles on the road also increased the potential for dangerous human-wildlife interactions, since it would be easier for someone to venture too close to a bear, or a wolf, or a moose, with either the human or the animal suffering dire consequences. The shuttle bus system was instituted in 1972, following the example set in Yosemite Valley. There were growing pains at first—and a devastating accident in 1974, when a bus rolled off the roadway, killing one passenger and injuring a number of others—but today visitors understand, and welcome, the opportunity to enjoy the park's viewscapes while leaving the wheel in the hands of an experienced professional.

And there is still the opportunity for a slow meander up the Denali Park Road in the shoulder season, when the crowds disappear. The lucky lottery winners get to go all the way to trail's end, if they choose and the weather permits. For others there is a window of time when the gate at the Savage River swings open and passage to the Teklanika River is allowed. On those days a driver can count the cars coming and going on fingers and toes; a camaraderie is built with the lonely car that appears up ahead or the lonely car way back in the rearview mirror.

The Alaska Railroad

In the early years the easiest way to reach Mount McKinley National Park was by rail. Starting in 1923, when President Warren G. Harding drove a golden spike that ceremonially completed the line in Nenana, passengers could board the Alaska Railroad in Anchorage or in Fairbanks and travel in relative comfort to McKinley Park Station, located right outside the park boundary.

The Alaska Railroad, like railroads in the Lower 48 serving Yosemite, the Grand Canyon, and other national parks, proved a big proponent of Denali, since promoting the park translated to promotion of the railroad. McKinley Park Station was Denali's commercial hub in those days, the "Glitter Gulch" of the early twentieth century. But the glamour was distinctly that of the frontier; aside from a handful of taverns and roadhouses, the town was populated by trappers, hunters, miners, and a few park rangers. The tourists who made the scenic journey from Anchorage could find lodging at Maurice Morino's McKinley Park Hotel, which opened for business on Thanksgiving Day in 1921, four years after the park was established. According to park literature, the station also encompassed a post office and a schoolhouse, as well as the park's first headquarters. With two million acres to patrol, Superintendent Karstens decided it made sense to concentrate administrative functions near the depot, as that was where the visitors would disembark. The railroad served more than just tourists; it also transported survey teams dispatched to delineate the fledgling park's boundaries and crews from the ARC charged with building the new park road.

When the park road reached the Savage River in 1925, and Savage Camp was established by the park's concessioner, railroad officials "jiggered their schedules to allow daytime stops at McKinley Park Station in both directions," according to historian Frank Norris. The result was a threefold increase in visitation from just over sixty souls in 1924 to more than two hundred in 1925, with, of course, a corresponding increase in ridership. The railroad also erected a welcome arch for the park in 1926; the arch was closer to the depot than the actual park boundary at the time, but served its purpose. Norris notes that the railroad's "advertising brochures and its boxcars soon began to proclaim that the Alaska

McKinley Park Station in 1924.
PHOTO COURTESY OF THE NATIONAL PARK SERVICE, DENALI NATIONAL PARK AND PRESERVE MUSEUM COLLECTIONS. PHOTO BY FRITZ NYBERG.

Railroad was 'the Mount McKinley Route,' and for years afterward the railroad prominently mentioned both the park's beauty and the rewards of a park visit."

The railroad took on an even bigger role in the national park's ability to attract visitation when it acquired the park's concession in the 1940s. Chief among its duties was operation of the McKinley Park Hotel, a visual "monstrosity" that struggled during the war years and was used as a recreational site for army personnel in World War II. Business picked up after the war, as did park visitation, but the railroad never made money on the enterprise due to the short tourist season. The railroad also ran tours through the park, mostly on demand, since visitation was unpredictable and sporadic. When a private company bid on the concession in the early 1950s, the railroad was happy to step away.

Today, the railroad still folds the park under its marketing umbrella, offering trips on the Denali Star throughout the summer tourist season.

Planes

Without air travel, Denali would be a different mountain.
—Denali mountaineering ranger Tucker Chenoweth

The history of flight in the park begins with Carl Ben Eielson. The young bush pilot flew mail runs between Fairbanks and gold camps in the Kuskokwim River drainage, north and west of Denali, and was "always making emergency landings without the benefit of a field," as ranger Grant Pearson relates in *My Life of High Adventure*. Eielson's most memorable feat near the park involved transporting a miner, Jack Tobin, to his cabin near Kantishna in 1924. According to an account published in the *Fairbanks Daily News-Miner*, Eielson "did not fly to the field which had been prepared near the Quigley properties [in Kantishna], but traveled direct to Copper Mountain, which saved his passenger a tramp of about fifteen miles." Once at the destination, according to Pearson, Eielson "set his little plane down in a skillful though bumpy landing on the floodwater-constructed landing field." After the pioneering pilot was killed in an accident on a rescue mission in Siberia in 1929, Congress renamed

A small plane flipped on the McKinley Park airstrip in 1930.
PHOTO COURTESY OF THE NATIONAL PARK SERVICE, DENALI NATIONAL PARK AND PRESERVE MUSEUM COLLECTIONS.

Copper Mountain (now Mount Eielson) and the Eielson Visitor Center in his memory.

No pilot, no matter how skilled, is immune to the hazards of flying in Denali. The weather is notoriously dangerous; the mountain generates its own storm systems, and winds funneled through gaps in the ridgelines can exceed 150 miles per hour. The literature of mountaineers and researchers is littered with harrowing tales of sketchy landings on glaciers, in camps, and on rescues. Pilots need both experience and nerve to negotiate the hazards.

Don Sheldon's skill as a pilot in Denali is legendary. Called the "first and most famous" of Talkeetna's Denali Flyers, he ferried climbers and their outfits to and from the Kahiltna and other glaciers on the mountain for more than two decades. According to journalist Bill Shernowit, Sheldon, arguably, "knew the mountain better than any bush pilot past or present." The writer also maintains that Sheldon's work made Denali accessible to "the masses," whether aspiring summiters or flightseers.

Stories of Sheldon's expertise made him much sought after; the pilot of choice for climbers seeking a drop on the Kahiltna, and for rescuers hoping to pluck climbers off the mountain when disaster struck. In *Minus 148°*, the story of Denali's first successful winter ascent, climber Art Davidson recounts asking the pilot if he could land the expedition on the mountain in winter. "He answered, 'Yowza, no problem. What you want to do, Art, is get yourself a hundred-pound sack a beans, fire yourself up, and climb that old mountain.'" When it came to actually depositing the climbers on the Kahiltna Glacier in February 1967, Davidson described the twilight descent to base camp this way:

> *We had resigned ourselves to returning to Talkeetna for the night and coming back the next morning, but suddenly we felt that weightless sensation which meant the plane was losing altitude fast. Since it seemed impossible that Sheldon might be heading down for a landing, I shouted over the roar of the prop to ask him what was wrong. He clicked on a headlight and yelled, "Let's give her hell, boys!" Shiro and I exchanged worried glances and braced ourselves for the crash. Sheldon hollered, "Geronimo!" The glacier rushed up toward us. Sheldon stared straight ahead, and I watched him so closely that I almost failed to notice when the plane's skis touched the snow and skimmed smoothly along the surface.*

Sheldon wasn't the first pilot to make memorable or historic landings on Denali's glaciers. The first flights ferrying climbers and caches onto Denali occurred in 1932, when pilot Joe Crosson of Fairbanks deposited members of the Cosmic Ray expedition on the Muldrow Glacier. According to Shernowit, Crosson "[delivered] his passengers to the Muldrow at an elevation of about 6,000 feet as though it were a routine matter, not an aviation first." That's not to say the flight didn't have its challenges; Shernowit goes on to describe how, after attempting takeoff and failing to clear a ridge, Crosson was forced to put his plane down on the glacier just out of sight of the camp. The pilot snowshoed back down to ask for help freeing the plane from snow and ice higher up on the glacier and then tried again, this time with success.

After two members of the Cosmic Ray team became the first climbing fatalities on the mountain, Crosson was called upon to rescue other members of the team who had succumbed to illness. It was spring at the Fairbanks airfield where the pilot was based, and to get a plane outfitted with skis airborne, the runway was inundated with water by the local fire department. On the return to Fairbanks, Crosson executed a memorable landing, "probably the only one on record ever accomplished in a manmade mud pie," ranger Grant Pearson remembered.

Pilot and University of Alaska president Terris Moore would follow in Crosson's pioneering glacier-landing footsteps, depositing a climbing party on the Kahiltna Glacier for the first time in 1951. Aerial supply drops were also part of that memorable first ascent of the West Buttress route via the Kahiltna, setting another precedent that would continue into modern times. Those aerial deposits resulted in Moore setting another record; his landing at 10,000 feet on Kahiltna Pass to ferry the Washburn party off the mountain was, at the time, the highest landing ever made by a plane in Alaska.

For Denali wolf biologist Gordon Haber, air travel was integral to his work. For years he flew with pilot Troy Dunn, who knew the mountain, his passenger, and where to find the park's wolves. Dunn was not at the controls for Haber's final flight in 2009, when the small plane he was riding in crashed into a mountainside on the East Fork. Speculation about what caused the crash swirls around a number of issues. Fickle wind is a prime suspect: In *Among Wolves*, author Marybeth Holleman describes the experience of a pilot who encountered an updraft in Denali that shot him from 8,000 feet in altitude to 13,000 feet—"it was like riding an elevator." Another suspect is the new pilot's lack of experience flying in the region; Holleman notes that Haber expressed some reticence about that on the day of the accident.

But the story of the long hike that Haber's pilot, Dan McGregor, made after the crash epitomizes the instinct for survival that Denali can evoke. After attempts to pull the unconscious (and possibly already dead) Haber from the wreckage of the plane resulted in McGregor's being severely burned, and after spending the night near the wreckage, the pilot reportedly hiked nearly twenty miles to a campground near the Denali

Grant Pearson's Swallow aircraft is parked on the McKinley Park airstrip in 1932. PHOTO COURTESY OF THE NATIONAL PARK SERVICE, DENALI NATIONAL PARK AND PRESERVE MUSEUM COLLECTIONS.

Park Road, where he hoped to initiate a rescue for Haber (which, as it turned out, was already under way).

Air support of mountaineering and scientific expeditions has long been tradition on Denali. It's a necessity given the distance and difficulty of making overland approaches and transporting supplies to base camps. Air travel is also good business as far as concessioners and related tourism industries are concerned: Airstrips at McKinley Park Station and Kantishna, as well as the airport in Talkeetna, have seen brisk activity for decades.

But planes have also sparked controversy in the park. Sound pollution is an issue; the sound of a prop can rend the spell of silence in Denali's remotest reaches. There are also impacts at the popular landing sites—on the Kahiltna in the height of the climbing season, for example, where air traffic renders any illusion of wilderness moot. Once the park's Wilderness boundary was established in 1980, landing planes became illegal in the park's highest and most remote locations. This ensures that adventure and challenge, as well as undisturbed enclaves for wildlife, endure in those areas.

Talkeetna

Located on the south side of the Alaska Range, at the confluence of the Susitna, Talkeetna, and Chulitna Rivers, Talkeetna is Denali National Park and Preserve's air hub. The tiny town's airport, longer and wider than its main street, is where most of Denali's aspiring summiters launch their assaults, using small planes piloted by expert fliers to transport their teams and gear to the mountain's base camp on the Kahiltna Glacier. Though it is located miles from the boundaries, the park's mountaineering rangers speak of the town as if it is part of the park.

The town's evolution from Alaskan bush outpost to mountaineering central began in 1951, when Brad Washburn and his team established the West Buttress route. Relying on air support is the only way that route can be climbed (in a reasonable amount of time), and as its popularity grew, so did Talkeetna's. With more than a thousand climbers attempting to summit Denali each climbing season, the place hums with energy. All climbers begin their expeditions at the Walter Harper Talkeetna Ranger Station, located a block off the main street and a block away from the banks of the Susitna—and iconic views of Denali and Mount Foraker, when the weather permits. The unincorporated town's historical society museum contains the NPS's spectacular, room-sized scale model of Denali, with the most popular climbing routes and camps mapped and flagged, and oriented to floor-to-ceiling photographs by Bradford Washburn illustrating the different faces of the mountain.

Before its transformation into climbers' central, Talkeetna was an Athabascan village, a place where fish and other wildlife, as well as fruit, wood, and willow, provided a sound foundation for subsistence living. A history published by the town's chamber of commerce records that in the language of the local Dena'ina band, Talkeetna translates to "river of plenty" or "place where food is stored near the river."

In 1905 gold was discovered in the hills above the confluence. Prospectors and miners descended on the village to work the placers and also established gold mines west of the growing town. But Talkeetna remained sleepy until 1915, when it was designated the Engineering Commission Headquarters for the Alaska Railroad. The townsite was established the following year and lots were platted, with the railroad auctioning parcels in the township for $14.25, according to the chamber history, which also notes that "none of the buyers elected to use the easy payment plan that was offered."

Over the years such an investment would prove as profitable as any gold claim, as Talkeetna's star continued to rise. The railroad was a lifeline to larger towns to the north and south, and access to the village also improved upon completion of the George Parks Highway in 1971.

By then the climbing industry had moved into Talkeetna, and air taxi services served as park concessioners, transporting climbers and their kits to and from base camp on a regular basis. When the climbing season wanes, the focus shifts toward flightseeing tours, which extend through the summer season and beyond, weather permitting.

ONE ROAD IS ENOUGH

The park service mandates have been met. More than 400,000 visitors travel to, from, and within the park annually via plane, train, and automobile. In recent years cruise ships have also entered the mix: Passengers can end their sea journeys by climbing aboard a bus or train in Anchorage for three- to five-day excursions to the park. The only accessibility limit faced by park administrators now is how many people can find seats in the fleet of shuttle buses that run up and down the Denali Park Road in the May-to-September high season.

Though the buses ferry hundreds of sightseers from scenic point to scenic point along the park road each day, and air taxis ferry climbers to base camps and flightseers to other destinations, the bulk of the park remains an "unimpaired" wilderness as originally envisioned. All other travel is powered by foot or paw. In winter, sled dog teams enable rangers to patrol the backcountry and visitors explore on skis or snowshoes. In summer, hikers may travel cross-country anywhere they desire; Denali remains a place where wandering shoes (but not wandering minds) are encouraged.

Why just one road? Because one road is enough. In a wilderness park like Denali, access is a privilege, and at the whim of the elements.

The park's remoteness and the logistical challenges of moving around once inside are central to its mystique and allure. And blessedly, when the season changes, that one road becomes essentially invisible, a shadow track beneath a blanket of snow, discernible only to dogs, wildlife, and the thoughtful human explorer.

Chapter Twelve

Denali's Natural History

They're called the Big Five. Sheep, wolves, bear, moose, and caribou have drawn people to Denali for thousands of years. They've been studied, admired, and revered; they've been hunted for food and sport; and now they are the stars of photo shoots, films, and vacation memories.

But Denali's natural history is about more than its charismatic megafauna. The Arctic ground squirrel, the snowshoe hare, and the lowly mosquito may not be as photogenic or tasty, but without them Denali's ecosystems couldn't flourish. And none would thrive without the flora—the berry bushes of the tundra, the black spruce of the taiga, the willowy stream sides and boggy lake bottoms. These are ties that bind: The willow needs the moose as much as the moose needs the willow; the berries need the bears as much as the bears need the berries. One can't do without the other.

Studying the complexities of Denali's ecosystems and habitats predates the park, and as is the case with mountaineers, Denali can't be defined without exploring the exploits of its naturalists. Charles Sheldon made the first extensive observations of the park's wildlife on his long field trips between 1906 and 1908. His are the earliest studies of the creatures that make up Denali's animal kingdom: how they are born, how they live, how they die. His work was transformative; there wouldn't be a park without it.

The National Park Service's (NPS) pioneering wildlife biologist George Melendez Wright (who would later head the NPS's Wildlife Division), along with colleague Joseph Dixon of the University of California,

Berkeley, conducted a survey/transect in the park in 1926. Over the course of nearly three months, the two men traversed five hundred miles on foot, staying close to the routes traveled by tourists. The biologists obtained what Dixon called a "bird's eye view of the animal life as it would be seen by most visitors." The two men identified 86 bird species and 25 different mammals, collected more than 160 bird specimens and 80 mammal skins for research, took 350 photographs, and compiled nearly 300 pages of field notes.

Dixon returned to the park in 1932 to finish what he and Melendez Wright had started, logging another 250 miles and revisiting sites from the first survey, as well as sites that Charles Sheldon had frequented during his Denali field days. "On this expedition the known list of mammals of the McKinley region was brought up to 34 species, and the bird list was increased to 107 species," Dixon wrote in *Birds and Mammals of Mount McKinley National Park, Alaska*, part of the NPS's *Fauna of the National Parks* series and published in 1938.

This work, and the work of other biologists and resource managers, has helped define the nature of Denali. The animals have stories to tell, and people help them do it.

The Handsomest Grizzly

> *[Its coat is of] a graduated blond-to-brown hue, much like a surfer's hair that has been bleached by longtime exposure to sea salt and sun. The long summer days of sun paint the bear's upper fur with a golden hue. Their deep brown-to-black legs lead up to the sunlight-bleached coat—a contrast that makes these bears the best looking I've ever had the pleasure of observing.*
>
> —Author, photographer, and naturalist Kennan Ward describing the Toklat grizzly

The grizzly bear (*Ursus arctos horribilis*) is a massive animal in any setting. A full-grown male can weigh up to eleven hundred pounds, stand five feet tall at the shoulder when on all fours and seven feet tall when upright, and leave tracks in mud or snow measuring a foot long. It attains these massive proportions mostly by consuming berries, insects, and small prey and by scavenging carcasses left by other predators. Opportunistic and omnivorous, the grizzly is supremely adapted to consuming whatever nature serves up.

The grizzly bears of Alaska's Interior are a distinct subspecies of the brown bears (*Ursus arctos*) that inhabit the coastal regions. Coastal brown bears are generally recognized as larger and more aggressive toward humans. The bears of Katmai National Park and Preserve, often featured in film and video standing at the top of Brooks Falls snatching spawning salmon midair, are brown bears. The Kodiak bear, isolated on islands with no opportunity to breed outside the population, is another brown bear subspecies (*Ursus arctos middendorffi*).

Denali is home to a subset of the subspecies, called the Toklat grizzly, which writer Kim Heacox aptly describes as having "striking blond coats set off handsomely by dark ears and legs." The number of grizzly bears thought to roam the north side of the park ranges from 300 to 350.

A grizzly bear forages on the tundra (1967).
PHOTO COURTESY OF THE NATIONAL PARK SERVICE, DENALI NATIONAL PARK AND PRESERVE MUSEUM COLLECTIONS. PHOTO BY PETER SANCHEZ.

On the south side, with its abundance of salmon streams, the density is thought to be greater.

Grizzlies are mostly solitary but also travel in small family groups: a mother and her cubs, or young adults (siblings) still learning the tricks of survival. Their main mission is to find food: Denali's bears thrive on the bounty of the short summer season, when they gorge themselves—called "hyperphagia"—to bulk up for their long winter torpor. Berries are a prime source of calories. When they are in season, the Toklat grizzly feasts on blueberries, soapberries, and cranberries. But the bears truly eat anything. Charles Sheldon examined the stomach contents of several grizzlies; inside he found pea vine, mice, ground squirrel, worms, "meat," and grass. Leave it to a scientist to do that kind of unsavory work.

Most of Denali's bears roam freely, without strict territories, though some are more dominant than others and will defend food sources—and their young—if threatened by another bear or some other animal. The spreading of hundreds of bears across thousands of square miles of terrain means that sighting one is fairly rare, but grizzlies leave signs of their passing in big ways, including prints like dinner plates, musk and hair on trees and signposts that they've used as back-scratchers, and decimated berry patches.

In winter the bears enter a state of torpor, which is not technically the same as hibernation. They slumber, and their physiological functions (metabolism, respiration, heart rate) slow, but according to ranger Sarah Hayes they can wake up, unlike a true hibernator such as the Arctic ground squirrel, which, as one ranger described, you could "toss across the tundra without them twitching." Females give birth during winter; former park superintendent Grant Pearson describes the mother-cub denning tableau this way: "Mamma doesn't even know she has had them until she wakes up in the spring to find her children placidly feeding at her breasts." She usually has twins, each weighing about a pound and "about the size of a man's fist" when they are born. The family stays together through the following winter; by the end of the following summer season, the mother has turned her twins "loose to shift for themselves," as Pearson puts it. Once the cubs are on their own, the female is free to mate again.

Black bears (*Ursus americanus*) also call Denali home. Though they are generally smaller than grizzlies, neither size nor color—their coats can range from black to brown to cinnamon to blond—is a reliable identifier. Rangers caution backcountry travelers to home in on two key distinguishing features: the face, which is "dish-shaped" on a grizzly, while a black bear has a longer snout, or "Roman nose"; and the grizzly's hump, a mass of muscle on the shoulders. These are important to remember since a human should employ different tactics to stay safe in encounters with the different animals. Safe travel in bear country is complicated, and as ranger Sarah Hayes explains, travelers within the park should "become students of bear behavior before venturing into bear habitat." With proper education, people can determine whether an animal is "curious, defensive, or predatory," and how best to handle a given situation. While the rule of thumb in the event of an actual attack by a black bear is that people should fight back, and that people attacked by a grizzly should fall to the ground and play dead, protecting the head and neck with the hands or a pack, proper behavior in a bear encounter is just not that simple

The best tactic is to avoid a close encounter altogether by making noise while hiking and keeping plenty of distance between yourself and any bear. With grizzlies and black bears in Denali, that's three hundred yards (three football fields). The park also advises visitors to carry (and know how to use) bear spray, which is a proven, effective deterrent in the event of an attack. Maintaining a healthy separation from any wild animal is sound practice for backcountry travelers. In Denali, park regulations call for a twenty-five foot separation from any wildlife, but if you are affecting behavior, even from a greater distance, then you are too close.

These days the park's wildlife biologists and rangers are careful to avoid disruptive encounters with the wildlife they are studying or observing. But close encounters have occurred, such as one recounted by Dixon in *Birds and Mammals of Mount McKinley National Park*: "When I approached to within 25 feet of the bear the animal ceased feeding and gave a warning cough or grunt. Once it made a pretense as if it were going to rush in my direction. I interpreted this behavior of the bear as its way of warning me to keep at a safe distance and I took the hint. As soon as I withdrew a few feet the bear resumed its feeding."

Unlike black bears in Yellowstone and Yosemite, Denali's grizzlies are not habituated to humans and human food. If a person maintains a safe and proper distance of three hundred yards from a bear, the bear likely poses little danger to backcountry travelers. Still, educating visitors about how to deal with an up-close encounter occupies a healthy chunk of park literature and park rangers' time.

Unfortunately, there have been issues, the most recent in 2016, when a grizzly had to be euthanized after a series of close encounters with hikers on the trail at Savage River. According to news reports, a hiker attempted to distract the bear by throwing a day pack with food in it at the bruin. The maneuver helped the hikers escape, but it also caused the animal to associate food with humans. The park attempted to handle the delicate situation by closing the area to visitors and using "aversive conditioning," including shooting beanbags at the animal to drive it away, but the efforts weren't successful. When the bear approached another group of hikers, they played dead—not the proper tactic in this instance—and the bear, in the process of investigating the group, bit one person. The rangers who eventually trapped the animal found it both injured and thin, factors that may have prompted the young male to seek out food from humans. Despite what could be considered a mitigating circumstance, rangers were forced to comply with park policy, which dictates a bear that's bitten a human must be put down.

Wolves

> *I have listened to wolves howl across these mountains, valleys, and tundra expanses, summer and winter, under almost every condition imaginable, and yet each time I hear another of their wilderness serenades it thrills and delights me.*
>
> —Gordon Haber in *Among Wolves*

Unlike most animals in Denali, the story of the wolf is more about how it is threatened than how it thrives.

Wolves pose a conundrum. They are ruthless, efficient, and persistent hunters. People have long witnessed their expertise and battled their

A wolf carries the hindquarter of a caribou carcass.
PHOTO COURTESY OF THE NATIONAL PARK SERVICE.

depredations on livestock and wild game. Ranchers and hunters on the American frontier, marching westward across the continent and north into Alaska, were diligent about ensuring that wolves (and coyotes and big cats) were trapped and hunted to the brink of extinction, thinking this would preserve their livelihoods. For a time the trapping and hunting of wolves was also policy within the national parks, the thought being that removing the predators would conserve other wildlife resources.

In Alaska the territorial legislature enacted a bounty on wolves in 1915, hoping to increase caribou and moose populations, key to subsistence and market hunting in the region. Over the years wolves have been poisoned, trapped, and shot both on the ground and from the air; even the radio collars used by biologists to track wolves' movements within the parks could be used by hunters in aircraft to track the animals for sport and profit.

The mindset began to shift in the mid-twentieth century, and Denali's wolves were the pivot point. Wildlife biologist Adolph Murie's groundbreaking work on predator-prey relationships, which documented the role wolves play in maintaining healthy prey populations, changed national park policy across the board. Instead of being persecuted, wolves were now preserved.

But while some minds were changed, others were not. Outside the boundaries of Denali and other national parks, wolves remain subject to hunting and trapping. In Alaska, where the wolf population is challenged by living conditions in general—the sub-Arctic is not an easy place to survive, no matter the skill set—adding human predation makes their survival more precarious.

Revising the wolf-hunting mindset—a job not yet complete, by any stretch—was the life work of both Murie and wildlife biologist Gordon Haber. Throughout most of the twentieth century and into the twenty-first, these two men (and others) have carefully documented the complex truths of the natural history of wolves, studying them for extended periods in the field; locating their dens and watching them raise their pups; following them on hunts; as well as observing how they interact with each other and with other animals, including their prey. Because wolves have been part of Interior Alaska's ecosystem for millennia—Haber thought at least a million years, making them contemporaries of extinct megafauna including woolly mammoths and mastodons, as well as the caribou, moose, and sheep that occupy Alaska's tundra today—biologists maintain that prey and wolf have developed durable mechanisms for coexisting, which in turn keep the populations in balance through time.

Both Murie and Haber recognized family groups among Denali's wolves, led by an alpha male and female (the mating pair) and consisting of extended families. These family relationships, based on "cooperative breeding and cooperative hunting," are profound: "The intimacy of a family group is often comparable to, and sometimes exceeds, the degree of intimacy found within a typical human family," Haber wrote. And the bonds between alpha males and females "easily rival or exceed the typical human marital bonds in their strength."

Haber also observed a number of interactions between wolves and grizzlies. Wolves sometimes harassed bears—nipping at their rear ends—to drive them off a kill the pack hoped to scavenge, and bears batted back with giant, clawed paws that could easily lay a wolf out. On the other end of the spectrum, he describes a pair of pups that "approached [a grizzly bear] to within one hundred feet and watched the bear intently for about twenty minutes; they seemed fascinated." The bear ignored the pups, and the alpha male and female, not far off, "kept a casual watch on the bear." No conflict; no harm done. Still, Haber believed that bears and wolves maintain "an age-old rivalry that I am convinced includes some genuine dislike for each other, beyond the normal aggression of other competitive and predator-prey relationships."

Intimate communication extends beyond the alpha pair and their immediate families. Haber found that wolves howl not to frighten humans but to communicate with other members of their family group and "to advertise their territorial boundaries." He also believed that wolves howl to "express emotion." This is poignantly illustrated in a passage from *Among Wolves*: "Wolves call-howl to family members who have been trapped or shot. They howl in obvious pain and distress while still alive in traps or snares, and so do any other family members on the scene who might be trying to help them." If the wolf that's been trapped or shot is an alpha female who is pregnant or nursing, more than just that single animal is lost to the park and pack; the pups are lost as well.

To promote further understanding and better track population fluctuations, Denali's wolves have been systematically surveyed since 1986, using radio collars as well as aerial reconnaissance. According to park literature, there were an estimated 170 animals in eleven packs in 1990. By April 2014 "there were approximately 51 wolves in the 13 packs regularly being monitored by park biologists," and as of winter 2016 the park documented 49 wolves in nine groups.

Haber argued that hunting and trapping outside the park was responsible for these losses and that only by providing buffers around park boundaries could wolf populations—and by extension the opportunity for visitors to see and appreciate wolves—be maintained. Buffers were briefly in place in the early 2000s, but removed in 2010 by the Alaska Department of Fish and Game, which is answerable not only to park biologists, vocal advocates like Haber, and other conservationists but also to a hunting and trapping constituency with a long history in Alaska.

The state has a checkered record when it comes to policy and wolf hunting. Writers have documented disturbing accounts of a former Alaska state biologist, nicknamed "Machine Gun Kelleyhouse," who was a proponent of aerial hunting of wolves to protect moose and caribou populations and reportedly had a machine gun mounted on his own plane. Despite the Airborne Hunting Act passed by Congress in 1971, Alaskan hunters continued to kill wolves from helicopters; even when they were caught, punishment was minimal. Author Jon Waterman describes the 1993 fish and game department policy whereby wolves were collared so packs could be tracked for aerial hunting. When the story hit the *New York Times*, outraged opponents flooded the agency's phone lines. A threatened tourism boycott hit Alaska in the financial underbelly, and the collaring-hunting program was banned . . . only to be overturned by the state's legislature later. Today, aerial hunting is permitted on public lands surrounding Denali and other national parks.

But the work goes on. The park had proposed reestablishing the buffer zone in the Wolf Townships north of the boundary, with the desire to increase park visitors' chances of observing wild wolves along the park road, but the proposal was rejected in February 2017. A bill that would establish the Gordon Haber Denali Wolf Special Management Area is up for consideration in Alaska's state legislature in its 2017-2018 session.

Hope remains that, through better understanding of the symbiotic roles played by predator and prey in any environment—including Denali's—wolves will no longer be seen as purely destructive but as productive and manageable members of a healthy ecosystem, even by those who seek to hunt them.

The Big Game: Moose, Caribou, and the Dall Sheep

It was late September, during the rut, and hardly anyone was in the park. But a few cars were parked alongside the Denali Park Road, not far above the park's headquarters, where the spruce is still thick. Waiting, waiting . . . and finally the moment came. A big bull moose stepped up onto the roadway, sporting an impressive rack and a casual, made-for-Hollywood strut. The tourist paparazzi tumbled from their vehicles, camera lenses thumping against their chests as they ran toward him. The moose was oblivious, which was a good thing. He stepped off the far side of the road and, amazingly, given his size, quickly disappeared into the woods.

Moose

Moose, along with the caribou and the Dall sheep, don't inspire the instinctive fear in people that Denali's wolves and grizzlies do. But they should. Sure, these vegetation consumers lack claws and canines, but like all wild animals they may react to a perceived threat with fight rather than flight. A tourist suddenly facing off against a startled moose—say an angry, rutting male in the prime of life, weighing close to sixteen hundred pounds and standing seven feet high at the shoulder, with a rack weighing eighty pounds—stands a healthy chance of suffering serious injury in any confrontation.

Not that a female moose is anything to be trifled with. Grant Pearson, Denali's superintendent in the 1950s, shared a cautionary tale describing his encounter with a mother during the calving season in his memoir, *My Life of High Adventure.* He was running the telephone line along the park road. (For a time an overhead line linked park headquarters and facilities deeper in the park. The line came down in 1955 for the reasons you might expect: weather and wildlife toppling tripods and shredding the wire.) While he was working through prime moose habitat on the approach to Savage River, a snap in a willow thicket alerted Pearson to danger:

> *I turned my head. Charging me was a cow moose. She was a frightening sight, her hackles raised, looking twice her normal size. Her eyes were flaming red, ugly as the devil. She really meant business.*

I dashed to the nearest spruce tree and practically ran up it with my climbing irons, just barely getting out of reach before she caught up with me. When I got up there I saw below me twin moose calves, spindle-legged and awkward, only a few hours old. I had walked within fifteen feet of them. Mamma moose kept me up in that tree for fifteen minutes before going away with her babies.

When treated with respect and given their space, moose are fine to behold. The largest members of the deer family, moose range throughout Alaska, thriving in areas where prime forage—willow, aspen, and birch—can be found, especially on plateaus approaching timberline and along river drainages. In Denali they have also been observed feeding on aquatic grasses in the park's lakes and ponds, and rarely on moss, lichens, and grasses in the tundra.

A lot of energy goes into growing antlers, which the males employ in jousting matches during the rut. They are covered in velvet most of the year, but that layer is shed in fall so that nutrients are diverted to packing on weight for the lean winter months. But nothing goes to waste in the Alaska Range: naturalist and writer Kennan Ward noted that wolves eat the bloody velvet shed by the moose, which is rich in protein. Though sparring generally doesn't result in physical injury, battling bulls have been known to knit antlers; unable to separate, they perish of wounds, starvation, and exhaustion.

Park biologists estimate that roughly fifteen hundred moose abide on the north side of the Alaska Range; about half that number are thought to occupy areas of the park on the south side of the range. Though they are subject to predation by wolves and the occasional grizzly, and hunted for subsistence and sport where permitted within the preserve, moose numbers are stable, making it a good bet that visitors will see one at some point on their travels in the park.

Caribou

Caribou are also members of the deer family. Called a "Stone Age" animal by Dixon, they are sub-Arctic survivors. Not as massive as moose, full-grown bulls average between 350 and 400 pounds, and cows between 175

A caribou bull eyes the photographer (1967).
PHOTO COURTESY OF THE NATIONAL PARK SERVICE, DENALI NATIONAL PARK AND PRESERVE MUSEUM COLLECTIONS. PHOTO BY PETER SANCHEZ.

and 225 pounds. They maintain that weight by eating any plant matter they can find on the tundra, including lichens and mosses, and also forage on willow and birch. Members of Denali's herd also frequent mineral springs, like the one in the Igloo Creek area, to bolster their nutrition.

Caribou are wanderers. Like all caribou herds, Denali's is migratory, heading to lowlands outside of the park in winter, where the grazing is easier, and returning in spring, climbing into the high country to bear their calves where the pests—mosquitoes and flies—aren't as noxious. Dixon noted that Denali's caribou trails, created by animals traveling single file from range to range, have been worn into the landscape over generations.

Both males and females sport antlers, though the antlers of cows are smaller than those of bulls, which can reach five feet in length before they are shed in winter and can grow as much as an inch each day. A bull's antlers are coated with velvet for much of the year; that velvet is rubbed off for the autumn rut, when he must spar with rivals for mating rights.

The size of Denali's herd fluctuates depending in part on how many calves survive to be "recruited" into the adult population from year to year. Estimates of its size have ranged from 3,100 in 1990 to 1,960 in 2002, and Alaska's fish and game department estimates the 2016 herd size at 2,100. Females typically bear a single calf in May, and according to biologist Dixon, parenting is relaxed, with calves frequently wandering from their mothers, a tendency he thought contributed to a high mortality rate. "The young caribou wanders far from home and seemingly depends upon its mother to hunt it up. Charles Sheldon has pointed out that the cows constantly lose their young and run about excitedly trying to find them," Dixon wrote.

The eyesight of the caribou, like that of the moose, is notoriously bad. Mountaineer Belmore Browne, taking a break on his third attempt to ascend Denali, described encountering an old cow, "a great-great grandmother at least," who failed to notice the reclining man until he sat up and said, "Hello, Carrie, where are all the bulls?" The animal assumed a "ludicrous look of surprise, combined with outraged dignity," Browne wrote, and then, "with a deep grunt of disapproval," turned and ambled away.

Dixon relates a similar encounter. One day while on survey, he sat down to rest and watched a small herd draw near: "When the main band had approached within 40 yards, they stopped and began to graze," the field biologist wrote. "The old bull caribou which was leading the band came straight on toward us and passed quietly within 10 feet of our resting place on the open hillside. The wind had been blowing directly from the feeding animals and in our direction, but as soon as the old bull leader reached a point behind us he got our scent and nearly exploded in his frightened attempt to escape the previously unobserved danger."

What a caribou lacks in sight it makes up for with its sense of smell. Dixon also writes about a small herd that picked up his scent more than a mile away and bolted. "Caribou are as keen to scent danger as mountain sheep are to see it," he observed.

Interpretive ranger Dan Irelan related another interesting story about Denali's caribou, the Legend of the Rainbow Herd, a small but "bizarre" slice of park history. Starting in June 1998 a small cluster of bull caribou would gather at the Eielson Visitor Center and hang out there for about six weeks. Eielson is a hub of human activity in the summer months, so having a group of wild caribou choose that site as a place to congregate was unusual. The rangers' "best guess" for this strange behavior, according to Irelan, was that the caribou found some relief near breezy Eielson from the mosquitoes and parasitic flies that can torment them in the summer season. Another possibility is that the caribou were being fed and became habituated, losing their caution around humans as a result of getting handouts.

The caribou presented a "management hassle," however, and officials did their best to run the animals off, hoping to avoid potentially dangerous human-caribou encounters. To get a handle on whether the same individuals were returning year after year—and this went on for several years—wildlife technicians marked the visiting caribou with paintballs; hence the name Rainbow Herd.

In the end, rather than manage the animals, Denali's rangers "decided to manage the people instead." Hikes were rerouted away from the herd; visitors were advised to keep their distance; the caribou were left to their own devices. And a year later they didn't return. Perhaps, Irelan mused, the lack of human interest reduced Eielson's desirability. Whatever the reason, the Rainbow Herd hasn't been seen since.

Dall Sheep

Dall sheep are the wise old souls of Denali. They are at home on the tundra and on the rocky ridgelines, and like the rest of the park's big game, they are survivors, having adapted to the environment over millennia. They also survived the depredations of market hunters at the turn of the twentieth century by inspiring hunter and naturalist Charles Sheldon to initiate the conservation effort that led to the establishment of Mount McKinley National Park. Sheldon takes center stage, but the sheep were his implacable supporting cast.

More than two thousand sheep roam the north slope of the Alaska Range in the park. Aside from their spectacular white coats, the sheep are also known for their distinctive horns, short, slim, and slightly curved on the ewes, and massive curling appendages on the rams. Unlike male

Dall sheep catch some sun on Cathedral Mountain.
PHOTO COURTESY OF THE NATIONAL PARK SERVICE, DENALI NATIONAL PARK AND PRESERVE MUSEUM COLLECTIONS. PHOTO BY VERDE WATSON.

caribou and moose, rams retain their headgear year after year (thus the distinction between a horn and an antler), adding to their bulk annually in concentric rings that can be used to accurately determine an animal's age. The males butt heads to establish dominance during the rut in autumn, though the clashes may be witnessed year-round.

Ewes give birth to a single lamb each year in spring, climbing into the rocky high country—called the lambing cliffs—to bear their young in relative safety. For the lambs the first few weeks of life are precarious, and in some years losses due to falls and predation can be severe. Lambs begin to graze almost immediately, foraging on tundra plants in the summer and on mosses and lichens in winter, as do adults. Sheep also visit the park's mineral licks in the spring, supplementing their nutrition by eating the mineral-rich soils found at these sites.

For all their apparent implacability, sheep are subject to the harsh realities of life in Denali. Pearson relates the story of one bitter winter, when heavy snowfall, combined with a melting wind, was followed by a freeze that "sealed [the sheeps'] grazing ground into a sheath of ice." The sheep hacked at the ice with their hooves, cutting the flesh on their legs, to get at nourishment, to no avail. Hundreds died of starvation and injury. "Nature never permits herself to be sentimental," Pearson observed. "This stark tragedy for the Dall sheep was what could only be called a boom year for the wolves, foxes and wolverines."

The Little Ones

The list of players that back up Denali's wildlife superstars is rich and varied: foxes, weasels, martens, lynx, snowshoe hares, red squirrels, beavers, voles, porcupines, pikas, marmots, wolverines, Arctic ground squirrels, ravens, owls, hawks, golden eagles, Canada geese, ducks, gray jays, ptarmigan, songbirds, grayling, salmon, whitefish, char, botflies, mosquitoes, and more.

Most of the park's smaller wildlife go about their business without fanfare. They eat and are eaten, burrow and fly high overhead, breed and give birth, play, explore, build homes, and hibernate. But a few have generated notable mentions in the studies and memoirs of Denali's rangers, biologists, and naturalists.

Take the wolverine, for example. Grant Pearson called these mighty carnivores "the most destructive animals for their size in the whole area, their flashingly efficient hunting technique giving them a somewhat unwarranted reputation as wanton killers." That said, the ranger noted that wolverines "are no varmints to play games with."

A pair of early mountaineers broke from observations on climbing, weather, and crevasses to ruminate on the snowshoe hare. There's this, from Hudson Stuck of Denali's first ascent team: "A rabbit followed us up the glacier to an elevation of ten thousand feet, gnawing at the bark from the willow shoots with which the trail was staked, creeping around the crevasses, and in one place at least, leaping such a gap. At ten thousand feet he turned back and descended, leaving his tracks plain in the snow." And this from Belmore Browne, who would have relied on hares for dog food during his summit expeditions but could not, given that "the Alaskan rabbits die off about every seven years. The character of this epidemic is not known for certain . . . were it not for this wise provision

Living dangerously: A man holds a porcupine (circa 1930).
PHOTO COURTESY OF THE NATIONAL PARK SERVICE, DENALI NATIONAL PARK AND PRESERVE MUSEUM COLLECTIONS.

of nature there would not be a willow bush left in Alaska inside of fifteen years."

A surprising amount of literature is dedicated to one of Denali's smallest creatures, the Arctic ground squirrel. It's adorable, with a rich coat of brown and gray fur and sharp black eyes. Just about every carnivore and omnivore in the park eats these little beasties, which are referred to as everything from "Arctic hamburger" to Snickers candy bars. Whether staple or snack food, the remains of squirrels have been reported in wolf scat, the pellets of golden eagles (writer Kim Heacox calls them the "staff of life" for Denali's raptors), and the bellies of bears (Heacox notes that "a single bear might eat upward of two hundred ground squirrels each summer").

No wonder, then, that Arctic ground squirrels are ferocious breeders, with females producing up to ten young each summer season. They are also exceptional hibernators, retreating to their underground burrows in August and September and remaining there for the next eight months. During the long season their body temperatures plummet to about 27 degrees Fahrenheit, below freezing without freezing. Periodically they rouse themselves and shiver to bring their temperatures up and make sure all the synapses still fire; then they shut it all down again to conserve their energy stores. As one of Denali's writers-in-residence, Yelizaveta P. Renfro, described it: "If hibernation were an extreme sport, the arctic ground squirrel would be world champion."

Black-capped chickadees are another champion cold-weather survivor. Heacox recounts the observations of a friend and ranger who noted that the chickadees' body temperatures drop nearly twenty degrees Fahrenheit each night "to slow their metabolism to help survive the cold." In late summer the size of the birds' hippocampus, responsible for memory, enlarges so that come winter they can remember where they've cached the tens of thousands of seeds that will sustain them through the long season.

Chickadees are among the estimated 165 avian species that have been observed in Denali park, many passing through on a flyway that takes them from wintering sites to summer breeding grounds. "In June," Grant Pearson observed, "the tundra is as crowded with nests as a city tenement, almost all of migrating birds." However, the migrants need to keep moving; if unlucky enough to be caught in the Alaska Range during a storm, they can become lost, starve, or freeze to death. The migration of sandhill cranes from summer nesting grounds in the Arctic southward to warmer wintering grounds is a harbinger of fall in Denali, according to ranger Sarah Hayes. The big birds are an impressive sight: With calls that evoke prehistoric pterodactyls, they "fly in large flocks that are frequently circling around overhead as they ride the thermals to higher altitude," Hayes notes.

Among those that reside in the park year-round, ravens earn their share of press. As journalist Bill Sherwonit notes, quoting from the *Mt. McKinley Climber's Handbook*: "These tough, intelligent and powerful birds can wreak havoc on a cache, consuming an amazing amount of food and scattering much of the rest." Capable of foraging above 16,000 feet, ravens have been recorded pillaging climbers' caches year-round. In *Minus 148°*, Art Davidson's account of Denali's first winter ascent, the climber describes the mess made of a cache at a high camp: "We found the snow littered with torn plastic bags of jello and potato flakes, scraps of cardboard, and bits of candy, cheese, and beef jerky. A bank of ravens indicated their annoyance at being disturbed by cawing indignantly as they flapped off over Kahiltna Pass . . . though ravens are notorious for their thievery among the caches of climbers in the summer, we had naively assumed that these bandits wouldn't be marauding about the upper reaches of the Kahiltna during the winter months."

And then there are the bugs. During the brief summer season, mosquitoes and other swarming insects plague Denali's wildlife and humans alike, sucking copious quantities of blood, burrowing into exposed patches of skin, and swarming into open mouths and noses. Naturalist Kennan Ward writes about "crazy caribou," driven mad by botflies that burrow into their noses, causing infected animals to "rear up and jump around in circles, chasing away some invisible demon."

Writer Jon Waterman recorded his observations of another creature driven mad in the park by a more notorious plague: the mosquito. "I have witnessed otherwise gentle alpinists—people steeped in the art of suffering stoically—who stooped to petty vengeance by sitting behind tent bug screens for hours at a time, luring mosquitoes to the screen, then plucking out their tormentors' probocises with tweezers."

Mountaineers aren't the only ones tormented by what have been half-jokingly referred to as Alaska's state bird. The story Grant Pearson shares about a Kantishna miner's encounter with a swarm of mosquitoes resonates with hyperbole, but is entertaining nonetheless. Having just finished a new sluice box, the placer miner was attacked by a cloud of mosquitoes "about the size of crows." To save his life, the man overturned the sluice box and crawled underneath. But that didn't stop the bugs: "They rammed their stingers right through the inch-thick boards, probing for dinner," Pearson relates. "This naturally made the miner furious. The pesky insects were ruining a brand-new sluice box. So he picked up his hammer, and every time a stinger came through, he clinched it on the under side." This didn't prove a good solution, however. "After he had cinched twenty-five stingers, those mosquitoes revved up their wings and flew away with the box . . . [l]ast the miner saw of his sluice box it was heading for tidewater at a 75-foot altitude."

For the record, mosquitoes are not Alaska's state bird: The ptarmigan has that honor. And mosquitoes do have a purpose beyond being crazy-making: They are food for birds and bats, wild creatures that most humans look upon with fondness and appreciation, and their larvae support aquatic creatures including fish and the wood frog. The wood frog is Denali's only amphibian, and it too has evolved with a remarkable technique for survival over the long sub-Arctic winter: It freezes solid.

A LAND OF LITTLE STICKS

> *Among the flowers blossoming along the hike are lupine, cinquefoil, harebells, monkshood, moss campion, Labrador tea, wild roses. Delightful.*
>
> —A TWEET FROM GORDON HABER DATED JUNE 21, 2009; FROM *AMONG WOLVES*

Tree line in Denali is at 3,000 feet. The bulk of the Alaska Range rises above that level, with tundra slipping up to where the ice and rock becomes too inhospitable to support most kinds of life. While vertical relief like that in Denali might support four or five life zones at a lesser latitude, there are essentially only two zones within the park, the Arctic and the sub-Arctic.

In the highest reaches of the Arctic zone, where the glaciers rule, nothing grows and wildlife is transient. The only permanent inhabitant is the iceworm, a creature that thrives at freezing temperatures and is thought to survive by harvesting snow algae and windblown pollen grains. But summertime visitors from lower elevations may include grizzlies, Dall sheep, caribou, ravens and other birds (some of which breed up high), and small mammals including hares, pikas, and marmots.

There is greater diversity in the sub-Arctic zone. Ecosystems include taiga, subalpine or boreal woodlands, meadows, scrub tundra, and more. Broken fields of talus are home to pikas, marmots, and Dall sheep, which also wander down into the tundra, where more fruitful habitats include shallow lakes and ponds, the gravel bars of rivers and creeks, bogs and marshes, and thickets of alder and willow. This is where the berries grow; other plants include Labrador tea, a variety of grasses and sedges, and wildflowers including mountain heather and buttercups, fireweed and larkspur, frigid shooting star and frigid arnica.

At timberline scattered stands of black spruce find purchase in the permafrost, buckled down against the wind and cold. They are short and spindly, resembling what would be considered saplings in forests farther south; hence the "land of little sticks," or the taiga. These trees, however, can be a century or more old.

Descend farther, and the spruce forests grow more crowded, interspersed with alpine meadows, small lakes, and kettle ponds carved by glaciers in eons past. Called the boreal lowlands, the forests also harbor stands of white spruce and paper birch, as well as aspen and balsam poplar on south-facing slopes, according to park literature. Willow and alder thrive near the water, and on drier slopes sagebrush and juniper can be found. Wildflowers include wild rose and cinquefoil, lupine, geranium, and cow parsnip.

Wildlife roams between tundra and forest, moving with the bloom and fruiting of berries and other food sources. But each creature has a favorite, being matched by constitution to the resource most abundant in that locale. Wildlife may also prefer a particular locale for its shade or camouflage. As Grant Pearson noted, "The dense shade of the higher white spruce groves form a protective coloration for black bears and timber wolves alike."

A patchwork quilt, created by the Denali Quilters and on display in the Murie Science and Learning Center in 2016, provides a visual illustration of Denali's complex vegetation types and ecosystems. Based on satellite images of the park's ground cover, the Denali Landcover Quilt's "pixel" patches represent four kinds of spruce habitats, habitats of scrub, alder, willow, and peat; aquatic habitats from snow and ice to silty water

Wilderness meets machine: A car "pushes" a grizzly bear across the Teklanika Bridge (circa 1930).
PHOTO COURTESY OF THE NATIONAL PARK SERVICE, DENALI NATIONAL PARK AND PRESERVE MUSEUM COLLECTIONS.

and clean water; burns and bare ground—twenty-three land cover types in all. A kaleidoscope of color, the quilt is a stunning and unique snapshot of Denali's ecological complexity and diversity.

THE HUMAN FACTOR

> *Every human population explosion brings with it a corresponding menace to the population of wild creatures . . . making conservation and wildlife management increasingly needful.*
>
> —GRANT PEARSON

Stewards of national parks throughout the system must contend with visitors who don't understand how important it is for wildlife to stay wild. Perhaps that's because memories are long. After all, in the early days of the NPS, rangers fed the deer; concessioners built lighted platforms so that visitors could watch bears forage through a park's refuse; elk and bears and wildcats were corralled into zoos for the entertainment of tourists.

Such interactions—particularly those with potential predators—posed dangers for people and, as it turns out, even greater dangers for wildlife. For example, when black bears became habituated to humans in Yosemite, breaking into camps and cars to get at the tasty morsels brought by visitors, the first mitigating strategy was to transport them far afield. But the bears often returned (the picnic baskets, after all, were still on the picnic tables), and when they did, they'd be deemed problem bears and exterminated. The issue of wildlife becoming dependent on human handouts had less obvious, but just as devastating, consequences as well—the ground squirrel adorably snacking on Cheetos in front of the visitor center was destined to have a hard time surviving the long, cold winter, particularly in snow country, when the tourists and their snacks were tucked snug and warm in homes far away.

Denali doesn't have the bear problems that Yosemite or Yellowstone must cope with, which is a good thing given that a close encounter with a grizzly is much more likely to result in serious injury or death. Still, as visitation increases, the park will have its issues, as 2016's grizzly-visitor interaction at Savage River illustrates.

For Denali's wolves habituation works in reverse: Animals that ordinarily might not show fear or curiosity toward people have, as a result of hunting and other management tactics, become wary, which not only diminishes the chance that a visitor might see a wolf in the wild but also increases the probability that a lone animal, or an entire pack, will stray outside the protection of park boundaries and into traps or snares.

"Any wolf-people problems in Denali are most likely to originate from avoidable people mistakes, not unnatural, dangerous wolf behavior," Gordon Haber advised in *Among Wolves*. For rangers in Denali and elsewhere, using education to stave off avoidable human mistakes has become the modus operandi. The tactic is now to show the public how they should behave around wildlife, which is to let the wildlife remain wild.

Travelers in Denali's backcountry and front country carry the responsibility to maintain what wildlife biologists now know are safe distances between animal and observer. The Savage River grizzly event was, hopefully, an aberration; interactions with the park's wildlife should never result in the death of an animal. In a wilderness truly untouched by human influence, the ultimate fate of a bear or moose or wolf would be unknowable, because its demise would take place far removed from camera, boot print, or binoculars . . . and it would certainly be far distant from a wildlife biologist, who should never have to make a decision to put a wild animal down.

Denali's preservation as a game reserve is sometimes overshadowed by Denali itself. The mountain looms larger than any collection of megafauna when the sun shines brightly on its shining slopes. But the stories of the animals, and the people who've lived with them, are integral to the park experience. Lower the sky to hide the peak, and the viewer's eyes are drawn down, across a world that's low and green and brown, a world that may actually be looking back at her.

Chapter Thirteen

Rock and Ice: A Mountain of Science

In the jargon of the National Park Service (NPS), what's been documented by scientists over the last century are Denali's "resources." More romantically, scientific inquiry walks with the Dall sheep on the mountain, stares with curiosity into the bowels of glaciers, lugs barometers to mountaintops, and hunkers in the tundra with notebook and magnifying glass. The curious and scholarly hail from any number of government agencies and institutions of higher learning, focusing eye and mind on every aspect of the park, from its geology to its wildlife, from climate change to the tracks left by creatures that roamed Alaska eons ago. The vast body of research that's been generated—the product of University of Denali—informs management decisions on how to protect those resources, from the tiniest tundra bloom to the massive glaciers that flow down the mountain's slopes. Scientific inquiry and the literature it generates are the wellsprings of collaboration and, occasionally, conflict in the park.

Science at the Top

> *No one had lived on North America's highest ridges in the winter twilight. No one knew how low the temperatures would drop, or how penetrating the cold would be when the wind blew. For thousands of years McKinley's winter storms had raged by themselves.*
>
> —Art Davidson, *Minus 148°*

Rocks and ice are in perpetual union on Denali's South Peak.
PHOTO COURTESY OF THE NATIONAL PARK SERVICE, DENALI NATIONAL PARK AND PRESERVE MUSEUM COLLECTIONS. PHOTO BY BRADFORD WASHBURN.

Those who climb Denali get asked the question all the time: Why? There is truth in the clichéd response, "Because it's there," but there are a multitude of nuances. Dig a little deeper, and each answer becomes deeply personal, as individual as the mountaineers themselves. Answering the other questions climbers have carried on their summit quests is more objective, subject to testing and proof. How high is Denali, exactly? What forces have shaped the terrain? How does the human body react at extreme altitude? How do cosmic rays behave at altitude? How cold does it get up there? How hard can the winds blow?

Even the earliest expeditions carried aloft scientific inquiry as well as crampons, pemmican, and ambition. The Stuck expedition, first to the top in 1913, spent an hour on the summit taking measurements to confirm the peak's height. A whole chapter in Archdeacon Hudson Stuck's account of the climb, *The Ascent of Denali*, describes the method and mathematics involved in making those calculations. Considering the era, the conditions, and the instruments, which were rudimentary by modern standards, his conclusion was remarkably accurate, proposing a South Peak summit elevation of 20,374 feet (officially, the mountain's height is 20,310 feet). Otherwise, the archdeacon's technique and philosophy were a bit wonky. He struggled to lug a mercurial barometer to the summit; in the end another expedition member shouldered that load, and ultimately Stuck himself had to be hauled aloft, where he "fell unconscious" for a spell before recovering breath. The churchman also rants about the ungodliness and "dogmatic" arrogance of scientists in another passage.

On the descent the Stuck expedition deposited a "spirit thermometer" at Denali Pass, hoping it would shed light on how far temperatures could drop four miles high at sub-Arctic latitudes. The thermometer was recovered by the Lindley-Liek expedition in 1932 and showed that the temperature had plummeted to the lowest recordable on the device. If nothing else, this meant future expeditions would have to figure out another way to see if it got colder than –95 degrees on Denali at 20,000 feet.

The Lindley-Liek expedition was one of two on the mountain in the early summer of 1932; the other was the ill-fated Cosmic Ray expedition, which, true to its name, sought to shed light on how cosmic radiation functioned at altitude. The party employed park service dogsled teams to haul equipment to its base camp on the Muldrow Glacier; while this practice would not become policy, it did mark the start of an ongoing, if sometimes troubled, partnership between scientists, mountaineers, and park administrators. In the end the Cosmic Ray team wasn't able to produce useful science, as its lead researcher and a colleague would perish on the Muldrow in a tragic crevasse accident.

Operation White Tower

The lifework of Bradford Washburn on Denali blurred the lines of art, science, mountaineering, and advocacy. He used photography to create detailed maps of the mountain and deepen the scientific understanding of its geography. His images are profoundly beautiful and completely functional, used over time as baselines for opening mountaineering routes, defining the mountain's architecture, and tracking changes to glaciers and other features over time. His first expeditions, starting in 1936, were sponsored by *National Geographic* magazine, which employed the young explorer to take aerial photographs of the mountain. A classic image of Washburn shows him seated at the open door of an aircraft, enveloped in cold-weather gear, his camera on his knees. A number of classic images would follow, taken by Washburn from the sky and on the slopes of the mountain, which he summited several times.

Operation White Tower, staged in 1947, embodied the merger of art, science, and mountaineering in ways the park had never seen before. One goal, of course, was to get to the top, which the expedition did in memorable fashion, with Barbara Washburn making the first ascent by a woman. Another was filmmaking: The expedition shot footage for a mountaineering film for RKO Pictures. The third prong was science. Washburn headed up the New England Museum of Natural History at the time and, according to park service literature, sought input from a number of scientists "to suggest how many ways [the] expedition might make a real scientific contribution." Cosmic ray research was one way; surveying was another. The party lugged ten thousand pounds of scientific and filmmaking equipment onto the mountain, and when some of that equipment was damaged or destroyed in what was dubbed the "Great Storm," a "research hut" and replacement equipment were delivered via airdrop to Denali Pass, above 18,000 feet on the mountain. Washburn envisioned a permanent research facility on the pass, touting the mountain's high, remote ridgelines as ideal sites not only for cosmic ray research but also for "use as radar stations, weather observation points and centers of nuclear research." In the end Denali's remoteness would thwart Washburn's vision, but science and mountaineering remained paired in the decades to come.

The Physical Toll

In the years following the opening of the West Buttress route in 1951, the summit of Denali became more accessible and more popular. The park service monitored climbing parties attempting the summit much

Brad Washburn (left), shown here with park superintendent Grant Pearson, merged three disciplines on Denali: science, art, and mountaineering.
PHOTO COURTESY OF THE NATIONAL PARK SERVICE, DENALI NATIONAL PARK AND PRESERVE MUSEUM COLLECTIONS.

more rigorously in those days, requiring minimum party sizes, detailed plans, and medical examinations, among other things. Teams that promised to add to the park's scientific reservoir of knowledge had an edge on the competition: By carrying new and better tools to measure temperature, altitude, wind speed, and the effects of radiation, climbers could secure permission to make airdrops high on the slopes, expediting access to the summit. Superintendent Grant Pearson was among the park administrators who began to question climbers' scientific motivations. As documented by historian Frank Norris, Pearson suspected that climbers were using science as a "subterfuge." His answer was to allow each party "one air drop of equipment and supplies . . . at the base of the mountain."

The scientific hook was still in play in 1967, when an eight-man expedition made the first winter ascent of Denali. Climber Art Davidson, one of three who reached the summit in that bitter season, exposed some raw mountaineering truths in his memoir *Minus 148°*, pulling back the veil on the double-edged sword of the mountaineer's ego, the mortal dangers posed by Denali's weather and geography, and the toll that extreme climbing takes on body and mind. To document physiological impacts, members of the expedition submitted to a battery of tests at the Institute of Arctic Biology in Fairbanks before beginning their climb. Davidson collected blood samples from his teammates while on the mountain. And after a brutal storm trapped Davidson and two comrades in a snow cave at 18,200 feet for a week, nearly killing them, a follow-up examination revealed that the climbers had lost an average of thirty-five pounds each (Davidson recalls attempting to "rectify" this loss by supplementing a second breakfast with nineteen eggs). It took weeks for expedition members to recover from frostbite to their extremities. As for mental wear and tear, when the scientists "hooked our heads back up to the electroencephalograph, [they] recorded mental patterns common for a person sleeping lightly."

Collection of these kinds of data on the mountain—about its height and weather, about the effects of altitude on climbers, on the performance of gear in extreme conditions—is ongoing. The University of Alaska Anchorage's High Latitude Research Group maintains a study station at

14,200 feet on the Kahiltna Glacier, collecting data on the effects of altitude on climbers as well as helping in the event of a medical emergency. And harkening back to what the Stuck expedition grappled with on its first ascent, scientists continue to recalculate Denali's height: in 2015 the number was revised downward from 20,320 feet to 20,310 feet, as new instrumentation provided still greater accuracy.

On the Rocks

> *The recipe is to place the sediments of the Grand Canyon, the plutonic rocks of Yosemite, and the volcanics of Mount Rainier in a blender, and turn it on briefly to "chop." Then layer as a parfait, and serve with large quantities of ice from the likes of Glacier Bay National Park!*
>
> —Phil Brease, Denali National Park and Preserve's geologist from 1986 to 2010, as quoted in Denali's *Geology Road Guide*

A "ring of fire" encircles the Pacific Ocean, a fractured and chaotic assemblage of volcanoes, fault and rift zones, and buckled mountain ranges that mark the boundaries of several of the tectonic plates that comprise the earth's crust. Activity on the ring, where plates floating on a molten subterranean ocean of rock collide, subside, and slide against each other, is often violent, punctuated by earthquakes and eruptions. Most notably from the American perspective, the volcanoes of the Cascades, including Mount Rainier and Mount St. Helens, and fault lines like the San Andreas, which ruptured in 1906 and resulted in the destruction of much of San Francisco, lie along the Pacific Ring of Fire.

Denali and the Alaska Range, along with other spectacular ranges along the state's coastline, were raised by these tectonic forces. Seven major and many minor "terranes"—blocks of crust broken off the major plates—collide within Alaska and have been "suturing" together for millions of years, shaping the geography. In Denali park, geologists have mapped the intersection of four minor terranes—the McKinley, Yukon-Tanana, Farewell, and Pingston.

What underlies Denali directly is a fault zone that follows the west-to-east arc of the Alaska Range. According to Denali's *Geology Road Guide*, a terrane known as the Yakutat Block and the massive Pacific Plate rotate counterclockwise along the Denali Fault. Within the park "some of the fault's energy manifests as compressional forces that fold and crumple the plates, causing the rocks to be uplifted," the guide's authors explain. Denali soars above the other peaks in the crumple zone by virtue of a "kink," or "restraining bend," that has forced the uplift at this particular point to exceed that manifested elsewhere in the range.

Another factor in Denali's height: its granitic composition. The peak is what geologists call a "pluton," part of a granite batholith, a giant bubble of magma formed far below the earth's crust, that has slowly risen to the surface. In the case of Denali, the pluton "sort of 'popped' up to the surface, much like a cork held under water will pop up when released," according to one report. The mountain's granite composition also means it is resistant to the forces of erosion—water, ice, and wind. The glaciers spilling down its flanks are doubtless carving Yosemite-style monoliths, but they aren't making a big dent in the peak's height.

Rather than diminishing, Denali continues to grow, albeit at the proverbial glacial pace. Geologists estimate that the peak is rising at a rate of a half millimeter each year; they estimate that in two million years the mountain will have added another kilometer, or 3,280 feet, which more than makes up for the loss of 10 feet as calculated in 2015.

Though the mountain's great height can't be directly attributed to the volcanics that have shaped other iconic mountains in Alaska, that's not to say volcanoes haven't played a part. The 1912 eruption of Novarupta, in what is now Katmai National Park and Preserve, is a case in point. The event, called the "largest volcanic eruption in the twentieth century and one of the five largest in recorded history," drained the magma supporting Mount Katmai's summit and caused its collapse; jettisoned ash more than twenty miles into the atmosphere; and generated pyroclastic flows that traveled at speeds exceeding one hundred miles per hour, creating what is now poetically known as the Valley of Ten Thousand Smokes. The eruption took place hundreds of air miles southwest of Denali, but had dramatic consequences on the frozen anatomy of the mountain and its neighbors. Members of the Browne expedition, who were in retreat from a summit attempt when the eruption occurred, experienced a subsequent earthquake and witnessed an avalanche of massive proportions on a neighboring peak.

What they couldn't see was that, in addition to being earth-shattering, the distant event was also ice-shattering. When the Stuck expedition reached what is now known as Karstens Ridge the following summer, team members found the smooth slope of snow and ice described by Browne's party transformed into a confused jumble of frozen rubble. It took Harry Karstens and Walter Harper weeks to grapple with the route-altering mess, carving a staircase up to more predictable terrain.

Its location on a fault line means Denali is routinely rattled by earthquakes, most very small in magnitude. According to park literature, about three thousand temblors are recorded within the park's boundaries each year, most too small for visitors to feel. Many of those quakes occur within what's called the Kantishna seismic cluster, located in the foothills north of the mountain.

But a few of those quakes have been large enough to make an impression, including one with a magnitude that registered 7.9, the largest recorded in Interior Alaska. According to the *Geology Road Guide*, "This single earthquake released more energy than all of the earthquakes that have occurred in the lower 48 US states over the last 30 years combined."

While some earthquake impacts are lasting, like those that rent Karstens Ridge in 1912, others are ephemeral. A temblor in 1953 caused a landslide on rainfall-saturated hills; the flow dammed the Stony Creek drainage north of the park road. Bergh Lake (known colloquially as Quake Lake) took almost a month to fill. Historian Jane Bryant records that when it overflowed the dam, Bradford Washburn paddled out in a canoe to measure its depth, pegged at seventy-two feet. The lake was around long enough to make the U.S. Geological Survey (USGS) maps, but by 1988 the earthen dam had eroded away and the lake was history.

As was the case with the 1912 Katmai eruption, Denali has also been affected by major quakes occurring on plate boundaries far distant from the park. On Good Friday in 1964, far below Prince William Sound, the Pacific Plate abruptly lunged northward into, and under, the neighboring North American Plate. The break triggered a magnitude 9.2 quake, which the USGS has deemed the second largest ever recorded worldwide and the largest quake to occur anywhere in America. The temblor demolished Anchorage and other towns along the coastline and generated tsunamis that ranged south to Oregon and northern California and southwest to Hawaii. Though mention of the quake's immediate effect on Denali is minimal, a subsistence report written by Richard Bishop in 1978 notes that water levels in ponds and lakes in the bogs and black spruce forests along the Muddy and Kuskokwim Rivers began to drop, a phenomenon attributed to the 1964 event.

In the aftermath of the Good Friday quake, scientists began to unravel the mysteries of plate tectonics. With the recognition that the forces at work along the tectonic boundaries reached inland to the Alaska Range, and that the range itself lay atop the Denali Fault, the park has since been outfitted with seismic monitoring systems, and cataloging of earthquake activity continues to the present day. Four seismometers lie along the Denali Fault within the park and just outside its borders, gathering information about how the forces that underlie the range work, and possibly helping predict when the next major rupture will occur.

Paleontology

The rocks of Denali have revealed more than just information about the mountain's geologic components. Folding and lifting along the Denali Fault has also exposed something unexpected: the remnants of dinosaurs that roamed a different Alaska in distant times.

The variety of fossilized plant matter preserved in the rocks of the Cantwell Formation illustrates an ancient Alaskan "wonderland," according to Denali's *Geology Road Guide*. Despite its northerly latitude, at the time the formation was laid down seventy million years ago, the region was a much more temperate place, with "short, warm, dry summers and long, comparatively mild, and probably wet winters." Coniferous forests and shallow lakes and rivers with associated floodplains, where ferns and horsetails thrived, dominated the landscape.

It was prime dinosaur country, but no evidence of the long-extinct beasts was discovered until July 2005. According to park literature, a study group from the University of Alaska Fairbanks was conducting a survey along Igloo Creek when the professor, Paul McCarthy, leaned up against an outcrop from the Cantwell Formation and explained to his students that this was just the type of rock where one might expect to find dinosaur tracks. Student Susi Tomsich "immediately spied the dinosaur track not far from McCarthy's gesturing hand and asked, 'Like this one?'"

The track, laid down by a theropod, marked the beginning of a Late Cretaceous period fossil bonanza. Tracks of more theropods (bipedal carnivores; think *Velociraptor*), hadrosaurs (giant herbivores; called "duck-billed" dinosaurs), ceratopsians (horned herbivores; think *Triceratops*), and pterosaurs ("winged lizards"), as well as "bird tracks, fish traces, crayfish burrows, and insect trackways," have been uncovered at hundreds of sites. Among the finds: mudflats trampled by herding hadrosaurs, creating what has been dubbed a "dinosaur dance floor." One of the discoveries, an "extinct marine brachiopod" found only in Denali, was named *Myirospirifer breasei* in memory of longtime park geologist Phil Brease.

As with geologic studies, paleontological research is ongoing in the park. In 2016 paleontologists from the university and the park service unearthed fossilized hadrosaur bones, the first to be found in Denali. Examples of the park's dinosaur legacy comprise a popular display in the Murie Science and Learning Center.

Science on Ice

> *It seems probable that this one glacier covers an area equal to the combined area of all the glaciers in Mount Rainier National Park.*
>
> —Joseph Dixon, reflecting on the immensity of the Muldrow Glacier in *Birds and Mammals of Mount McKinley National Park*

The statistics, as compiled by the NPS, are impressive. Denali National Park and Preserve encompasses forty named glaciers and hundreds of unnamed glaciers—in 2010 the park service counted 881 glaciers covering about one million of Denali's six million acres (more than 1,540 square miles; about 17 percent of the park). Glaciers reach from near the top of the peak, at more than 20,000 feet, to lows at about 800 feet above sea level. On the north side of the Alaska Range, the longest glacier is the Muldrow, at 34 miles. On the south side of the range, the Kahiltna is longest—and longest in the park—at 44 miles. The Ruth Glacier, also on the south side, is more than 30 miles long and is the deepest glacier in the park, at about 3,800 feet. The Great Gorge of the Ruth features cliffs soaring 5,000 feet above the glacier's surface. With nearly 4,000 feet of its walls under the grinding ice, if the glacier were to melt today, the gorge would dwarf Yosemite's glacier-carved monoliths and exceed the vertical relief of the Grand Canyon by more than 2,000 feet.

These glaciers are just remnants of massive glaciations that took place in the past, the last engulfing the Alaska Range about ten thousand years ago. The retreat of those glaciers left signs of their passage in the form of glacial erratics, immense boulders deposited by the receding ice; kettle ponds; and distinctive, U-shaped valley floors. These grinding forces are still in play today as Denali's rivers of ice flow slowly downhill, a powerful, gravity-driven locomotion that peels rock from mountainsides, tumbles it into boulders, and then pulverizes the boulders into silt and gravel deposited in the beds of massive, milky streams.

The story goes that glaciers move at . . . well, a glacial pace. But that's not necessarily true. Denali's glaciers, notably the Muldrow, have been known to "gallop," or surge. When the Muldrow went for a gallop in 1957, moving 6.6 kilometers in a matter of months, according to park literature, it altered the long-established climbing route that followed the glacier up Denali's north slopes, making it much less accessible and shunting climbers to the south side, where the Kahiltna offered easier access. Surges on the Muldrow are thought to begin higher up on the Traleika Glacier, with research pointing to at least three other surges over the past two hundred years.

The crevasses created by both a glacier's slow creep and, if it happens, a surge pose significant obstacles to travel. Mountaineers on Denali exercise extreme caution when crossing any glacier, roping up so that if

The Muldrow Glacier was the route of choice for mountaineers prior to the ascent of the West Buttress route and a "galloping" event.
PHOTO COURTESY OF THE NATIONAL PARK SERVICE, DENALI NATIONAL PARK AND PRESERVE MUSEUM COLLECTIONS.

someone plunges into a hidden crack, a teammate can (hopefully) arrest the fall, anchor in, and haul the victim out. Likening glaciers to "obstacle courses," Grant Pearson reflected on the care the 1932 Lindley-Liek expedition took as members sought safe passage up the Muldrow, prodding with ice axes and marking safe ground with willow wands. "What with this constant poking and prodding about, we must have looked as if we were out on the Muldrow hunting for clams," he wrote.

For Belmore Browne there were three kinds of crevasses. Some crevasses "sink to the very bowels of the glacier—great blue chasms that are so deep that you can see nothing but a blue void." Others cradled "icy stalagmites upon which a falling man would be impaled." And finally, there were "crevasses that fall sheer to subglacial torrents, the bellowing of which between the deep ice walls sends cold shivers down a man's back."

Seracs loom above an observer on the Muldrow Glacier (1957).
PHOTO COURTESY OF THE NATIONAL PARK SERVICE, DENALI NATIONAL PARK AND PRESERVE MUSEUM COLLECTIONS. PHOTO BY JOSEPH MEEKER.

Glaciers gone vertical are called ice falls, which are the sources of yet another terrain-sculpting force: avalanche. Again, mountaineers have long stood in awe of the impressive, transformative power of Denali's avalanches. There's this from Dr. Frederick Cook in *To the Top of the Continent*: "McKinley is one of the severest battlegrounds of nature, and warfare is impressed with every look at its thundering immensity. The avalanches fire a thousand cannons every minute and the perpetual roar echoes and re-echoes from a hundred cliffs. The pounding of the massive blocks from ledge to ledge in their mad descent makes the whole mountain world quiver with battle spirit."

And this from Belmore Browne's *The Conquest of Mount McKinley*: "Sliding snow has a nasty look and sound—there is something sinister about it—like the noise of a snake in dry grass." Browne should know: The earthquake-induced collapse on Mount Brooks in 1912, which he witnessed, created a cloud of ice that rose four thousand feet into the air and generated winds clocked at sixty miles per hour as it collapsed.

And anyone who has approached the Wickersham Wall, from the judge that the formidable cascade of rock and ice is named for to the climbers who finally scaled it in 1963, has stood in awe of the number and size of the avalanches that regularly roar down the face when Denali is softened by the sun.

When They Become Water

The powerful, terrain-sculpting forces of Denali's glaciers don't cease where the ice stops. The rivers issuing from their termini define the lowland landscapes. The riverbeds become more massive as they descend, collecting the flows of subsidiary streams as they drop toward the sea. The Yukon is the penultimate river of the Interior, fed by streams originating on the north side of the Alaska Range, on the south side of the Brooks Range, and deep in Canada's Yukon Territory. The Tanana River, fed by many of the creeks and rivers draining Denali's north, east, and west faces, is a major tributary of the mighty Yukon.

Within the park the Toklat and its East Fork, the McKinley, the Teklanika, the Sanctuary, and the Savage Rivers are linchpins on the landscape culturally as well as physically. Their wide beds are, at times

Aufeis barricades the Denali Park Road in 1960.
PHOTO COURTESY OF THE NATIONAL PARK SERVICE, DENALI NATIONAL PARK AND PRESERVE MUSEUM COLLECTIONS.

of lower flows, classically braided, with gravel bars separating channels of cold, swift-moving, silt-laden water. Come spring or storm, the rivers flood: The literature is strewn with stories of mountaineers and explorers, along with their horses, sleds, or boats, stymied, nearly drowned, or swept away by high water.

The park's administrative history highlights stories of how rivers in flood (as well as creeks) have remodeled the landscape and the man-made structures imposed upon it. Bridges, for obvious reasons, take a regular beating, and not just because of flowing water, but also because of ice. Archival images show earth worn from bridge buttresses, culverts filled with river gravel, and aufeis (pronounced *OFF-ice*; sheets of ice that form up on top of Arctic waterways over the long winter months) building up against the spans and flowing down the park road. Images from 1964 show aufeis being blasted off the roadway not far from park headquarters.

Climate Change

In recent years, science on Denali's glaciers has focused on the effects of climate change. Though climate has helped define flora, fauna, geology, and glaciology in Alaska for eons, the difference now, according to researchers with the NPS, "is that the changes are happening faster—fast enough for people to sense and recognize."

Mapping the retreat and thinning of glacial ice sheets in Alaska's national parks is one way to track the effects of climate change. Glaciologists are using comparative photography to document the diminishing and retreat of the mountain's ice rivers, and are also measuring changes in glacial volume using laser altimetry, satellite imagery, radar depth measurements, and other tools. In Denali researchers have found that the rate of retreat on the Middle Fork Toklat Glacier has increased by 37 percent since 2010, as compared to the rate of retreat over the previous half century or so. On the East Fork Teklanika Glacier, the park reports "~980 feet (300m) of obvious thinning and associated retreat," with a number of the park's smaller "pocket" glaciers retreating even farther and faster. Monitoring of change on the Kahiltna Glacier has been ongoing since 1991, with researchers concluding that "despite being fed by significant snowfall from the highest peak in North America, the Kahiltna Glacier has been losing mass in warming temperatures, leading to gradual but visible changes in the Denali National Park landscape." None of Denali's glaciers are presently thickening or advancing.

Climate change is also taking a toll on Denali's infrastructure. The stability provided by permafrost, the permanently frozen soil that underlies as much as 80 percent of Alaska, is lost as it melts, or as it freezes and thaws. A longtime Denali road maintenance worker, Tim Taylor, is quoted in park literature about the impacts of melting permafrost on the Denali Park Road. He notes that in some areas the road is in constant motion due to thawing permafrost, which wasn't a problem back in the 1970s and 1980s. "Now," Taylor observed, "every time we rebuild a section of the park road we have to account for thawing [to] keep the road structurally sound for the future."

Melting permafrost near the roadway can have drastic effects. In October 2013 thirty thousand cubic yards of destabilized earth slipped onto the road near Igloo Creek in an event the park viewed "as a case study in climate change-induced hazards." The permafrost layer had separated from the underlying clay, depositing chunks of frozen ground the size of "small houses" on the roadway. Though slides of all kinds are part of Denali's geologic anatomy, a rise in their incidence over the long term is not only worthy of observation as part of climate study but also crucial to the park's ability to monitor hazards. No one was on the Denali Park Road when the Igloo Creek slide occurred, but had a bus been present, there would have been losses.

Melting permafrost has also affected Denali's flora. As the soil beneath them destabilizes, some of the park's black spruce get all tipsy, creating "drunken forests." Another effect: As the climate warms, insects like the spruce bark beetles are able to gain ground in forests, compromising their health. The number of wildfires also increases, impacting plant life and wildlife. While fire and beetles are part of natural cycles in forests, scientists continue to monitor the frequency and severity of blazes and infestations. It's part of an ongoing effort to understand and mitigate the impacts of climate change, which also includes the NPS's Long-Term Glacial Monitoring program and Citizen Science Expeditions sponsored by Alaska Geographic.

Poop

Yes, poop. It turns out that scientific inquiry across disciplines on Denali has, in the most intriguing way, coalesced around poop.

Climbers have been pooping on Denali for a century. And it hasn't been pretty: As writer Jonathan Waterman recollected from his days on the mountain, in some places "snow for cooking had to be chosen carefully from the wasteland of brown turds." Since the opening of the West Buttress route in 1951, the NPS estimates that between 152,000 and 215,000 pounds (or 69 to 97 metric tons) of poop have been deposited on, or in, the Kahiltna Glacier. There was a protocol: For decades the mountain's crevasses served as its latrine. Mountaineers were encouraged to dump their dumps into deep yawning breaks in the glaciers where they camped.

And that's where the science comes in, merging the study of climate change, the impacts of human use on the mountain, and the effectiveness of Leave No Trace ethics. As glaciers flow and retreat, things that have been frozen in ice—from pollen to fallen climbers—get spit out, dropped like erratics at the glacial toe. This detritus contains artifacts with the potential to shed light on many aspects of Denali's human and natural history. The mass of human waste tossed into what was thought to be the impermeable container of a crevasse will, like bodies, garbage, and discarded mountaineering gear, eventually flow toward the toe and then melt out. As the melt-out is studied and documented, researchers and park officials have the opportunity to reconsider sustainable climbing practices and study an unexpected consequence of climate change.

Researchers from the NPS and Alaska Pacific University also have been trying to time when poop dropped into a Kahiltna crevasse might reemerge in what's known as the "ablation zone," as well as measure the potential effects of that human waste on water quality downstream. On the Leave No Trace side, innovative waste collection technology known as the Clean Mountain Can (CMC) was developed by longtime Denali mountaineering ranger and climber Roger Robinson. The cans, which can hold the fecal output of a single climber for the course of a typical expedition, have slowly become the gold standard of waste removal on the mountain. It's an expensive program and one that requires ongoing education, but in the end, carrying poop off Denali's glaciers rather than depositing it in its crevasses could save ecosystems in ways not yet documented. The cans aren't required equipment yet—mountaineering regulations presently only require climbers to maintain clean zones around camps and use biodegradable bags when they toss their poop into a crevasse. But if these practices prove detrimental, use of CMCs could become standard on the peak, and elsewhere.

A Scientific Summit

It all goes back to 1902, when Alfred Brooks of the USGS worked in the hills north of Denali, near the mining enclave of Kantishna, surveying an unknown geography. Stephen Capps, another geologist with the USGS, continued those surveys, writing an article for *National Geographic* magazine that bolstered calls for the area's preservation as a national park. Charles Sheldon immersed himself in study of the park's wildlife, the first in a long, passionate line of biologists and naturalists that includes Adolph Murie and Gordon Haber, George Wright and Joseph Dixon, and many others. Denali's flora has been studied by botanists since the 1920s, though the names—Inez Mexia and Frances Payne; Aven Nelson and Ruth Ashton Nelson; Leslie A. Viereck—are less familiar. So too are the names of Denali's more modern researchers, like Phil Brease and Susi Tomsich. And another small army has also contributed to the pot of knowledge. When the mountain unveils itself, camera shutters snap like rounds of applause. Journalists, poets, and advocates record experiences and revelations, capturing moments in time. This is the stuff of citizen science. To define Denali as a mountain for climbers doesn't begin to cut it; Denali is also a mountain of science.

Chapter Fourteen

Defining Wilderness: A Different Kind of National Park

Where an Alaskan town ends wilderness begins.
—Belmore Browne, *The Conquest of Mount McKinley*

Beauty is a resource in and of itself. Alaska must be allowed to be Alaska, that is her greatest economy.
—Margaret Murie

When Mount McKinley National Park was established in 1917, Americans were not far removed from real wilderness. In its first hundred years, the nation had been preoccupied with conquering the sprawling wildlands that separated the East Coast from the West. Armed with manifest destiny, they had charged forward and subdued that wilderness, along with the peoples and animals that had, for thousands of years, forged sustainable relationships with the prairies, mountains, and deserts they called home.

Fast forward a century, and wilderness is as rare in America as it once was dominant. Even the territory of Alaska has been transformed, from last frontier to war front to oil hub and, most recently, to tourist trap. Its remotest regions have been opened to exploitation. But there's been backlash: The same impulse that created the first national parks in the late 1800s was revived when the threats to Alaska's remaining wilderness were recognized in the late twentieth century. Just as the commercialism that sullied the natural beauty of Niagara Falls prompted preservation of Yosemite Valley in 1864, in 1980 the specter of commercial development prompted the United States to set aside millions of acres in Alaska as new national parks, preserves, and wildlife refuges.

Denali, of course, had been set aside as a national park and game reserve nearly sixty years earlier. But with passage of the Alaska National Interest Lands Conservation Act (ANILCA) it burgeoned, and the original park, some two million acres surrounding the highest peak on the North American continent, was given even stronger protections, set aside as designated Wilderness.

Denali's identity as a wilderness park continues to evolve. What was once a natural state is now a state subject to policy and political will. Those who live and work in the park know something that the tourist has little chance of fully grasping in a week's vacation. They know that as vast and untouchable as Denali's wilderness appears, it can be tarnished and must be defended.

The two mandates of the National Park Service come into conflict here. Building roads, trails, campgrounds, and visitor centers fulfills one mandate, which is to make parks accessible for the enjoyment of the people. Designating Wilderness with a capital W, where nothing mechanized—not a bicycle, not a chainsaw—is permitted by law, satisfies the other, which is to preserve natural features unsullied for posterity. There are labels for these ideals: conservation as the "proper use of nature" and preservation as "protection of nature from use." Which mandate should be primary has been debated since the national park idea began to take form. Conservation, as championed by Gifford Pinchot, first director of the U.S. Forest Service, calls for management of natural resources to promote their best and highest use. Preservation, as championed by John Muir, the father of the National Park Service, calls for protection of landscapes and resources in their natural states.

Denali, at this point in its evolution, mostly reflects the Muir ideal. Some argue that even the thirty or so miles of trails that exist around the park's most heavily utilized areas—near the visitor center and park entrance, at headquarters, at the Polychrome rest area, at the Eielson

Denali's winter wilderness in 1975.
PHOTO COURTESY OF THE NATIONAL PARK SERVICE, DENALI NATIONAL PARK AND PRESERVE MUSEUM COLLECTIONS. PHOTO BY WILLIAM GARRY.

Visitor Center, and at Wonder Lake—constitute a violation of the park's status as a trailless wilderness; a place set aside specifically for "wilderness recreation."

But as Denali's backcountry management plan undergoes revision, and as visitation continues to rise, one of the items on the table is whether additional trails should be built. It is a subject that is, and will continue to be, hotly debated.

"I wish that people and the park would understand what a trailless wilderness means," says interpretive ranger Laura Wright. She disagrees with the idea that the park should cater to visitors by building trails for them. Denali, she argues, could be known as "the place where you walk without trails." But for many, she acknowledges, that would require a huge mind shift.

Wright's viewpoint is echoed by other Denali rangers. There is something special, and precious, in their trail-free ideal. South District

More than thirty years after it was built, Charles Sheldon's Toklat River cabin slowly subsides back into the wilderness.
PHOTO COURTESY OF THE NATIONAL PARK SERVICE, DENALI NATIONAL PARK AND PRESERVE MUSEUM COLLECTIONS.

mountaineering ranger Tucker Chenoweth calls Denali a "deprivation chamber," a place where climbers and other visitors must turn off their cell phones, a place where societal chaos falls away. That helps make Denali "a place of amazing creativity," he says. In this park a person has the time to "tell a story without fact-checking. The art of storytelling is still alive here because of this essence of wilderness."

Defining wilderness is profoundly personal. Charles Sheldon and Harry Karstens experienced the wilds of Denali on the Toklat in a way that can never be replicated. The trails they followed were created by hooves and paws, by water and ice, by their desires. But they understood that others would follow, and they understood that was good. They protected their beloved wilderness as a national park, opening it to future generations of seekers with needs and desires they couldn't have imagined.

Denali's wilderness is now managed, observed, recorded. It is wilderness with history. It is wilderness brought home in digital images and souvenirs. Those who work to protect Denali today will write its next chapter, for seekers they also can't imagine. It is already far removed from the place that inspired Sheldon and Karstens, but that's the promise that trailless wilderness inspires in today's conservationists—a chance to see what the founders saw, perhaps feel what they felt, walk in their footsteps without following the same path . . .

. . . a chance to experience the wilds of the High One as nature intended.

Chapter Fifteen

Denali by the Numbers

Here are some statistics for Denali National Park and Preserve, as of the end of 2016. Some will be history soon.

Highest point = Denali at 20,310 feet above sea level
Lowest point = Yentna River at 223 feet (at the Denali National Park and Preserve boundary)

Visitation = 599,822
Budget = $14.3 million

1917 = Established as Mount McKinley National Park
1976 = Designation as an International Biosphere Reserve
1980 = Redefined and expanded as Denali National Park and Preserve

Total acreage (park and preserve) = ~6 million
Designated Wilderness = ~2.1 million acres

Employees = 113 permanent; 170 seasonal
Campgrounds = 6 (3 for tent camping only); 232 total sites
Official trails = 35.5 miles
Denali Park Road = 92 miles

Shortest day = December 21 with 4 hours, 21 minutes of daylight
Longest day = June 21 with 20 hours, 49 minutes of daylight

Weather averages at park headquarters
- Rainfall = 15 inches
- Snowfall = 80 inches
- Average temperature in January = 2°F (–17°C)
- Average temperature in July = 55°F (13°C)
- Coldest recorded temperature = –54°F
- Warmest recorded temperature = 91°F

Species
- Amphibians = 1
- Birds = 172 (most migratory; some "incidental")
- Fish = 14
- Mammals = 38
- Mosses, lichens, and liverworts = 941
- Trees = 8
- Vascular plants (including coniferous and flowering) = 758

Denali ascents
- 2016 attempts = 1126
- 2016 summits = 675 (60% success rate)
- Total attempts (1903–2015) = 41,976
- Total summits (1903–2015) = 21,906 (52% success rate)

Glaciers
- Largest = Kahiltna (44 miles long)
- Deepest = Ruth (3,805 feet)
- ~15% of park (~1,422 square mile) covered by glaciers

Acknowledgments

My gratitude to all of the Denali National Park and Preserve rangers and employees who took the time to guide me through the park's legacy and review my work, including historian Erik Johnson, ranger Sarah Hayes, interpretive ranger Dan Irelan, subsistence and cultural resource manager Amy Craver, archaeologist Phoebe Gilbert, environmental specialist Andrea Blakesley, kennels manager Jennifer Raffaeli, backcountry ranger John Brueck, wilderness planner Kristin Pace, backcountry monitoring ranger Jessica Toubman, and backcountry ranger Monica Morin; Gordon Olson, former chief of Denali's Division of Research and Resource Preservation; and Tucker Chenoweth, Maureen Gualtieri, and Laura Wright at the Walter Harper Talkeetna Ranger Station.

Special thanks to Denali museum curator Kim Arthur. Without her support, direction, and kindness, this book never would have happened.

I pulled from a number of sources—books, articles, online publications, movies, and documentaries—in the compilation of these essays. The works of historians Frank Norris (*Crown Jewel of the North: An Administrative History of Denali National Park and Preserve*), Jane Bryant (*Snapshots from the Past: A Roadside History of Denali National Park and Preserve*), and Tom Walker (*Kantishna: Mushers, Miners, Mountaineers and The Seventymile Kid*) were invaluable guides and reservoirs of information. The Denali National Park and Preserve website was another rabbit hole of information and guidance.

The editors at Lyons Press and FalconGuides have been most excellent partners for much of my career as a writer. Thanks to Holly Rubino for asking me to work on this project, to Sarah Parke for a thoughtful copyedit, and to Alex Singer for ushering the book (and me) through the editing process. Thanks also to Mike Urban, who asked me to write my first set of historic essays for Yosemite National Park. If I'm lucky, I'll get to do more.

A special thanks to my core cadre of fellow wordsmiths for their ongoing support: Patrice Fusillo, Arthur Dawson, Jim Shere, Kate Williams, and Ann Peters.

Special thanks also to Sara Bergendahl. My Alaskan base camp is her Sitka home; my sounding board for all things Alaskan—and so much more—is her able, inventive mind. Here's to years and more years of exploring together.

As always, my thanks and love to my parents, Jesse and Judy Salcedo, and to my sons, Jesse, Cruz, and Penn, who never fail to support me, pester me, and remind me not to take myself too seriously.

Resources and Further Reading

General

Anyone curious about Denali National Park and Preserve should first visit its website, www.nps.gov/dena. Start digging around and, as with every National Park Service website, you'll find links that will either satisfy your curiosity or direct you to another resource that can. Pages dealing with Denali's wilderness, planning your visit, mountaineering, and cultural and natural histories are all particularly enlightening.

Additionally, the park publishes a newsletter twice annually. It's available at the park or online at www.nps.gov/dena/learn/news/newspaper.htm.

For publications, including reports, books, original legislation—heck, anything in the public domain that's been published by the government, whether documenting the history of Denali National Park and Preserve, another park, or any variety of subjects, the National Archives maintains a massive, searchable, online database at archives.gov.

Excellent resources are located at the University of Alaska Fairbanks, including exhibits at the Museum of the North and in the Alaskan Polar Regions Collection Catalog. The Fairbanks Public Library hosts abundant resources as well, including microfiche editions of the *Fairbanks Daily News-Miner* dating back to the turn of the twentieth century. The Alaska Public Lands Information Center in Fairbanks also provided useful background information. The museum and library at headquarters in Denali National Park and Preserve is a repository for historic photographs and additional resources, and houses bound volumes of superintendent's reports dating back to the park's founding.

Alaska Geographic is a park partner and offers access to educational programs as well as books and merchandise relating to not only Denali

National Park and Preserve but other Alaskan parks, preserves, refuges, and public lands. The website is akgeo.org.

For an entertaining and comprehensive look at the history of the national parks, Ken Burns's documentary series *The National Parks: America's Best Idea* can't be beat. Sections of episodes 3 and 6 focus on Denali National Park's founding and evolution.

Books

Bauer, Erwin, and Peggy Bauer. *Denali: The Wild Beauty of Denali National Park.* 2000. Sasquatch Books, Seattle, WA.

Berten, Pierre. *The Klondike Fever: The Life and Death of the Last Great Gold Rush.* 1958. Carroll & Graf Publishers, New York, NY.

Brands, H. W. *The Age of Gold: The California Gold Rush and the New American Dream.* 2002. Random House Inc, New York, NY.

Brown, William E. *A History of the Denali–Mount McKinley Region, Alaska: Historical Resource Study of Denali National Park and Preserve.* 1991. US Department of the Interior, National Park Service, Santa Fe, NM.

Brown, William. *Denali: Symbol of the Alaskan Wild.* 1993. Alaska Natural History Association.

Browne, Belmore. *The Conquest of Mount McKinley.* 1913. G. P. Putnam's Sons, New York, NY.

Bryant, Jane. *Snapshots from the Past: A Roadside History of Denali National Park and Preserve.* 2011. National Park Service, US Department of the Interior, Santa Fe, NM.

Cook, Frederick Albert. *To the Top of the Continent.* 1908. Originally published by Hodder & Stoughton.

Davidson, Art. *Minus 148°: The First Winter Ascent of Mount McKinley.* 2013 (revised edition); first published 1969. The Mountaineers Books, Seattle, WA.

De Laguna, Frederica, ed. *Tales from the Dena.* 1935. University of Washington Press, Seattle, WA.

Dixon, Joseph. *Birds and Mammals of Mount McKinley National Park.* 1938. US Government Printing Office, Washington, DC. https://babel.hathitrust.org/cgi/pt?id=pst.000018374032;view=1up;seq=21.

Dunn, Robert. *The Shameless Diary of an Explorer.* 1907. Outing Publishing Co, New York, NY.

Ewing, Susan. *The Great Alaska Nature Factbook.* 1996. Alaska Northwest Books, Seattle, WA.

Follows, Don S. *Denali: The Story Behind the Scenery.* 1997; reprinted in 2016. KC Publications Inc, Wickenburg, AZ.

Haber, Gordon, and Marybeth Holleman. *Among Wolves.* 2013. University of Alaska Press, Fairbanks, AK.

Hall, Andy. *Denali's Howl: The Deadliest Climbing Disaster on America's Wildest Peak.* 2014. Dutton, New York, NY.

Hall, M. C. *Welcome to Denali National Park.* 2007. The Child's World, Chanhassen, MN.

Hampton, Bruce. *The Great American Wolf.* 1997. Henry Holt & Company, New York, NY.

Heacox, Kim. *Rhythm of the Wild: A Life Inspired by Alaska's Denali National Park.* 2015. Lyons Press, Guilford, CT.

Kari, James, and James A Fall. *Shem Pete's Alaska: The Territory of the Upper Cook Inlet Dena'ina.* 1987. University of Alaska Press.

Muir, John. *Travels in Alaska.* 1914.

Murie, Adolph. *The Wolves of Mount McKinley.* 1944; reprinted in 1985. University of Washington Press.

Norris, Frank. *The Crown Jewel of the North: An Administrative History of Denali National Park and Preserve*, volumes 1 & 2. 2006. Alaska Regional Office of the National Park Service, Anchorage, AK.

Orth, Donald J. *Dictionary of Alaska Place Names.* 1967. Geological Survey Professional Paper 567; US Government Printing Office, Washington, DC. https://archive.org/details/bub_gb_0y48AQAAMAAJ.

Pearson, Grant, and Philip Newill. *My Life of High Adventure.* 1962. Prentice-Hall Inc, Englewood Cliffs, NJ. Available online at archive.org/details/mylifeofhighadve012794mbp.

Ritter, Harry. *Alaska's History.* 1993; reprinted in 2002. Alaska Northwest Books, Portland, OR.

Service, Robert. *The Best of Robert Service.* 1940. McGraw-Hill, Ryerson, Toronto, Canada.

Sfraga, Michael. *Bradford Washburn: A Life of Exploration.* 2004. Oregon State University Press, Corvallis, OR.

Shernowit, Bill. *To the Top of Denali.* 1990. Alaska Northwest Books, Portland, OR.

Snyder, Howard. *Hall of the Mountain King: The True Story of a Tragic Climb.* 1973.

Stuck, Hudson. *The Ascent of Denali: A Narrative of the First Complete Ascent of the Highest Mountain in North America.* Originally published in 1914 by Charles Scribner's Sons, New York, NY.

Tabor, James. *Forever on the Mountain: The Truth Behind One of Mountaineering's Most Controversial and Mysterious Disasters.* 2007. W. W. Norton & Co, New York, NY.

Walker, Tom. *Kantishna: Mushers, Miners, Mountaineers—The Pioneer Story behind Mount McKinley National Park.* 2005. Pictorial Histories Publishing Co Inc, Missoula, MT.

———. *The Seventymile Kid.*

Ward, Kennan. *Denali: Reflections of a Naturalist.* 2000. NorthWood Press, Minnetonka, MN.

Waterton, Jonathan. *In the Shadow of Denali: Life and Death on Alaska's Mt. McKinley.* 1994. Bantam Doubleday Dell Publishing Group, New York, NY.

Wickersham, James. *Old Yukon: Tales, Trails, and Trials.* 1938; reprinted in 2009. University of Alaska Press, Fairbanks, AK.
Wilcox, Joe. *White Winds: America's Most Tragic Climb.* 1981.

Online Resources, Reports, Articles, Publications, and Miscellany

The resources listed below were among many used as background for these essays. I've organized them as they were associated with specific essays, but the information contained in each may also provide background for a different essay.

1. The Native Name

https://geonames.usgs.gov/apex/f?p=138:1:0::::
Brian Clark Howard, "McKinley vs. Denali: Who Decides Names on a Map?" *National Geographic*, August 31, 2015, http://news.nationalgeographic.com/2015/08/150831-denali-mount-mckinley-name-change-geography-maps/
Alaska Native Language Center, "The Name 'Athabascan,'" https://www.uaf.edu/anlc/resources/athabascan/
Roger W. Pearson and Marjorie Hermans, ed., *Alaska in Maps: A Thematic Atlas*, University of Alaska Fairbanks, 1998–2003
Craig Medred, "McKinley or Denali? How About Mount Big High One in Any Language?", adn.com, April 23, 2013, https://www.adn.com/voices/article/mckinley-or-denali-how-about-mount-big-high-one-any-language/2013/04/24/
http://ukpreservation.com/native-place-names/

2. Denali's First People

https://www.nps.gov/dena/learn/management/upload/Subsistance%20Management.pdf
http://www.archaeologicalconservancy.org/archaeology-in-the-ice-patches/
https://www.nps.gov/articles/denali-crp-archaeology-surveys.htm
https://www.nps.gov/articles/denali-prehistoric-upland-hunting-site.htm
https://www.nps.gov/articles/painted-bison-skull.htm
http://www.ankn.uaf.edu/npe/culturalatlases/yupiaq/marshall/raven/DotsonSa.html
Alaska Humanities Forum: Alaska History and Cultural Studies, http://www.akhistorycourse.org/alaskas-cultures/alaskas-heritage/chapter-2-3-athabaskans
Nicholas Wade, "Pause Is Seen in a Continent's Peopling," *New York Times*, March 12, 2014, http://www.nytimes.com/2014/03/13/science/linguistic-study-sheds-new-light-on-peopling-of-north-america.html?ref=science&_r=0
https://en.wikipedia.org/wiki/Daniel_Carter_Beard
https://en.wikipedia.org/wiki/Arthur_Harper_(trader)
https://en.wikipedia.org/wiki/Alaska_National_Interest_Lands_Conservation_Act
http://mtnt.net/index.php

https://www.tananachiefs.org/about/communities/lake-minchumina/
Ahtna, Inc., Ahtna History and Culture, http://ahtna-inc.com/about/history-and-culture/
Alaska Native Heritage Center, Athabascan Cultures of Alaska, http://www.alaskanative.net/en/main-nav/education-and-programs/cultures-of-alaska/athabascan/
https://www.culturalsurvival.org/publications/cultural-survival-quarterly/subsistence-and-cultural-survival-athabascan-people
https://genographic.nationalgeographic.com/land-bridge/
https://www.nps.gov/stateoftheparks/dena/DENA_StateOfThePark.pdf
https://www.sba.gov/sites/default/files/files/ANC%20FAQ_final.pdf
https://www.propublica.org/article/what-are-alaska-native-corporations
John Noble Wilford, "Entirely Preserved Inca Mummies Found," *New York Times*, April 7, 1999, http://www.nytimes.com/1999/04/07/us/entirely-preserved-inca-mummies-found.html
Richard H. Bishop, "Subsistence Resource Use in the Proposed North Addition to Mt. McKinley National Park," Anthropology and Historic Preservation Park Studies Unit, University of Alaska Fairbanks, 1978.
Brenda Rebne, *Cantwell Native Village History*, National Park Service and Alaska Department of Fish and Game's Division of Subsistence, 2000.
Raymond Collins, *Dichinadnek' Hwt'ana: A History of the People of the Upper Kuskokwim Who Live in Nikolai and Telida, Alaska*, 2000, https://www.nps.gov/dena/learn/historyculture/upload/Dichinanek%20Hwtana.pdf
The Legend of Denali, https://www.nps.gov/dena/learn/historyculture/legend-of-denali.htm
https://www.nps.gov/subjects/alaskasubsistence/denali.htmhttps://www.facebook.com/AlaskaNPS/videos/vb.162797840436892/1234797466570252/?type=3&theater

3. Mountaineering: First to the Top and
7. Mountaineering: The Second Wave

http://jukebox.uaf.edu/denali/html/people.htm
Craig Medred, "Belmore Browne Was the FIrst to Nearly Climb Alaska's Mount McKinley. Then He Got Lost," adn.com, October 30, 2012, https://www.adn.com/features/article/belmore-browne-was-first-nearly-climb-alaskas-mount-mckinley-then-he-got-lost/2012/10/30/
Andrew Szalay, "Belmore Browne against Denali," *The Suburban Mountaineer*, November 20, 2015, https://suburbanmountaineer.com/2015/11/20/belmore-browne-against-denali/
John Graham, "Climbing the Wickersham Wall," *Harvard Magazine*, August 29, 2013, http://harvardmagazine.com/2013/08/climbing-the-wickersham-wall
Alaska Department of Natural Resources, Division of Parks and Outdoor Recreation, Wickersham State Historic Site, http://dnr.alaska.gov/parks/units/wickrshm.htm
https://www.nps.gov/akso/nature/science/ak_park_science/PDF/2011Vol10-2/science-on-the-slopes-of-mount-mckinley.pdf
http://www.rockandice.com/lates-news/charlie-porter-we-hardly-knew-you

http://www.cascadeimages.com/images/main/cassin.pdf
https://www.adn.com/alaska-news/article/guides-50th-summiting-mckinley-probably-record/2011/07/20/
http://www.summitpost.org/the-tragedy-of-the-1979-korean-mckinley-expedition/434125
https://www.adn.com/uncategorized/article/1992-was-deadliest-alaska-range-climbing-season/2011/05/27/
http://www.smithsonianmag.com/history/who-discovered-the-north-pole-116633746/
http://www.dioi.org/vols/w73.pdf
https://www.nps.gov/katm/planyourvisit/exploring-the-valley-of-ten-thousand-smokes.htm
http://futurism.com/mckinleydenali-the-tallest-land-based-mountain-on-earth-yes-taller-than-even-everest/
https://www.ncbi.nlm.nih.gov/pubmed/18331224
https://www.nps.gov/dena/planyourvisit/upload/OVERALLCLIMBERS-thru-2015.pdf

4. Kantishna

https://www.nps.gov/klgo/planyourvisit/chilkoottrail.htm
https://www.kantishnaroadhouse.com
http://www.alaskacollection.com/lodging/denali-backcountry-lodge/
http://www.katair.com
http://campdenali.com
https://www.nps.gov/articles/aps-v5-i2-c6.htm
http://postalmuseum.si.edu/gold/nome.html
http://www.explorefairbanks.com/explore/gold-rush-history/
http://fairbanks-alaska.com/gold-rush-history.htm
https://www.nps.gov/klgo/learn/historyculture/tonofgoods.htm
http://www.historynet.com/klondike-gold-rush
http://www.akhistorycourse.org/northwest-and-arctic/1897-1920-gold
https://www.nps.gov/articles/aps-v4-i2-c8.htm
http://www.newsminer.com/news/local_news/denali-park-considers-last-unpatented-mining-claim/article_c55c3026-1427-11e6-8d35-4bf685eb36ec.html
Public Law 94-429; 94th Congress; "Mining in the National Parks Act", https://www.gpo.gov/fdsys/pkg/STATUTE-90/pdf/STATUTE-90-Pg1342.pdf

5. Denali in Two Steps: Defining and Redefining a National Park

https://en.wikipedia.org/wiki/George_Vancouver
https://en.wikipedia.org/wiki/William_Healey_Dall
https://history.state.gov/departmenthistory/people/seward-william-henry
http://www.history.com/topics/world-war-ii/lend-lease-act
http://www.pbs.org/wgbh/americanexperience/features/general-article/alaska-building/

http://www.pbs.org/wgbh/americanexperience/features/timeline/alaska/

https://www.nps.gov/media/photo/gallery.htm?id=3B0E8723-CC14-7C0A-768BDE0A0950FE7A

https://irma.nps.gov/Stats/SSRSReports/Park%20Specific%20Reports/Annual%20 Park%20Recreation%20Visitation%20(1904%20-%20Last%20Calendar%20 Year)?Park=DENA

http://www.akhistorycourse.org/modern-alaska/oil-discovery-and-development-in-alaska

http://ngm.nationalgeographic.com/2016/02/denali-national-parks-text

http://alyeska-pipeline.com/TAPS/PipelineFacts

http://www.akhistorycourse.org/modern-alaska/oil-discovery-and-development-in-alaska

http://www.akhistorycourse.org/modern-alaska/anilca

https://www.youtube.com/watch?v=fGeI-9cLoDg

https://www.adn.com/commentary/article/thirty-five-years-ago-carter-drew-wrath-many-alaskans/2013/12/01/

https://www.nps.gov/parkhistory/online_books/williss/adhi6.htm

http://dnr.alaska.gov/commis/opmp/anilca/more.htm

http://dnr.alaska.gov/mlw/factsht/land_fs/land_own.pdf

William E. Brown, *Denali: Historic Resource Study*, www.nps.gov/parkhistory/online_books/dena/hrs0a.htm.

Denali Summer Times 2016, Northcountry Communications Inc, Anchorage, AK

Chance Finegan, "The Alaska Lands Controversy: A Fight Bigger Than the Last Frontier," *The George Wright Forum*, vol. 32, no. 3, 290–98; 2015

6. *Of Sheep, Wolves, and Men: Charles Sheldon, Adolph Murie, and Gordon Haber*

http://www.wilderness.net/NWPS/Murie

http://www.nytimes.com/1994/12/03/us/tv-pictures-lead-alaska-to-suspend-wolf-killing.html

https://www.adn.com/alaska-news/article/pilot-tried-save-wolf-biologist-after-crash-denali-park/2009/10/16/

http://archives.evergreen.edu/1988/1988-01/full_text_projects/Group_Contracts/SOS/Swanberg_C-Case_Study_Spec_Reintro.pdf

http://www.anchoragepress.com/news/searching-for-gordon-haber-and-the-wolves-he-loved-/article_5bfa7be9-38f7-5255-9854-936158817844.html

http://articles.latimes.com/2005/mar/05/nation/na-wolves5

https://www.youtube.com/watch?v=EBjzYjXiz98

http://www.arlis.org/docs/vol1/B/224593500.pdf

Gordon Haber, "Socio-ecological Dynamics of Wolves and Prey in a Subarctic Ecosystem," University of British Columbia, 1977, www.arlis.org/docs/vol1/B/224593500.pdf

8. Supermen: Harry Karstens and Grant Pearson

https://www.nps.gov/dena/learn/photosmultimedia/station06a.htm
http://c498469.r69.cf2.rackcdn.com/1956/112_farquhar_karstens_aaj1956.pdf

9. On Denali's Skirts: Superwomen

http://campdenali.com/blog/133576
https://www.gilderlehrman.org/history-by-era/development-west/essays/women-west
http://www.newsminer.com/features/sundays/sketches_of_alaska/the-colorful-true-life-story-of-the-famed-fannie-quigley/article_99800062-e690-11e2-b295-001a4bcf6878.html
http://alaskamininghalloffame.org/inductees/quigley.php
https://www.adn.com/alaska-news/article/barbara-washburn-dead-99/2014/10/08/
https://jukebox.uaf.edu/denali/html/bawa.htm
https://www.adn.com/alaska-beat/article/louise-murie-last-original-alaska-conservation-family-has-passed/2012/05/25/
http://www.newsminer.com/louise-murie-who-helped-catalog-denali-national-park-s-flowers/article_603d1429-7f27-56cd-aa3e-af2f47da6557.html
http://www.jhnewsandguide.com/news/environmental/murie-clan-botanist-macleod-dies-at/article_36a55cc3-b39e-556f-a916-49a1b7f2ea2a.html
http://campdenali.com/about/history
http://rememberthewasp.blogspot.com
https://www.adventure-journal.com/2015/07/alaska-conservationist-ginny-wood/
http://alaskaconservation.org/achievement-awards/alaska-conservation-hall-fame/
http://www.history.ucsb.edu/labor/sites/secure.lsit.ucsb.edu.hist.d7_labor/files/sitefiles/ContinentalDivide-Ch6.pdf
http://371w8pt906u2838z82o8uy01.wpengine.netdna-cdn.com/wp-content/uploads/Weezy1.pdf

10. Let the Big Dogs Run

Zoë Sobel, "Denali's Dogs: Protecting the Environment and Preserving Heritage," KTOO Public Media, October 28, 2016, http://www.ktoo.org/2016/10/28/denali-national-park-sled-dog-kennel/
https://www.nps.gov/dena/planyourvisit/kennels-history.htm
http://www.nationalparkstraveler.com/2010/02/new-chief-musher-selected-denali-national-park-and-preserve5363
https://www.nps.gov/dena/planyourvisit/kennels-and-wilderness.htm
http://www.anchoragepress.com/news/dogs-of-denali/article_cbe746c8-8af6-5fe2-ab44-2b9ec2218e77.html

11. Planes, Trains, and Automobiles

https://www.nps.gov/dena/learn/photosmultimedia/station.htm
http://www.talkeetnachamber.org/history

https://www.boem.gov/uploadedFiles/BOEM/About_BOEM/BOEM_Regions/Alaska_Region/Ships/2011_Shipwreck.pdf
https://jukebox.uaf.edu/denali/html/temo.htm
https://www.nps.gov/dena/planyourvisit/walter-haper-trs.htm
http://www.talkeetnahistoricalsociety.org/?page_id=22
https://www.nps.gov/parkhistory/online_books/dena/dena_concession.pdf
Frank Norris, National Park Service, *Drawing a Line in the Tundra: Conservationists and the Mount McKinley Park Road.*

12. Denali's Natural History

http://www.newsminer.com/news/alaska_news/denali-rangers-euthanize-bear-that-caused-savage-river-area-closures/article_6f69a792-547e-11e6-8fe7-6797281a32f7.html
https://www.adn.com/alaska-news/article/grizzly-kills-san-diego-backpacker-alaskas-denali-national-park/2012/08/26/
http://ngm.nationalgeographic.com/ngm/0405/feature6/index.html
https://babel.hathitrust.org/cgi/pt?id=pst.000018374032;view=1up;seq=13
https://www.nps.gov/dena/learn/management/upload/South%20Side%20Denali%20DCP.pdf
https://www.nps.gov/dena/learn/management/upload/South%20Denali%20Implementation%20Plan%20&%20EIS.pdf
https://www.nps.gov/articles/rivers-and-streams-of-denali.htm
https://www.nps.gov/articles/denali.htm
https://www.nps.gov/articles/dena-muldrow.htm
https://placesjournal.org/article/the-view-through-the-crack/
https://www.nps.gov/dena/learn/nature/images/wolfmap2016_wPoints.jpg
https://www.nps.gov/articles/denali-animal-count.htm
https://www.nps.gov/katm/learn/photosmultimedia/brown-bear-frequently-asked-questions.htm#2
https://www.bear.org/website/bear-pages/brown-or-grizzly-bear/68-brown-grizzly-bear-facts.html
https://www.nps.gov/dena/learn/nature/wolfviewing.htm
http://journals.plos.org/plosone/article?id=10.1371/journal.pone.0153808
https://www.nps.gov/dena/learn/nature/upload/Wolf-Buffer-Proposal-2017.pdf
https://craigmedred.news/2016/07/29/denali-bear-dead/
https://craigmedred.news/2016/07/02/denali-bear-death-sentence/
http://www.newsminer.com/news/alaska_news/grizzly-bites-hiker-at-denali-national-park/article_9a60c0ea-40bd-11e6-a4d6-b782070bf083.html
https://www.adn.com/alaska-news/2017/02/24/alaska-game-board-shoots-down-bid-for-wolf-buffer-next-to-denali-national-park/
http://futurism.com/mckinleydenali-the-tallest-land-based-mountain-on-earth-yes-taller-than-even-everest/
https://www.nps.gov/dena/learn/nature/amphibians.htm

https://www.nps.gov/articles/denali-animal-count.htm
http://www.adfg.alaska.gov/index.cfm?adfg=species.main
https://www.nps.gov/dena/learn/nature/dallsheep.htm
https://www.nps.gov/articles/aps-v5-i1-c2.htm
http://www.akleg.gov/basis/Bill/Detail/30?Root=HB%20105
Freshwater Fish Inventory of Denali National Park and Preserve, Wrangell-St. Elias National Park and Preserve, and Yukon-Charley Rivers National Preserve; Central Alaska Inventory and Monitoring Network, 2004.
Kim Tingley, "Whisper of the Wild," *New York Times Magazine*, 2012, http://www.nytimes.com/2012/03/18/magazine/is-silence-going-extinct.html?_r=1&pagewanted=all&

13. Rock and Ice: A Mountain of Science

http://www.wilderness.net/NWPS/Murie
National Park Service, *Alaska Park Science: Climate Change in Alaska's National Parks*, vol. 12, issue 2, published in collaboration with the National Park Service, the National Parks Foundation, and Alaska Geographic, https://www.nps.gov/subjects/alaskaparkscience/index.htm or https://www.nps.gov/subjects/alaskaparkscience/archives.htm
http://onlinelibrary.wiley.com/doi/10.1029/JZ065i011p03703/abstract
https://www.nps.gov/articles/denali.htm
https://www.nps.gov/dena/learn/nature
https://www.nps.gov/dena/learn/management/upload/supt-report-2014.pdf
https://www.nps.gov/articles/denali-factsheet-debris-slide.htm
National Park Service, *State of Change: Climate Change in Alaska's National Park Areas*, https://www.nps.gov/akso/nature/climate/state-of-change.cfm.
DenaliNPS YouTube channel, www.youtube.com/watch?v=zc7jev3ri4c&list=UUyfk7EjiFzH49NnWq RyLC3w
http://news.uaf.edu/museum-exhibit-explores-1913-first-ascent-of-denali/

15. Denali by the Numbers

Sources: Denali National Park and Preserve; www.nps.gov/dena/learn/management/statistics.htm; www.nps.gov/dena/planyourvisit/upload/OVERALL CLIMBERS-thru-2015.pdf

Index

Accidental Adventurer, The (Washburn & Freedman), 142
aerial hunting, 184
Age of Gold, The (Brands), 58
Airborne Hunting Act (1971), 184
air travel/support, 93, 99, 167–72
Alaska
  explorers from Outside, 60–62
  purchase from Russia, 61–62
Alaska Conservation Foundation, 144
Alaska Department of Fish and Game, 89, 184
Alaska Dispatch News, 77
Alaska Geographic, 73, 217
Alaska Highway, 72–73
Alaska Humanities Forum, 77, 78
Alaska National Interest Lands Conservation Act (1980), 6, 21–22, 23, 55, 77–79, 221
Alaska Native Claims Settlement Act (1971), 24, 25, 76–77
Alaska pipeline, 75–76
Alaska Public Lands Center, 85
Alaska Railroad, 64–65, 165–67
Alaska Road Commission, 56, 67, 119–20, 161, 163, 166
Albright, Horace, 84, 162
Alcan Highway, 72–73
altitude sickness, 29, 42, 107
American Alpine Journal, 109–10
Among Wolves (Haber & Holleman), 6, 90–91, 170, 180, 183, 195, 198
Anderson, John, 49, 125, 146
Anderson, Pete, 35–38
Anderson, Polly, 49, 125, 146
Andrus, Cecil, 77
Aramark, 24–25, 56–57, 73
archaeology, 9–12
Arctic ground squirrels, 192–93
Arctic National Wildlife Refuge, 78, 88, 138, 144
Arctic zone, 195
Ascent of Denali, The (Stuck), 26, 38, 40, 41, 154, 201–2
Aten, Arthur, 39
Athabascans
  about, 13
  bears, 17
  construction work, 19–20
  endurance, 19–20, 24–25
  fish and fishing, 15, 21, 22–23
  folklore, 15–17
  food, 14–15, 22–23
  game, 14–15, 22
  hunting, 21–22, 23–24
  language, 12–13
  names for places, 1–2

plants, 15, 23
potlatches, 13–14
subsistence, 20–24
white man and, 18–20
women, 17, 131–32
aufeis, 215
avalanches, 29, 40, 214

Barrill, Edward, 33–34, 35
Batkin, Jacques "Farine," 101–2
bears, 17, 176–80, 183, 198
Beckwith, Edward, 96, 97
Been, Frank, 126, 156
Bergh Lake, 208
Bering, Vitus, 61
Bering Land Bridge, 9–10
Berton, Pierre, 46
Big Timber, 68, 125
birds, 193–94
Birds and Mammals of Mount McKinley National Park (Dixon), 176, 179, 210
Bishop, Richard, 20, 22, 209
black bears, 179, 198
Blomberg, Gregg, 101–2
Boone and Crockett Club, 64–65, 83–84
boundaries of park, 59–60, 67
Brands, H. W., 58
Brease, Phil, 206, 210
Brown, William, 19, 51–52, 84
Browne, Belmore
avalanches, 214
caribou, 188
crevasses, 212
dogs, sled, 153–54
mountaineering, 32–33, 33–35, 38–40
naming of places, 3–4, 5
as park advocate, 54, 63–64, 84
snowshoe hares, 191–92
wilderness, 220
Browne, George, 141
Bryant, Jane, 50, 68–69, 72, 137, 146, 161–62, 208
bugs, 194–95
buses, shuttle, 75, 165, 173
Busia, Johnnie, 49, 52, 53, 125
Butcher, Susan, 142, 158

cabins, ranger patrol, 68, 155
California gold rush, 46–47, 57
Camp Denali, 57, 74, 144
Cantwell, 23, 77
caribou, 186–89
Carpé, Allen, 6, 96, 97
Carter, Jimmy, 77–78
Cassin, Ricardo, 107
Chenoweth, Tucker, 167, 223
chickadees, black-capped, 193
Civilian Conservation Corps (CCC), 70–71
clean climbing policy, 111–12
Clean Mountain Can, 112, 218
climate change, 216–17
climbing. *See* mountaineering
Cole, Jerryne, 57, 144
Cole, Wally, 57, 144
Collins, Florence Rucker, 145
Collins, Raymond, 18–19, 24
concessioners, 24–25, 56–57, 71–72, 73
Conquest of Mount McKinley, The (Browne), 3–4, 33, 34, 38, 153–54, 214, 220
Cook, Frederick, 31–35, 214

Cosmic Ray expedition, 94–95, 96–97, 169–70, 202
Craver, Amy, 14
crevasses, 211–12
Crosson, Joe, 96, 169–70

Dall, William, 61
Dall sheep, 61, 63, 80, 81, 82–83, 189–91
Dalton, Joe, 48, 50
Davidson, Art, 101–2, 169, 194, 200, 205
deaths, mountaineering, 93, 110–11
de Laguna, Frederica, 17
Demientieff, Mitch, 16–17
Denali, Mount. *See also* mountaineering
  "discovery" by explorers from Outside, 60–61
  height, calculating, 201–2, 206, 207
  names for, 1, 2, 3, 6–7, 61, 62
Denali Fault, 207, 208, 209
Denali Landcover's Quilt, 196–97
Denali National Park and Preserve. *See also specific topics*
  boundaries, 59–60, 67
  establishment, 54, 59, 62–65, 84
  expansion, 59, 78–79
  funding, 66
  headquarters, 66, 67–68
  statistics, 225–26
Denali Park Road
  about, 67, 75, 119–20, 160–65, 173–74, 216–17
  photos, 5, 64, 215
Denali Pass, 102, 202, 203
Denali Subsistence Resource Commission, 145
Densmore, Frank, 62
Dichinanek' Hwt'ana (Collins), 18–19, 24
Dickey, William, 3, 62
dinosaurs, 209–10
Dixon, Joseph, 175–76, 179, 186, 187, 188, 210
Doege, Richard Loren, 109–10
dogs, sled
  about, 148–49
  breeding, 149–50
  history on Denali, 153–58
  legacy of, 158
  work done by, 151–52
Donnelly, Jack, 120
Doyon Ltd., 24–25, 56–57, 73
Dunn, Robert, 32
Dunn, Troy, 6, 91, 170–71

earthquakes, 208–9
ecosystems, 195–97
Edmunds, Chris, 56
Edwards, John, 101–2
Eielson, Carl Ben, 167–68
Eielson Visitor Center, 74, 75, 85, 188–89
Ercolani, Miri, 142–43
establishment of park, 54, 59, 62–65, 84
Everest, Mount, 28–29
expansion of park, 59, 78–79
explorers from Outside, 60–62

Fairbanks Daily News-Miner, 55, 134, 138, 139–40, 145, 167
Fake Peak, 35
falls, mountaineering, 95–96
Feral, Priscilla, 91

fish and fishing, 15, 21, 22–23
folklore, Athabascan, 15–17
food of Athabascans, 14–15, 22–23
Foraker, Mount, 44
Fredson, Johnny, 41, 43
Freedman, Lew, 142
funding, 66
fur trappers and trapping, 18–19

game, 14–15, 22
Genet, Ray (the Pirate), 101–2, 109–10, 158
Geology Road Guide, 206, 207, 208, 209
George, Esaias, 41, 43
George Parks Highway, 72, 164, 173
glaciers
  about, 29, 210–14, 216, 226
  Kahiltna Glacier, 100, 105, 106, 169, 170, 211, 216
  Muldrow Glacier, 36–38, 42, 95, 154, 169, 210–13
  Ruth Glacier, 33, 34–35, 211
gold rushes. *See also* Kantishna
  Athabascans, impact on, 19
  California, 46–47, 57
  independence, spirit of, 57–58
  Klondike, 47, 57
  tourism and, 55–57
Great Denali-McKinley Trespass, 77
Great Depression, 72
Griffith (musher), 153, 154
grizzly bears, 176–78, 179, 180, 183, 198
guides, mountaineering, 109–11

Haber, Gordon. *See also Among Wolves*
  air travel, 170–71
  flowers, 195
  naming of places, 5–6
  wolves, 89–91, 180, 182–83, 184, 198
  work and legacy, 81
Harding, Warren G., 165
hares, snowshoe, 191–92
Harper, Arthur, 61, 132
Harper, Walter, 38, 40–44, 117, 131–32
Haydon, Jack, 82
Hayes, Sarah, 149, 155, 178, 179, 193
Heacox, Kim, 31, 177, 192, 193
headquarters of park, 66, 67–68
Holleman, Marybeth, 6, 90, 170. *See also Among Wolves*
Howard, Johnny, 147
Howard, Lena, 146–47
human impact on wildlife, 197–99
Hunter, Celia, 143–44
hunting, 21–22, 23–24, 63, 83, 181–82, 184
hydraulic mining, 53

ice patches, 12
Ickes, Jane, 69–70
Igloo Creek, 160, 187, 210, 217
In the Shadow of Denali (Waterman), 109, 110
Irelan, Dan, 188–89

Jackson Hole News & Times, 138, 139
Jennie (mother of Walter Harper), 131–32
Jewell, Sally, 6
Johnson, Erik, 4, 52, 53, 61
Johnston, Dave, 101–2
Joseph, Abbie, 132

Kahiltna Glacier, 100, 105, 106, 169, 170, 211, 216
Kantishna
  gold rush, 47–50
  gold rush, after, 50–54, 63
  mining rights in park, 54–55
  tourism, 55–57
Kantishna (Walker), 51
Kantishna Hydraulic Mining Company, 53
Kantishna Roadhouse, 25, 57
Kantishna Roadhouse Backcountry Lodge, 57
Karstens, Harry
  dogs, sled, 155
  early life, 114–15
  as gold prospector, 115
  Karstens, Louise, and, 136–37, 138
  as mail carrier, 49, 114, 115–16
  mountaineering, 40–44, 117
  as park superintendent, 55, 66–68, 71, 73, 117–22
  Pearson, Grant, and, 122–23, 124
  personality, 113
  Sheldon, Charles, and, 63, 116–17
  wilderness, 223
Karstens, Louise, 136–38
Karstens Ridge, 3, 42–43, 117, 142, 208
Kennedy, Dan, 71
Klondike Fever, The (Berton), 46
Klondike gold rush, 47, 57
Kogl, Sandy, 157–58
Koven, Theodore, 6, 96, 97

latitude, 28
La Voy, Merl, 39–40
Legend of Denali, The (Demientieff), 16–17
Legend of the Rainbow Herd, 188–89
Lewis, Jerry, 104
Liek, Harry, 94, 96, 125, 126. *See also* Lindley-Liek expedition
Lindley, Alfred, 94, 96, 125. *See also* Lindley-Liek expedition
Lindley-Liek expedition, 94, 95–96, 97, 125, 155–56, 202, 212
Lloyd, Tom, 35–38, 49

mail carriers, 49, 114, 115–16
market hunters, 63, 83, 181–82
Mather, Stephen, 64–65, 119
McCarthy, Paul, 210
McFarland, Ranger, 121
McGonagall, Charley, 35–38, 49
McKenzie, Angus, 134
McKinley, William, 3, 6, 62
McKinley Flora (Murie), 139–40
McKinley Park Hotel, 69–70, 72, 73, 126, 165, 167
McKinley Park Station, 67, 68–71, 119, 121, 165–66, 171
Medred, Craig, 138
Meier, Tom, 91
Melendez Wright, George, 86, 175–76
migration, land-based, 9–10
Minchumina, Lake, 22–23
Mining in the National Parks Act (1976), 52
mining rights in park, 54–55
Minus 148º (Davidson), 102, 169, 194, 200, 205
Mission 66 initiative, 74–75, 85, 88, 163

Moore, Terris, 170
moose, 185–86
Morino, Maurice, 68–69, 165
Morino roadhouse, 67, 68–69
Morton, Rogers, 76
mosquitoes, 194–95
mountaineering
  about, 26–29
  air support, 93, 99, 171
  altitude sickness, 29, 42, 107
  ascent, first, 40–44
  ascent, first winter, 100–102, 205
  ascent, ski, 94, 95
  ascent/attempt statistics, 106, 226
  attempt, first, 30–31
  attempt, near, 38–40
  avalanches, 29, 40, 214
  Cosmic Ray expedition, 94–95, 96–97, 169–70, 202
  deaths, 93, 110–11
  Everest compared to, 28–29
  falls, 95–96
  firsts, 93–94, 107–8, 112
  guides, 109–11
  hoax, 31–34
  hoax, debunking, 34–35
  impact of, 111–12
  latitude, 28
  Lindley-Liek expedition, 94, 95–96, 97, 125, 155–56, 202
  motives for, 93–94
  regulations, 105, 108, 203, 205
  rescues, 108–9
  scientific inquiry, 201–3, 205
  Sourdough Expedition, 35–38
  trash and human waste, 111–12, 217–18
  vertical relief, 28–29
  weather, 28
  West Buttress route, 97, 98–100, 172
  Wilcox expedition, 103–5
  women, 140–42
Mountaineering Club of Alaska, 104
Mount McKinley Gold Placers Company, 53
Mount McKinley National Park. *See* Denali National Park and Preserve
Mount McKinley Park Hotel, 69
Mount McKinley Park Road. *See* Denali Park Road
Mount McKinley Tourist & Transportation Company, 71–72, 147
Mt. McKinley's Climber's Handbook, 193–94
Muckluck Pass, 5
Muir, John, 86, 221
Muldrow Glacier, 36–38, 42, 95, 154, 169, 210–13
Murie, Adolph, 80–81, 85–89, 163, 182
Murie, Louise, 138–40
Murie, Margaret, 85, 88, 220
Murie, Olaus, 85, 88, 120, 138, 163
My Life of High Adventure (Pearson)
  air travel/support, 167
  Denali, 122, 124, 126, 129
  dogs, sled, 148, 150
  moose, 185–86
  mountaineering, 94
  Quigley, Fannie, 134–35
  Sourdough Expedition, 35, 36
  Wonder Lake, 5

names for places, 1–7, 61, 62
National Geographic, 98, 203, 218
National Park Service (NPS). *See also specific topics*
  Alaska National Interest Lands Conservation Act, 78–79
  Denali Park Road, 161
  funding, 66
  mandates, 67, 113, 117, 159, 173, 221
  Mission 66 initiative, 74–75, 85, 88, 163
Nenana Daily News, 69
New York Times, 37, 90, 184
Nichols, Rufus, 120
Nishimae, Shiro, 101–2
Nome, Alaska, 47
Norris, Frank, 63, 65, 70, 156, 166–67, 205
North Peak, 35, 37, 38, 43, 95, 141
NPS. *See* National Park Service
Nyberg, Fritz, 68–69, 122, 125

Obama, Barack, 1, 6
oil, 75–76
Okonek, Brian, 110
Old Yukon (Wickersham), 31
Olton, Percy, 96, 97
Operation White Tower, 98, 126–27, 140–42, 203
Organic Act (1916), 117–18, 159

Pacific Ring of Fire, 206
paleontology, 209–10
Parker, Herschel, 34–35, 38–40
park superintendents, 113–14. *See also* Karstens, Harry; Pearson, Grant
Pearson, Grant
  air travel/support, 167, 170, 171
  bears, 178
  birds, 193
  Dall sheep, 190–91
  dogs, sled, 148, 150, 155, 156, 157, 158
  early life, 122–24
  glaciers, 212
  human population explosion, 197
  Karstens, Harry, and, 122–23, 124
  life after park work, 128–29
  mining, 51, 53
  moose, 185–86
  mosquitoes, 194–95
  mountaineering, 94, 95–96
  as park ranger, 68, 124–25, 126–28
  as park superintendent, 128, 204
  personality, 113, 122
  Quigley, Fannie, and, 132–33, 134–35, 135–36
  scientific inquiry, 205
  Sourdough Expedition, 35, 36
  wolverines, 191
  Wonder Lake, 4–5
Pearson, Margaret, 126
pemmican meatballs, 41, 42
permafrost, 162–63, 216–17
Philip, Jacques, 158
Pinchot, Gifford, 221
pipeline, Alaska, 75–76
place names, 1–7, 61, 62
placer mining, 52–53
planes, 93, 99, 167–72
plants, 15, 23
poaching, 120–21
Polychrome Pass, 161–62, 164
poop, 111–12, 217–18
Porter, Charlie, 107–8

potlatches, 13–14
predator-prey relationships, 86, 87–88

Quake Lake, 208
Quigley, Fannie, 49, 51, 52, 55, 56, 125, 132–36
Quigley, Joe, 48, 49, 51, 52, 125, 134–35, 136
quilt, 196–97

Raffaeli, Jennifer, 148, 150, 152, 156, 157–58
railroad, 64–65, 165–67
Rainbow Herd, 188–89
Raven (mythological figure), 15–17
ravens, 193–94
Rebne, Brenda, 1, 18
Redington, Joe, Sr., 158
Red Top, 51–52
Renfro, Yelizaveta P., 193
rescues, 108–9
Richardson Highway, 72, 114
rivers, 214–15
roads, 160–65, 173–74. *See also specific roads*
Robinson, Florence, 145
Robinson, Roger, 112, 218
rocks, 206–9
Roosevelt, Teddy, 83–84
Rumohr, John, 150–51, 155–56, 157
Russians, 18–19, 61
Ruth Glacier, 33, 34–35, 211

Savage Camp, 71–72, 147, 166
Schlichter, Paul, 104
scientific inquiry
  about, 218–19
  climate change, 216–17
  glaciers, 210–14
  mountaineering, 201–3, 205
  Operation White Tower, 203
  paleontology, 209–10
  poop, 217–18
  rivers, 214–15
  rocks, 206–9
Seventymile Kid, The (Walker), 116, 137
Seward, William, 61–62
Sfraga, Michael, 97
Shameless Diary of an Explorer (Dunn), 32
Shannon's Mine, 49
sheep, 61, 63, 80, 81, 82–83, 189–91
Sheldon, Bobby, 71–72
Sheldon, Charles
  bears, 178
  caribou, 188
  Dall sheep, 80, 81–84, 189
  Karstens, Harry, and, 63, 116–17
  naming of park, 4
  as park advocate, 19, 54, 63–65
  wilderness, 223
  wildlife, 116–17
Sheldon, Don, 37, 168–69
Shernowit, Bill, 36, 37, 168, 169, 193–94
shuttle buses, 75, 165, 173
ski ascents/descents, 94, 95
sled dogs
  about, 148–49
  breeding, 149–50
  history on Denali, 153–58
  legacy of, 158
  work done by, 151–52
Snapshots from the Past (Bryant), 72, 161

Snowball (dog), 154
snow machines, 157
snowshoe hares, 191–92
Snyder, Howard, 103, 104, 105
Sourdough Expedition, 35–38
South Peak, 95, 104, 201, 202
Spadavecchia, Nicholas, 96, 97
spruce, black, 196
squirrels, Arctic ground, 192–93
Stiles, Joe, 48, 50
Strom, Erling, 94, 95, 96, 125
Stuck, Hudson
  dogs, sled, 154
  mountaineering, 26, 38, 39, 40–44, 117
  naming of places, 3
  scientific inquiry, 201–2
  snowshoe hares, 191
Stumps, Mugs, 108, 111
sub-Arctic zone, 196
subsistence, 20–24, 54, 145, 209
Swanke, Denice, 147

Tales from the Dena (de Laguna), 17, 20
Talkeetna, 172–73
Tatum, Robert, 40–44
Taylor, Billy, 35–38
Taylor, Tim, 216
Teklanika East, 10–11
Teklanika West, 10, 11
temperatures, 202
Tige (dog), 150–51
Tobin, Jack, 167
Toklat grizzly bears, 176–78
Tomsich, Susi, 210
torpor, 178
To the Top of Denali (Shernowit), 37
To the Top of the Continent (Cook), 31, 32, 33, 214
tourism, 55–57
trails, 222–23
transportation. *See also specific roads*
  about, 159–60
  planes, 93, 99, 167–72
  railroad, 64–65, 165–67
  roads, 160–65, 173–74
trash, 111–12
Traveler (mythological figure), 17
trees, 196

Udall, Morris, 77–78
University of Alaska, 10, 139, 140, 142, 205–6, 210
U.S. Board on Geographic Names, 1, 6

Vancouver, George, 61
visitors, 119, 225
volcanic eruptions, 39, 40, 65, 207–8

Wags (wolf), 86–87
Walker, Tom
  on Kantishna, 50, 51, 53
  on Karstens, Harry, 114, 115, 117, 136–37
  on Wickersham, James, 30
Ward, Kennan, 176, 186, 194
Washburn, Barbara, 98, 126–27, 140–42, 143, 203
Washburn, Bradford, 94, 97–100, 126–27, 141–42, 172, 202–3, 204
waste, human, 111–12, 217–18
Waterman, Jon, 93, 109, 110, 184, 194, 217

Way, Ranger, 120, 121
weather, 28, 118–19, 202, 226
West Buttress route, 97, 98–100, 172
white man and Athabascans, 18–20
White Tower, Operation, 98, 126–27, 140–42, 203
Wichman, George, 101–2
Wickersham, James, 30–31, 48, 54, 62, 65, 84
Wickersham Wall, 29, 31, 107, 214
Wilcox, Joe, 94, 103, 104, 105
Wilcox expedition, 103–5
wilderness, 220–24
Wilderness Act (1964), 88, 151
Wilderness of Denali (Sheldon), 4, 63, 82, 116
wildlife, 175–76, 197–99. *See also specific animals*
Wilson, Woodrow, 65, 84
Wolf Townships, 90, 184
wolverines, 191
wolves, 80–81, 85, 86–87, 89–90, 91, 180–84, 198
Wolves of Mount McKinley, The (Murie), 85, 86
women. *See also specific women*
  Athabascan, 17, 131–32
  bears and, 17
  contributions of, 130–31
  equality and, 147
  fliers, 143–45
  hospitality, 146–47
  mountaineering, 140–42
Wonder Lake, 4–5, 73–75
Wood, Ginny, 143–44
Works Progress Administration, 69–70
World War I, 66, 84
World War II, 72–73
Wright, Laura, 112, 222
Wright, Miranda, 15–16

Yahoo (mythological figure), 16–17

About the Author

Tracy Salcedo is the author of *Historic Yosemite National Park* and has written guidebooks to a number of destinations in California and Colorado, including *Hiking Through History San Francisco*, *Hiking Waterfalls in Northern California*, *Hiking Lassen Volcanic National Park*, *Best Hikes Near Reno-Lake Tahoe*, and *Best Hikes Near Sacramento*. She has also written Best Easy Day Hikes guides to San Francisco's Peninsula, North Bay, and East Bay, as well as San Jose, Lake Tahoe, Reno, Sacramento, Fresno, Boulder, Denver, and Aspen. She lives with her family in California's Wine Country. You can learn more by visiting her website at www.laughingwaterink.com.